Developing Swimmers

Michael Brooks

Human Kinetics

Library of Congress Cataloging-in-Publication Data

Brooks, Michael, 1964-
  Developing swimmers / Michael Brooks.
    p. cm.
  Includes index.
  ISBN-13: 978-0-7360-8935-7 (soft cover)
  ISBN-10: 0-7360-8935-7 (soft cover)
  1. Swimming--Training. I. Title.
  GV838.67.T73B76 2011
  797.21--dc22
  [B]

                              2011006525

ISBN-10: 0-7360-8935-7 (print)
ISBN-13: 978-0-7360-8935-7 (print)

Copyright © 2011 by Human Kinetics, Inc.

Acquisitions Editor: Tom Heine; **Developmental Editor:** Heather Healy; **Assistant Editors:** Michael Bishop and Tyler Wolpert; **Copyeditor:** Alisha Jeddeloh; **Indexer:** Alisha Jeddeloh; **Graphic Designer:** Bob Reuther; **Graphic Artist:** Francine Hamerski; **Cover Designer:** Keith Blomberg; **Photographer (cover):** © Human Kinetics; **Photographer (interior):** David Haas; **Visual Production Assistant:** Joyce Brumfield; **Photo Production Manager:** Jason Allen; **Art Manager:** Kelly Hendren; **Associate Art Manager:** Alan L. Wilborn; **Illustrator:** © Human Kinetics; **Printer:** United Graphics

We thank York YMCA Graham Aquatic Center in York, Pennsylvania, for assistance in providing the location for the photo shoot for this book.

Human Kinetics books are available at special discounts for bulk purchase. Special editions or book excerpts can also be created to specification. For details, contact the Special Sales Manager at Human Kinetics.

Printed in the United States of America   10 9 8 7 6 5 4 3 2

The paper in this book is certified under a sustainable forestry program.

Human Kinetics
Web site: www.HumanKinetics.com

United States: Human Kinetics
P.O. Box 5076
Champaign, IL 61825-5076
800-747-4457
e-mail: humank@hkusa.com

Canada: Human Kinetics
475 Devonshire Road Unit 100
Windsor, ON N8Y 2L5
800-465-7301 (in Canada only)
e-mail: info@hkcanada.com

Europe: Human Kinetics
107 Bradford Road
Stanningley
Leeds LS28 6AT, United Kingdom
+44 (0) 113 255 5665
e-mail: hk@hkeurope.com

Australia: Human Kinetics
57A Price Avenue
Lower Mitcham, South Australia 5062
08 8372 0999
e-mail: info@hkaustralia.com

New Zealand: Human Kinetics
P.O. Box 80
Torrens Park, South Australia 5062
0800 222 062
e-mail: info@hknewzealand.com

                                                                         E5024

In Memoriam

Jackye Brooks (1940-2006)

Owen Jenkins (1927-2002)
Professor of English Literature, Carleton College

Contents

Acknowledgments

Albert Einstein is said to have quipped that he had only one original idea in his life. That warning alone should make any author soberly consider the predecessors, influences, and mentors who have contributed to his thoughts. I understand my debts, and they are numerous. Because a complete listing would be longer than the book itself, I must confine my acknowledgments to only a few of the major influences in my coaching.

I never met several of my most important mentors. Instead, I read and studied their books, thought about their ideas, took what I liked, and tried to apply their lessons and wisdom to my coaching. I owe a huge debt to John Wooden (UCLA men's basketball) and James "Doc" Counsilman (Indiana men's swimming), both deceased, and to Anson Dorrance (UNC women's soccer) and Keith Bell (sport psychologist), both still practicing their crafts.

I have also had the good fortune to share a deck with three great coaches: Murray Stephens and Bob Bowman at the North Baltimore Aquatic Club and Dennis Pursley at the Brophy East Swim Team in Phoenix. Most of my current ideas took form during the years I spent with them.

In the past few years, I have been involved with a small group of coaches at the York YMCA who are dedicated to building the best developmental swimming program ever. The help, advice, effort, and friendship of Andy Steward, Janet Borowski, Sandy Zamalis, Nate Gentzler, and Clyde Vedder have been invaluable in building a program, fashioning its principles, and writing about it.

But any thoughts, principles, or theories that inhabit a coach's mind are tried and tested by the swimmers in the water. It is cliché but true that any coach who is paying attention learns a lot more from his swimmers than they do from him. So, to all of my swimmers past and present, thank you for trying to teach me how to coach.

Introduction

Ever since I started coaching, I have been obsessed with the idea of development. How does an eight-year-old struggling to keep her head steady on backstroke become a national-level athlete over the course of six or eight years? What is the best way to take a swimmer from entry-level novice to national-level athlete, and what are the important steps along the way? What skills or talents do the elite athletes have; how do I best teach these to my age-group swimmers, and in what order should I teach them? How do I keep my swimmers continually improving and motivated to train hard and swim fast for years on end? This book is the fruit of struggling to find answers to these questions—in short, it is about developing swimming talent.

An obvious question arises: What do we mean by *age-group swimming*? Coaches argue about precise definitions here and never come to an agreement. In the absence of any consensus, I take the term to mean training programs for swimmers 14 years old and younger. Though some late-starting swimmers may be categorized as age-groupers when 15 or 16, most programs have their high school swimmers training in their senior programs. And even though some strong females will be at the national level and doing senior-level training by age 14, the large majority are still training and racing as age-groupers. Thus, though there may be some overlap at the boundary of age-group and senior swimming, 14 is a reasonable cutoff for discussing age-groupers.

When we watch elite athletes on television, competing at the Olympics, for example, we are rightfully impressed at their extraordinary physical and mental abilities. We marvel at what they can do, but we rarely think about how that phenomenal athleticism was developed. As viewers, we see only the last few minutes in a long developmental process that spanned 8 or 10 years of daily practices.

That long developmental process is crucial: As the twig is bent, so it grows. The likelihood that athletes will reach elite levels as seniors is much higher if they have participated in well-constructed age-group developmental programs. Teaching stroke skills to older swimmers who missed out on the early years of concentrated stroke development or building aerobic capacity in older swimmers who missed the early years of aerobic training is possible. However, in both cases, it is much more difficult and takes much longer. Swimmers who start late or who swim in poorly constructed programs have fewer options when they are older, and they generally have lower performance ceilings.

Good coaching is crucial to building a solid age-group foundation, and that fact is problematic. For better or worse, swimming is not a sport for the solitary; swimmers train with teams under coaches who develop training programs, and the swimmers on any team will largely be limited by the vision, aim, talent, and knowledge of the coaches who train them. At most swimming clubs, the age-group coaches are novice coaches with little experience. They may be enthusiastic, but they are not yet knowledgeable about coaching. The former collegiate swimmers among them may know swimming but not necessarily how to coach it. Coaching someone else to swim, especially hyperactive 10-year-olds, is very different from swimming yourself.

Unfortunately, the career path for most serious and ambitious young club coaches perpetuates this problem of inexperience. They plan on paying their dues for a few years, coaching age-groupers before they graduate to coaching seniors. By the time they have learned their craft, they are no longer developing young swimmers. Every time an experienced coach moves to the senior level, another novice coach comes in who will practice being a coach on younger swimmers during their crucial developmental years. This book is intended to accelerate the learning curve of these newer coaches to the benefit of the age-group swimmers training under them.

The most common sources of information about age-group swimming are inadequate. Swimming knowledge is available at the click of a mouse over the Internet. But the Internet has made everyone an expert, no matter how wise or foolish, and as a result, cyberspace is awash in bad information. Further, information tends to be limited in scope and scattered piecemeal across articles or Web sites based on conflicting assumptions and with conflicting aims. Making music out of this cacophony is nearly impossible, in particular for new coaches who cannot put each article or argument into context or properly evaluate it.

Much of the good information about swimming is not applicable. Most nationally known coaches have trained and developed Olympians and world-record holders—elite senior athletes—and most began coaching these athletes late in their development, guiding them the last few steps to the summit. Talks or articles by these coaches discuss that short but important climb. However, an age-group coach trying to teach a child to swim butterfly or train a talented 12-year-old doesn't need to know what Michael Phelps did when he was 22 and preparing to win eight gold medals. The needs of an age-group swimmer and age-group coach are different from those of the senior elite athlete and coach.

The last comprehensive book on age-group swimming, *Coaching the Young Swimmer* by Orjan Madsen, was published over 25 years ago and was based primarily on Eastern European research. A lot has changed, and it is time to incorporate what has been learned in the meantime. Further, Madsen seemed to assume an ordered world rather than real life with all its messiness, where coaches have to deal with inadequate pool time and space, kids getting caught between divorced parents, swimmers involved in multiple extracurricular activities, and some kids who pay attention and work hard and some who do not.

There is a desperate need for a practical manual for developing age-group swimmers—a book that is self-consistent, as simple as possible but no simpler, based on sound principles, and tested by experience. This book offers conclusions reached after much observation of my own and others' swimmers, many discussions with successful age-group and senior coaches across the United States, much reading and study, and years of experimentation in attempting to construct the perfect age-group developmental program. Realizing that what works with one situation or swimmer might not with another, I hope to be generous with suggestions and guidelines but modest with inflexible rules.

Part I explores recognizing and developing swimming talent. The concept of talent is usually misunderstood and equated with early success. I assume a more comprehensive idea of talent with many components; for instance, a swimmer can have a talent for technique, for speed or endurance, or for staying calm in stressful situations. All of these and more are necessary for high performance, all are separable, and all can to an extent be taught by the coach and learned by the swimmer. Skillful coaches have their eyes open all the time to discover what their kids do well and to build on those little victories. By creating good programs, coaches can create talent or at least uncover talent that had previously lain hidden.

We aim to develop talent over the course of a swimmer's career. Long-term development is the overarching strategy, and the coach must plan for years down the road. The ultimate goal is not speed right now but slow and patient building of the skills and capacities necessary for swimmers to be great when their bodies are mature. In this building process we take advantage of critical biological periods when the athlete's body is primed to make large gains relatively easily. We try to give kids what they need when they need it—mentally, technically, and physiologically.

Psychology is the underpinning of this developmental program. *Arete* is an ancient Greek word for all-encompassing excellence. This is what we are aiming to instill in our athletes. What is going on inside the heads of your swimmers determines what their bodies will do. Coaches can create a culture of excellence by setting properly high expectations and by ensuring that everything agrees with this message of excellence. Continual goal setting produces continual improvement. One of the secrets of great teams is that excellence, improvement, and mastery of skills are a lot more fun than mindless mediocrity, even for a 10-year-old.

Part II covers assessment and refinement of stroke technique. For most swimmers, the great obstacle to high performance is efficiency (technique) in the water. Though improving technique should be a main focus for swimmers at any step in the progression, the 10-and-under years are dominated by stroke technique work. For technique work to be effective, coaches must know what to teach. They must have models for each of the four competitive strokes while allowing for differences in how swimmers are built and for different combinations of strengths and weaknesses. Next, since it is one thing to know what a stroke should look like and quite another to get kids to look that way, the book examines how to teach technique so that the lessons stick from one day to the next and from practice to meet. Finally, the four strokes and the starts and turns are broken into fundamentals that can be taught to swimmers of any age.

Part III examines training and preparing swimmers to be their best. Training builds the physiological engine to power high performance. Age-group training emphasizes distance-base and individual medley training. Young children are facile at learning stroke skills, and their bodies are aerobic sponges, able to make huge gains with the right sort of training sets. The gains made in these developmental years will serve as the foundation for their senior swimming to come. Dryland training supplements water training to build basic strength, crucial flexibilities, and general athleticism. With the gradual demise of physical education in schools, more and more dryland training may be needed to make up for physical deficits in swimmers.

The basic goal of training is continual improvement. This is a tremendous challenge for both coach and swimmer. To get the most benefit from everything we do, we plan, monitor, and evaluate daily practices as well as the order and flow of practices throughout a week or season. We discuss how coaches steer a course and how they can keep their hands on the tiller so that their swimmers head in the right direction.

Supportive parents make the challenge of ensuring swimmers' continual development much easier. We discuss how to get the right families into the program and how to educate and communicate so that they stay supportive and remain in the program.

Part IV explores how to develop the competitive edge. It is frustrating for swimmers, coaches, and parents if athletes work hard and make progress in training, then get to a meet and fall flat. Unfortunately, most swimmers race inconsistently. Adopting proper racing attitudes can help swimmers overcome many of the challenges to consistent excellence. Further, physical and mental preparation for competitions take some of the chance out of racing and allow swimmers to use all they have. Finally, we discuss how coaches can systematize their meet scheduling and event choices to help swimmers improve more consistently.

I have been blessed in being able to coach for a living, which means that I get to work with a group of kids and watch them grow up before my eyes (and steer them in productive directions). Young swimmers drink in the lessons you try to teach them, just as their bodies are drinking in the training you give them, and the tremendous effect coaches can have on their charges is obvious from one season to the next. The time on the pool deck is easily the best part of the day. It is certainly satisfying to see a swimmer that you coached from the cradle make it to the national level. But it is just as satisfying to see the day-to-day improvement and growth in a group of kids and to imagine the mighty oaks that these little acorns can become.

PART I

Recognizing and Developing Talent

CHAPTER 1

Recognizing Swimming Talent

In thinking about talent, the starting point for just about every club coach is not a scientifically chosen group of seven-year-old children with exceptional motor skills and drive to excel but a disparate group with kids of varying sizes, ages, skill levels, fitness levels, and levels of interest and motivation. Some come to practice every day and are focused on swimming; others attend only a couple of times a week and participate in several different activities. Some do things right all the time; others only when the coach is standing over them nagging. Some are beautiful and easy in the water; others look like they are having convulsions. Some will gladly work themselves to exhaustion; others rarely get their heart rates north of 70 beats per minute. The daily process of talent development isn't a pretty, perfect laboratory world but rather a messy, imperfect world that coaches must make the best of.

My perspective as a coach conditions my thoughts on talent and talent development. Every day I am confronted with a group of kids and expected to do something with them. In order for me to do my job well, I must be attuned to as many kinds of talent in as many kids as I possibly can. Although I might wish every swimmer who walks on my pool deck to be genetically gifted and to have parents who are tall, coordinated, elite athletes, I have no control over what they come in with. My emphasis is on the factors that can change, not on those that cannot; I aim to improve my swimmers' fitness, technique, and competitive mentality. I attempt to maximize my swimmers' performance by constructing a program that develops what they have and brings out their potential.

A coach must assume that there are talents in the pool and that his job is to find and develop them. He must keep his eyes open for talent to show up in unlikely places. A seemingly unpromising swimmer may suddenly stretch out her stroke and achieve a long and beautiful body line, a nondescript racer may finally put his head down for the last 20 meters to win a relay, or a previously unmotivated swimmer may come alive and race her guts out in a 30-minute straight swim. These are the little sparkles of diamond amid the dirt and rocks, the glimpses of perfection that reveal something promising to build upon.

Having a broad view of talent helps more than just the coach. Pointing out the little daily excellences builds swimmers' confidence, feelings of competency, and motivation. Children like to do things they are good at and things they are able to improve upon, but they often aren't sure of their excellence until a coach tells them. When coaches define *success* correctly—not as winning but as getting better—every child can be on a long road to developing his talents.

Problems With Talent Discussions

Common discussions of talent are often dissatisfying. When quizzed about talent, many coaches respond that a talented swimmer is one who has good feel for the water, looks easy in it, is quick to learn new skills, and has good distance per stroke (meaning that when she pulls, her body moves forward a long way). Swimmers with this feel are rare and can be spotted instantly; their talent is on the surface. In this view, talent is confined to a physical gift, and more specifically, a neurological one.

Being easy and efficient in the water is important. Most coaches spend a lot of practice time trying to make their swimmers look beautiful, and I admit to saying a little prayer of thanksgiving when a new swimmer has great feel from the start. But we're not aiming at swimmers who are beautiful but slow, or who are beautiful but not interested in coming to practice and working hard. Beauty is necessary but not sufficient.

Other popular views of talent seem at best meaningless and at worst offensive. Talent is often equated with being fast. But simply defining fast people as *talented* begs the question of what talent really is. Worse, by calling any great performance the simple result of talent, we don't even try to understand how athletes become great. Instead, we just assume that fast now means fast forever, that slow now means slow forever, and that a swimmer has no hope without the right genes. Worst of all, talent is often used to rob great athletes of the credit for their accomplishments and the choices that created those accomplishments, including years of hard work, long and grueling practices, gradual refinement of technique, improvement of physical capacities, and excelling under enormous pressure. If great athletes are simply given their gifts, then they are not responsible for their successes, and their excellences are not true benchmarks by which the rest of us can evaluate ourselves.

> By calling any great performance the simple result of talent, we don't even try to understand how athletes become great.

Talent is often spoken of as a single quality that a person either has or doesn't have and that determines who will be successful and who will not. This distinction is often made when children are still young, and it is usually made on the basis of current performance levels. A fast 10-year-old is seen as talented and doted upon, while a slow 10-year-old is seen as untalented and not encouraged. This is highly problematic. The swimming world is littered with kids who were superstars when they were 10 or 12 but left the sport by 14 or 16. Conversely, there are many stories of kids who were plodders when young but who persevered and kept improving until they ended up at nationals.

Quite often, the fastest young kids are those who are early developers biologically. They are bigger and stronger than the rest of the kids their age, and they succeed because of that initial but temporary physical advantage. When their advantage disappears, usually between the ages of 14 and 16 as the late bloomers catch up, success is much harder attained, and they often stop enjoying the sport they no longer dominate. A swimming career is a marathon, not a sprint, and staying power is rewarded over a quick start. But if those who were slower off the mark leave the sport because they were considered hopeless, they aren't around to finish strong.

> A swimming career is a marathon, not a sprint, and staying power is rewarded over a quick start.

Talent predictions are usually wrong. Anyone who has paid attention to the annual drafts for professional sport leagues knows how unscientific and uncertain the process of trying to predict success is. This is the case even when billions of dollars hang in the balance, when scouts and general managers have mounds of data and videotape for each prospect, and when the athletes being evaluated are much older and closer to the next level than those we are discussing. How much more uncertainty is there when the athletes in question are 10 years old? We would be more often wrong than not, to the detriment of those kids selected for future greatness who do not pan out and of those rejected as having no potential. Because we cannot see into the future, we had better give the kids we work with the benefit of the doubt, and we had better use a big dragnet when trawling for talent.

A New Vision of Talent

In this book, we use the word *talent* broadly, comprehensively, pragmatically, concretely, and usually in the plural: talents. Certain skills, qualities, behaviors, habits, abilities, and attitudes that lead to success in swimming are talents. No one talent will make a swimmer a champion; conversely, there is no one talent whose relative lack will prevent a swimmer from becoming a champion. Just as no swimmer has every talent, no swimmer has none of them. Coaches can teach these talents, or at least most of them, and swimmers can develop them. These talents fall into three groups: psychological qualities or skills, physical qualities or capacities, and anatomical characteristics.

Psychological Qualities

Most people don't think of psychological qualities or skills as talents, especially not in an obviously physical sport such as swimming. Swimming is about getting from here to there faster than anyone else. However, the mind plays a great part in deciding how fast an athlete will swim. For instance, without toughness an athlete backs off when he starts to hurt or when put under pressure and thus chooses not to use his more physical capacities. Without persistence, an athlete will give up when he isn't instantly successful and again will not put in the time to develop his physical skills. These psychological skills

> You've got to think like a champion before you can swim like one.

provide the foundation for long-term development of the more physical talents, and they have as great an effect on an athlete's performance as aerobic capacity, stroke efficiency, or height. A mantra in our program is, "You've got to think like a champion before you can swim like one."

- **Drive to succeed.** Driven kids have a fire in the belly to be great. There is a close connection here with self-confidence—they think they *can* be great, and they *want* to be. They set high standards for themselves.

- **Competitiveness.** Competitive kids want to race and win at whatever they're doing, be it eating dinner, raking leaves, or swimming a set of 200 individual medleys (IMs). They hate to lose, and they will often ignore important considerations such as wise pacing or proper technique. These swimmers show up on race day; they are racers.

- **Focus.** Focused kids have a laser-beam attention to what they are doing, and they are not easily distracted. Most kids are more limited by their inability to pay attention than they are by physical deficiencies.

- **Self-confidence.** Confident swimmers expect to succeed. They have a positive attitude about their abilities, and they relish challenges where the results are in doubt because they enjoy proving themselves.

- **Self-reliance.** Self-reliant swimmers don't need their parents or coaches to walk them to the blocks. They pack their own swim bags. They figure out when they need to warm up for their races. They don't wait for things to be done for them; they take responsibility for their own success.

- **Poise.** Swimmers with poise remain unruffled under championship pressure, and the more important the meet, the faster they swim. They have access to all their physical capacities when it matters most; the mind does not get in the body's way. Poised swimmers can read themselves correctly, putting themselves in the right frame of mind to succeed.

- **Toughness and persistence.** Tough and persistent kids will not back off when under pressure or hurt, and they are willing to repeat a task after failing until it is mastered or until a goal is achieved. Psychological limits are brought closer to physiological limits; in most kids, these are far apart.

- **Work ethic.** Swimmers with a good work ethic love to work hard. They would rather die than miss a practice. Consistent hard work often reveals other kinds of talent.

- **Coachability.** Coachable swimmers trust the coach; they will make the changes a coach asks them to make. This requires an honest look at strengths and weaknesses and a willingness to fix problem areas. There is nothing more frustrating for a coach than working with swimmers who make the same mistakes at 16 that they made at 12. The underlying problem is more radical than just having bad turns or choppy strokes.

- **Courage.** Though obviously related to self-confidence, poise, and other psychological talents, courage deserves its own place at the table. A courageous swimmer can overcome the fear of pain, failure, and success.

These psychological skills can be practiced and improved, often concurrently with the physical improvements. By creating conditions that require certain psychological skills, coaches can give swimmers the opportunity to practice them. Toughness, for example, can be instilled by tiring out the swimmers and then ensuring that they finish strong on every set, no matter what. Persistent swimmers are created by not letting them quit on a skill that they are having difficulty mastering and by emphasizing the importance of doing the skill until it is perfected. By continually talking about these talents, highlighting swimmers who exhibit them, and linking mental attributes with swimming performance, coaches show athletes the importance of championship thinking.

Physical Qualities

This group of talents accounts for the swimmer's physiological engine, its efficiency, and its intelligent use. These qualities are what most people think of when they hear the term *swimming talent*.

- **Feel for the water.** This is kinesthetic sensitivity, in particular on the propelling surfaces of the hands, arms, and feet. Good feel produces long, smooth, efficient strokes. Swimmers with feel can do a new skill or change an old one on the first or second try, and they can keep doing it correctly. They intuitively understand how their bodies work in the water, and they can feel the difference between what works and what doesn't. At base, this is neuromuscular coordination and control.

- **Recoverability.** Swimmers who can recover quickly from one practice to another can work hard more consistently than the rest, and as a result, they get more benefits from training. A good aerobic base helps here.

- **Endurance.** Age-group swimming training is founded on endurance. Being able to maintain good speeds for long periods of time is crucial. Long-course swimming relies on endurance more than short course, and longer races rely on it more than short ones.

- **Speed.** We want to swim fast, we want to train fast, and we want to race fast. *Fast*, of course, is relative: Different races and strokes demand different amounts of endurance and speed, but all swimming speed depends on power and coordination more than on simple brute strength.

- **Pacing.** We want swimmers with a precise sense of pace who can allocate their resources for a race. This is the difference between the kids who fry and die, meaning those who go out fast and fade badly, and the Sammy save-ups, or those who have too much energy left at the end. This talent is allied with the ancient moral virtue of prudence: knowing how best to reach the goal. It requires self-control, which means that both physiology and psychology are important.

- **Health.** Swimmers who are sick or injured all the time cannot train consistently and have trouble improving.

Anatomical Characteristics

Certain sports give advantages to certain body types. An elite basketball center is not going to be an elite gymnast, and a wrestler is not built to be a diver. As swimmers move from one level to the next, the body types approach an ideal for the sport, and as a result, there is less variety at the Olympics than at a local dual meet. That said, the ideal swimming body changes slightly according to who is dominating the swimming world at the time. Before Michael Phelps came along, short legs were not seen as a virtue, but after his success, a hundred arguments arose for why short legs and a long torso were ideal.

- **Swimmer's body.** A coach's wish list would include swimmers who are lean, strong, and tall—long arms, long torsos, big hands and feet, wide shoulders, and slender hips are ideal. This talent encompasses the size of the body and its parts as well as their proportions: the swimmer's conformation. This does not mean that a swimmer not born to this ideal cannot be successful, and distance legend Janet Evans correctly stated, "I can swim fast even if I am little." But it is nonetheless true that having the ideal body for swimming helps. This talent is complicated with age-group swimmers since their bodies and proportions are changing as they go through puberty.

- **Flexibilities.** Flexible swimmers have optimal ranges of motions in the key swimming joints, especially the shoulders, back, ankles, knees, and hips. Often children are not uniformly flexible or inflexible; there can be big differences from one joint to another. Also, ranges of motion change as children grow because bones, muscles, ligaments, and cartilage do not grow in tandem and at the same rates.

Talent Profile

The preceding lists are not meant to be exhaustive. Further, many of these talents share components, complement one another, and blend on their fringes. On the whole, however, the proffered list is simple and can serve as a useful guideline for evaluating young athletes. A simple bar graph can be used to view a swimmer's talents at a glance. The various talents are listed down the side, and they are scored horizontally from 1 to 10. A score of 1 means that the swimmer at this moment has almost none of this particular talent, while a 10 means that the swimmer has ample talent. Most swimmers do not score 10s because almost everyone has room to improve.

The talent profiles shown in figure 1.1 highlight the fact that nobody has the complete package. Both of these swimmers are nationally ranked 11- to 12-year-olds that are strong at all four strokes. Swimmer A shows exceptional drive, competitiveness, endurance, and pacing but has relatively poor feel for the water, coachability, and speed. Swimmer B scores well in feel for the water, flexibilities, and coachability. Even excellent athletes have weaknesses, but weaknesses in one area can be mitigated by strengths in others. The higher on the ladder of performance

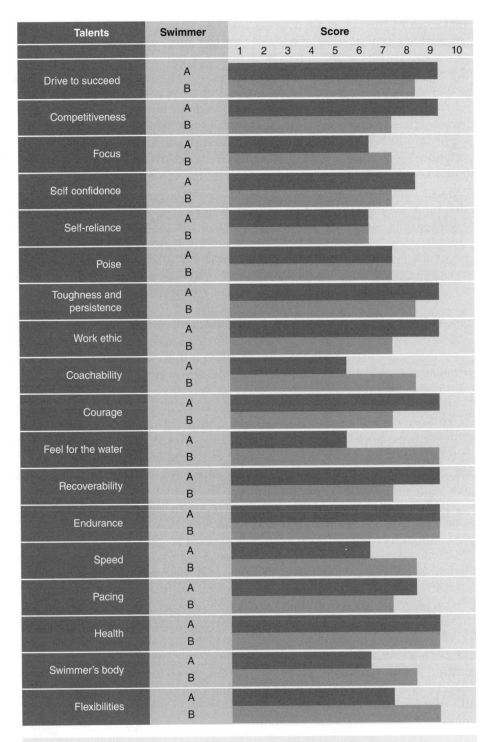

FIGURE 1.1   Talent profile for two nationally ranked age-group swimmers.

swimmers climb, the fewer weaknesses they can afford. Lower on the ladder (for instance, at the local or state level) or at younger ages, swimmers can hide many weaknesses if they have one or two skills that are comparably outstanding, if they work hard, or if they are big and strong.

In attempting to comprehend a swimmer with a bar graph, we are not trying to be scientifically exact but to gain a picture of relative strengths and weaknesses. No two coaches would score a single swimmer identically; one coach's score of 10 might be another's 8. Scoring partially depends on a coach's experience and expectations. Scores are arbitrary to some extent, but so long as they are consistent, that is acceptable. Again, you are looking for a profile that helps you see a swimmer's talents at a glance.

Also remember that no two swimmers are identical, not even Olympic gold medalists. There are many paths to the top of the podium, even in the same event. For several years Michael Phelps and Ian Crocker dominated the 100-meter butterfly, but they were very different swimmers. Physiologically, Crocker had tremendous speed that Phelps lacked, while Phelps had better endurance for the close of races. Psychologically, Phelps was hypercompetitive and relish the pressure and the limelight of being at the top more than Crocker. Anatomically, they were built differently, though both were tall and lean. Technically, Crocker's stroke was better suited to the sprint fly, Phelps' to the 200-meter event.

> There are many paths to the top of the podium, even in the same event.

Though all the talents are desirable and necessary, they are not always complementary. For example, swimmers with extraordinary range of motion in their shoulders can be more susceptible to shoulder injuries. A common situation with young boys is that they can be hypercompetitive swimmers who want to win every repeat and refuse to slow down and work on improving stroke technique because going slower would mean losing, and losing is unacceptable. Convincing them that one step backward at this moment will result in several steps forward later if they become more efficient is a hard sell, and a coach must be careful not to coach one virtue (competitiveness) out of a swimmer in order to get another one (beauty).

Children and adolescents are notoriously inconsistent. They will not consistently demonstrate the talents they seem to have, and they may not be interested in consistently developing their strengths or improving their weaknesses. Kids have their own priorities and make their own distinctions, and these are often hidden from parents and coaches. A swimmer who shows great poise at a big meet one weekend will have a meltdown a month later for no apparent reason. A swimmer who races her guts out in one race will seemingly not even try in another. This is frustrating for the coach, the parent, and often the swimmer as well. Plumbing the depths of these inconsistencies and trying to discover the rationale behind them—in other words, trying to find the psychological key to the swimmer—is an important part of the art of coaching.

Talent and Plasticity

The previous list of talents and the talent profile derived from it highlight the crucial idea that talent is not a single all-determining quality but rather several discrete qualities, each of which contributes to success. However, a bar graph can be misleading because it shows a snapshot of talents at a particular time and masks the importance of change, improvement, and development of talent. Talents are plastic, or capable of change, though to varying extents.

At one end of the spectrum are talents such as height, arm length, and hand size. These characteristics are set by our genes, and we cannot do much to change or improve them. Somewhat more plastic, speed is still difficult to improve; some kids are naturally fast, and others are not. This is primarily a function of the proportion of fast-twitch to slow-twitch muscle fibers in key muscle groups. In swimming, speed is probably also neurological; a complicated coordination of all the body parts is necessary. At the other end of the spectrum, endurance is capable of much improvement. Here again the proportion of fast- to slow-twitch muscle fibers plays an important role, but aerobic training can turn a weak swimmer into a strong one in a season or two. In a few years it can take a hard-working swimmer to nationals in the distance events.

More difficult to locate on the spectrum are the psychological talents. A swimmer can become more competitive or self-confident when placed in the right environment, but temperament and personality matter, too. One child is adventurous, afraid of nothing and looking for challenges; another is timid, sticking to routine and only trying things she knows she will succeed at. These differences affect a child's swimming in a thousand ways every day. Some swimmers will have a psychological profile that is naturally advantageous to swimming success, and others will not.

Some talents are more plastic at certain stages of a child's biological development. In brief, certain physical capacities are capable of large improvements when bodies are placed under the right kinds and loads of stresses at the right time in their development. For example, young swimmers aged 7 to 10 can make huge improvements in their technique, improvements that are much harder to come by if a child starts swimming as a teenager. Girls aged 11 to 13 and boys aged 12 to 15 can improve their aerobic capacities dramatically with the right kind of training. This aerobic foundation is crucial for their success as seniors; without it, swimmers place a lower ceiling on their future performance levels. Thus, what swimmers do in a training program is important. The right kinds of work in the right amounts, and at the right times, can slingshot their development.

Some talents are more plastic for some children than for others. The same training will result in huge gains for some swimmers and small gains for others. This can result from swimmers being at different places in their biological development, using varying levels of effort or attention, and having different temperaments or personalities. Frequently a genetic basis will account for these differences.

Some talents come naturally to some children. One swimmer dives into the pool for the first time and looks long, beautiful, and easy; another looks short, choppy, ugly, and inefficient even after years of technique work. One swimmer will be able to swim fast seemingly forever; another will be exhausted after a 50 or 100. Some children have a facility for a talent; others have to work a lot harder to reach the same levels, if they ever do. Anyone who has ever spent hours trying to solve math problems that the class genius figured out in seconds understands this situation. It is not fair—but it is life, and it is swimming.

Talent and Development

When you watch a 10-year-old swim, it's appropriate to predict where you think she can be at 16 or 18. If a young swimmer is fast, the immediate question is why. What makes her better than the others right now? What do you see now that can develop into something special later? Will these advantages last? Do these advantages mask other weaknesses that will slow her progression later? Are you being careful to help her develop the tools for national success later on, or are you content with her local success right now?

When age-groupers swim, do not be overly concerned with their current performance levels, whether high or low. Instead, focus on *talents over time*, aiming at sustained improvement. Plot your swimmers' improvement curves and note the slopes of those curves. Are they getting better and faster from meet to meet? What aspects of their races are improving to cause the time drops? Do they make reasonably sized jumps, or do they only improve .01 second in occasional increments? Are they improving across the board in all strokes and distances, or is their improvement scattered? Where were they a year ago, and where will they be a year from now?

The reason for focusing on the long term is that the present does not tell us much. You cannot tell what is going to happen to a young swimmer by seeing where she is at age 10, no matter how fast she may be. A 10-year-old phenom may be fast relative to his age group, but compared with competent senior swimmers, he probably is not fast. Biological and psychological maturity are necessary for international-level performance. Having a talent gives an athlete an obvious advantage, but the crucial question is, what will he do with that advantage? Even a child with a genetic predisposition to a phenomenal aerobic capacity, for example, will not become a great distance swimmer without consistent, long-term aerobic training. A knack is nothing without building the skills that you have a knack for. It takes time for a good young swimmer to become a good senior swimmer, for that early glimpse of talent to be realized in high performance. A swimmer needs the various talents and a long time to develop them fully. The idea of training is not to just take what we are given but to develop what we are given and get much better.

> The idea of training is not to just take what we are given but to develop what we are given and get much better.

Talent and Environment

Talents are for naught if they are not discovered and then placed in a nurturing environment to develop over the long term. A child does not develop the various swimming talents in a vacuum. In this respect, what happens at home is just as important as what happens at the pool. Parents, coaches, and swimming programs are all crucial to developing a swimmer's talents, and all three must dovetail.

Parents Matter

Parents have an enormous influence on their children's swimming. By setting high standards at home, expecting hard work and excellence, encouraging persistence, teaching accountability, and being supportive through the tough times and down to earth during the heady days, parents go a long way toward determining the basic mindset of their children.

Further, the parents must value swimming. They must be willing to make family decisions for the sake of the development of a child's talents. This may require rescheduling family vacations after championship meets, constructing the family's schedule around daily practice, or spending weekends at long meets and waiting hours for a few minutes of racing. With regard to the particular program their children represent, parents must trust the coaches and value the long process of developing talents. It doesn't matter how good the coach and the program are if the parents are continually undercutting or second-guessing them.

Dedicated parents who make choices to support their children, including spending hours at meets waiting for races, are essential to young swimmers' success.

Coaches Matter

Coaches vary enormously in their abilities to identify, nurture, and develop talents. Swimmers need a coach who can spot and develop talents and who has a vision of where swimmers can go and how to get them there. Before swimmers have expectations of excellence and goals of national-level performance, the coach must have them. As Proverbs says, "Where there is no vision, the people perish."

Programs Matter

Programs vary enormously in their cultures and expectations. There are few programs in each major swimming country that produce national- or international-level swimmers; these programs are obviously doing something better than their competitors. In these top programs, the various levels are designed to develop the requisite talents, and swimmers are taught to expect to succeed at national levels. There is a culture of excellence and high performance.

These programs are goal oriented to the point of obsession. Swimmers are challenged every moment to reach higher than they ever have before. This is especially important for the fast kids, who are likely to get bored with practices, sets, intervals, goals, and expectations that are geared toward the mean. Stuffing the fastest kid in a lane with 10 slower swimmers and treating everyone the same is not the way to get a good swimmer enthusiastic about becoming great. More advanced swimmers take more time, more attention, and more effort to develop, not less. Contrary to popular belief, you cannot just assume that talent will take care of itself.

> You cannot just assume that talent will take care of itself.

Characteristics of Top Programs

- Top training programs are systematic and developmental, working with a swimmer's biology and exploiting the critical periods for developing physical capacities.

- Top programs take psychology seriously. From a swimmer's first day in the program, they aim to build the mental or psychological talents. They teach their swimmers to think like champions, to set goals continually, and to expect a lot from themselves.

- In top programs, the focus on mental training helps create focus, drive, and self-confidence. These qualities underlie the technical and physical gains achieved through training. Thinking right leads to training right.

- Top programs see the 10-and-under years as the optimal time to focus on technique. Though swimmers are becoming faster and more aerobically fit and are laying the foundation of a training base, the overriding aim of training is to make the swimmers easy, efficient, beautiful, and adaptable in the water in all four strokes.

- Top programs view the ages of 11 to 14 as the aerobic years. Swimmers continue to improve technique, but the primary goal of these years is to construct the physiological foundation for later high-intensity training and high performance. They build the largest engine they can.

A program that gives its swimmers a variety of training gives a variety of talents an opportunity to show themselves and to be spotted by a sharp-sighted coach. Practices that focus on only one kind of training allow kids with a talent for that kind of training to shine and hence be noticed for their excellence and motivated to work hard and swim faster. Training all four strokes is important for the same reason: A swimmer with a strong breaststroke who trains nothing but freestyle will be less enthusiastic about working hard and less confident in his swimming abilities. Everyone needs a chance to shine.

CHAPTER 2

Developing Swimmers for the Long Haul

In this chapter, we survey the whole of a swimmer's age-group career. If we aim to give young swimmers the tools for senior success, we must know what those tools are. In discussing the talent profile in chapter 1, we outlined the talents necessary for high-level success. Knowing the end—the elite athlete, his characteristics, and his capacities—we reverse engineer. Beginning with the youngest swimmers, we slowly develop each of the desired talents season by season, taking into account that certain talents are more efficiently developed at particular ages or stages of development. The process takes a long time and requires a long-term view on the part of the coach as well as much patience from coaches and parents.

This point highlights the ambivalent position of age-group swimming and coaching. It is a means to an end (high-level senior swimming) as well as an end in itself (current performance levels). Wise coaches make decisions according to what they want to see in the future, but for the swimmers, their parents, and the team, right now counts, too. Swimmers must be successful enough right now to enjoy it and to stick with it so that they can reap the benefits of the coach's long-term planning. This is sometimes a difficult balance to achieve.

We must also remember that we are dealing with growing children. In particular, puberty and its biological and psychological changes, some advantageous to performance and some not, complicate the training process. The child you see before you today may be very different from the same child six months ago. Thus, biology must be taken into account when coaching children, in particular from ages 11 to 14. An optimal program for age-groupers is formulated for children and targets their needs—it is not just a watered-down version of a senior program.

A number of significant differences exist between an age-group program and a senior program. Age-groupers tend to do a lot more than just swim. Most are involved in multiple sports or activities, and all of these contribute to the swimmer's athletic package. Dryland programs tend to be less strength focused and more athletically focused. The water training is more general; usually all the swimmers in a training group will be doing the same thing every day without being divided into specialized subgroups (the breaststrokers here, the sprint freestylers there, the distance kids over there, and so on). Swimmers tend to train and race all strokes and all distances instead of focusing on what they do best. Age-group programs are more skill oriented, with a much higher proportion of technically focused work and with more feedback from the coaches. Age-group programs tend to be much more focused on aerobic training and individual medley, with much less of the high-stress sprinting seen in many senior programs.

Several influential research-based systems or plans of long-term athlete development are available. Tudor Bompa and Josef Drabik have written detailed books on general training and maturation. For swimming in particular, Orjan Madsen has been the dean of the subject since the early 1980s. In addition, Andrei Vorontsov, Istvan Balyi, and Brent Rushall have written numerous important articles on development. Institutionally, USA Swimming, Swimming Australia, British Swimming, and Swimming Canada have all published developmental progressions borrowing heavily from the previously mentioned authors, especially Balyi and Vorontsov.

Each plan has its own names for the stages or phases, as well as slightly different age ranges for the critical periods, but there are many similarities. All have the basic aim of determining exactly what kind, amount, and intensity of training to give children and adolescent athletes at each stage of their development in order to keep them in the sport, keep them improving, and maximize their performance levels when they are fully mature and their bodies are ready for high performance. In designing programs for my teams or training groups, I have freely borrowed from all of these sources, tweaking what I read according to what worked and what didn't with my swimmers.

Elite Training Triad

A successful long-term development program has three parts: the mental, the technical, and the physical. These three parts interact continually. Each of these parts of the training triad will be explained in much greater detail in later chapters. We discuss mental training in the following chapter, technique in the whole of part II (chapters 4 through 8), and training in chapters 9 and 10.

Mental

The mental training program aims to create a team culture based on a philosophy of *arete*, an ancient Greek term referring to all-encompassing excellence. It teaches swimmers to think like champions on the understanding that kids who think like champions act—and swim—like them. It teaches that fun results from improvement and that swimmers should aim to improve in as many ways as possible with each practice. We teach these lessons

> Kids who think like champions act—and swim—like them.

through almost daily meetings to discuss the way of a champion and even more through the understood expectations about our methods in our organization. In addition to the motivational aspects of this mental training, we also are concerned with the cognitive, namely the whys of the sport: getting the swimmers to understand why we teach the strokes the way we do, why we do the kinds of training sets we do, why we train all four strokes, and so on. We want swimmers to be students of the sport.

Technical

Work on technique all the time, even in main sets that have a physiological focus. Swimmers should never mindlessly swim up and down the pool. We use a stroke catechism that breaks down each stroke into its fundamentals, and we refer to these stroke points continually. Efficiency in the water matters. Beauty matters. Ugly strokes replete with thrashing and splashing signify that a swimmer is expending too much effort for the results she is getting.

Physical

The program in the water emphasizes building an aerobic base through training all four strokes and individual medley. Usually each day's practice has one major focus and one major stroke, and you want to cycle through the strokes daily. For out-of-the-water training, work on general athleticism (coordination, agility, quickness, core strength, flexibility in key joints) and play. Precisely what you do depends on the time of the year (and whether you can be outside), the part of the season, and the ages and developmental levels of the swimmers.

Development and Critical Training Periods

As swimmers age and develop, their training needs to change dramatically. What is proper training for a 10-year-old is not appropriate for a 14-year-old or a high school senior, and the level of commitment expected of an older athlete training for senior nationals cannot be expected of a novice learning the rudiments of freestyle. The team as a whole is split into distinct training groups to meet swimmers' changing needs. Although all of these training groups develop the training triad, they use different types of training, volumes and intensities of training, speeds of training, and levels of commitment to swimming, all of which are developmentally determined. Generally, as swimmers age and develop, the demands, skill levels, and performance levels rise gradually.

The groups also take advantage of physical and mental critical periods as children grow. These are times when children can make the greatest gains in a particular ability with well-directed training focused on that ability. In the literature of developmental biology, these critical periods are often assumed, but they have not been proven to exist, which is unsurprising given the difficulties involved with organizing long-term scientific experiments with children. However, most of the top age-group coaches, who daily run their own informal scientific experiments with training and its effects on children of varying ages, agree that these critical periods exist and that they are fundamental to formulating the parts and priorities of a long-term training progression.

These sensitive periods are general guidelines, not ironclad rules. Coaches are working with groups of children, usually girls and boys combined, and within a group each individual is on his own maturational timetable. Theories positing precise critical periods for so-called normal children will be in error for most of the group. Further, the critical periods often differ for boys and girls, though they overlap significantly. Because we are dealing with life, not a laboratory experiment, the training program aims at the sensitive periods in a general sense. For instance, the 10-and-under years are critical for developing good technique, coordination and rhythm, and the beginning of an aerobic base. The years from 11 to 14 are valuable for refining neuromuscular control, but they are most important for increasing the athlete's aerobic capacities. The growth in heart and lung size and function, or cardiorespiratory capacity, that can occur with the right kind, intensity, and consistency of training is staggering.

Beyond physiology, these keystone years in a swimmer's development help form her competitive psychology, which is highly transferable to other areas of life. In these years we are teaching them to be swimmers, to think like champions, to understand hard work and commitment, to think correctly about failure and success, to expect a lot from themselves and to set high standards, to build confidence in their abilities, to enjoy their strength and toughness, and so on. These psychological qualities affect everything a swimmer does, both in and out of the pool, and they are much easier to instill at the ages of 10 or 12 than they are at 15 or 16. Bad psychological habits are as hard to change as bad technical habits.

> Age-group swimmers are building the training foundation daily for their performances as seniors in high school or as collegians.

The gist of the discussion so far is clear: What kids do and how they do it when they are young matters a lot. It raises or lowers their ceiling for performance when they are seniors. The skills you see at 17 were slowly created from ages 8 to 14. Age-group swimmers are building the training foundation daily for their performances as seniors in high school or as collegians. It is a coach's job to give kids the foundation they need, even if they don't always want it and would rather goof around so that later on they can reach as far as their dreams. Someone has to be planning ahead, and that someone is rarely the swimmer.

Program Goals for Each Age Range

Each step in the developmental process is important. Swimmers cannot go back and make up missed steps, so they need to do things correctly from the beginning. The following section summarizes the most important goals for swimmers at each age range. Additionally, table 2.1 provides an overview of the suggested training progression. Specifics about daily training and methods of technique work are discussed in later chapters.

TABLE 2.1

Suggested Age-Group Training Progression

Age (and level) of swimmer	Sessions per wk	Time in water per session	Time for dryland work	Average volume per session	Break between seasons
8	2-3	45-60 min	15 min	N/A	2 wk spring, 2 wk fall
9-10	3-4	75 min	15-30 min	N/A	2 wk spring, 2 wk fall
10 (advanced)	4-5	90 min	30 min	5,000 m	2 wk spring, 2 wk fall
11-12 (slower track)	5-6	90 min	30 min	5,000 m	2 wk spring, 2 wk fall
11-12 (advanced)	5-6	105 min	30 min	6,000 m	1 wk spring, 2 wk fall
13-14 (slower track)	5-6	105 min	30 min	6,000 m	1 wk spring, 2 wk fall
13-14 (advanced)	6-8	120 min	30 min	7,000-8,000 m	1 wk spring, 1-2 wk fall

8-Year-Olds and Under

These are the youngest novice swimmers on the team, most of them fresh out of lessons, and they are initially only able to swim a little backstroke and freestyle. Their attention spans are brief, their energy levels are high, and their control over their bodies in the water is low. But their daily improvement is noticeable; to a good coach, they are as moldable as soft clay to a potter.

- **Teach love of swimming.** Teach them that racing is fun, win or lose; that working hard and getting better is gratifying; that learning and refining skills is enjoyable; and that doing things well is great. These youngest swimmers should be excited about coming to practice, bugging their parents to let them come more.

- **Teach all four strokes, starts, and turns.** Most comments from coaches at meets and practices should concern technique, not winning or times. We want these swimmers to gain control over their bodies in the water and to learn and be comfortable with many movements, rhythms, and speeds. They should learn the rules of the four competitive strokes and be able to swim and race legally.

- **Help them become swimmers.** Kids at this age need to learn the basics of swimming, including how to use a pace clock, how to start on time, how to get their times on repeats (preferably all repeats), how to do elementary sets, and how to behave at swimming meets. If novices can master these behaviors, it saves a lot of time for the coaches at more advanced levels of the program, and they will not need to go back to the first step in the progression.

9- and 10-Year-Olds

Most swimmers in this group began in the novice program, so they have a background in technique; they know how to do the four strokes legally; they know how to read the clock (in theory), and so on. They are still high energy and low focus, but they have more control over their aquatic selves compared with the younger swimmers. At this age, girls tend to learn technique quicker and focus better than the boys.

- **Keep them happy.** Be sure they are getting better and more skilled, and make sure they know it. As with younger swimmers, you want them excited about coming to practice and nagging their parents to let them come more.

- **Teach team culture.** "How we do things here" is an important statement because it includes the idea of *arete*, the love of competition, the goal of continual improvement, the setting of high expectations, the value of hard and consistent work, the love of challenges, the focus on performance, the continual goal setting, and the importance of doing things well. These attitudes underlie all the physical training.

- **Emphasize skill development as the primary focus of training.** These years are a sensitive time for many of the abilities underlying good stroke technique, including agility, balance, coordination, flexibility, and rhythm. The training program should emphasize working on and mastering all four strokes with many stroke drills and much variety to maximize the size of the swimmer's motor-pattern arsenal. Swimmers should learn and practice a variety of rhythms and timing, such as six- and two-beat-kick freestyles, straight-arm and high-elbow recoveries on freestyle, catch-up and oppositional timing on freestyle, various breathing patterns, and using pull-buoys with free and back to spotlight the timing between the arms and the body roll. We also want swimmers who are accomplished at the various *details*—starts, turns, and finishes—in all four strokes and individual medley transitions. Coaches should frequently give swimmers positive feedback to quicken learning.

- **Emphasize aerobic development as the secondary focus of training.** Since most technical work and improvement should occur while swimming short aerobic sets with relatively short rests between repeats, technical gains are mirrored by gains in aerobic endurance. Young kids have short attention spans and will not pay attention to long speeches, so keep them moving, keep their heart rates up, and vary the stroke emphases to keep their minds attentive. Backstroke can be effective for aerobic training. It is also important that swimmers learn to be good kickers. Kicking sets are serious for development, not social occasions for chatting. Set goals for the swimmers, and expect a lot. Have them kick on fairly tight intervals, and praise those who are working hard and kicking fast.

- **Coaches may need to increase the aerobic work for many of the girls to take advantage of their earlier critical period for aerobic development.** The girls can swim longer sets with longer repeat distances, though still focusing on technical points. The boys can do more skill work, perhaps more kicking, and definitely less volume. One simple way to boost the girls' mileage is to keep them in the water an extra 15 minutes every day for a short aerobic set.

- **Target certain events.** For both physiological and psychological reasons, you can target certain events for your swimmers' training, namely the 100s of the form strokes (backstroke, breaststroke, and butterfly); the 200-yard, 500-yard, and 400-meter freestyles; and the 200 individual medley. We pay little attention to the 50s. We are aiming to develop well-rounded swimmers who are good at every stroke and who have the technical skills and aerobic conditioning to excel at the longer events.

- **With dryland work, emphasize coordination, flexibility, core strength, and quickness.** You want to develop better athletes, and dryland training can supplement swimming. This training need not be complicated, nor does it require expensive equipment. Bodyweight exercises, simple core-strengthening work, basic stretches, and games will do just fine. When the weather permits, playing games outside and keeping score also helps develop competitive kids. At this age, you can begin special breaststroke leg stretches to create the flexibility needed by the 99 percent of the swimmers who are man-made breaststrokers.

- **Continue teaching them to be swimmers.** Coaches should aim at making the 9 and 10s swimming veterans, experts at using the pace clock on involved and complicated sets, starting on time consistently, getting their times correctly, setting goals for sets and for repeats, and taking care of their equipment.

11- to 14-Year-Olds

These are the most important years for creating future national-level senior swimmers. With their training, swimmers are determining what level of athletes they will be later. During this time, there is a gradual and progressive buildup in the intensity and volume of training. Also, we begin to differentiate in the training groups between those swimmers who are more advanced, more committed, and higher performing (the fast-track swimmers) compared with the others (the slower-track swimmers).

- **Place greater emphasis on team culture and swimmers' responsibilities**. Because peer influence is huge at this age, coaches must ensure that the group ethos is strong and positive, and they must protect the team culture. Swimmers are expected to behave like champions and set a good example for the younger swimmers who look up to them. Swimmers are treated as future national-level athletes and are assumed to have lofty goals. Continual goal setting is stressed.

- **Focus on aerobic development**. Swimmers can make huge gains in aerobic capacity with the right kind of endurance work. Compared with the 10-and-under program, training sets get progressively longer, repeat distances get progressively lengthened, send-offs get tighter, and performance and consistency of performance are more closely monitored. You should do serious work in all four strokes and individual medley, and the training program should be geared toward long-course competitive success (though this does not mean that teams must train in long-course pools).

■ **Target certain events for training.** For this group, the target should be longer events than those for the younger group. Focus on the 200s of the form strokes, the 500-yard or 400-meter freestyle and the mile, and the 400 individual medley. Do not allow swimmers to specialize in certain strokes or distances. Training is more frequent and more consistent with shorter breaks between seasons, and swimmers are expected to stay active during breaks. Toward the end of this phase, some of the more obviously distance-oriented swimmers will increase their mileage.

■ **Continue technical improvements.** Everything you do should have a stroke focus; never just swim. Because most swimmers are growing at furious rates during this time, and the proportional lengths and strengths of limbs and trunk are changing in the process, it is important to maintain coordination and control during this biomechanical restructuring. Training is not a question of technique *or* yardage; instead, do both. Adding super-short-course work in a 12- or 15-meter pool or diving well improves speed. This is mostly for neurological reasons since speed is a function of coordination before maturation sets in.

■ **Emphasize the connection between training and racing.** As swimmers mature physically and psychologically, continual progress in training performance should be expected. Further, there is a greater focus on tying together technique and physiology as you condition the racing stroke.

■ **Continue with general dryland training.** Most work still involves bodyweight exercises, core-strength exercises, stretching for flexibility, and games for coordination, agility, quickness, and competitiveness. However, you also want to build specific strength to prevent injuries to susceptible joints such as knees and shoulders.

■ **Account for gender and individual differences in maturation and development.** Girls are generally one to two years ahead of boys biologically during this period, and because of this, more is required of girls earlier. Without a good aerobic base, their athletic career is stunted. This is an important argument for encouraging girls to focus on their swimming earlier than boys if they have aspirations of high performance. Some of the faster-track girls will be at a national level by 13 or 14. It is important to proceed carefully and not squeeze the lemon dry. As long as these faster girls keep getting better, there is no need to bump up their training radically and treat them as if they were senior swimmers. It doesn't matter how fast they are when they are young if they don't improve after that. Give them a way to get better when they are 16 or 18. With boys, you can afford to move slower. Toward the end of this phase, some of the boys will be growing fast and developing muscles; they are ready to take off.

11- to 14-Year-Olds and the Challenges of Puberty

Puberty complicates things. You would think that because kids are getting bigger and presumably stronger, they would necessarily be getting faster. However, in the end, puberty is highly beneficial to almost all boys and more ambiguous for girls. As boys become men, they lose fat and gain muscle, getting bigger and stronger. As girls become women, they gain height and strength, though not nearly to the extent that boys do, and they add fat deposits. With proper nutrition (which does not mean starvation diets or eating disorders) and proper training (lots of consistent aerobic work), any adverse effects of these biological changes on swimming can be kept to a minimum.

In the short run, kids are growing during puberty, but they are growing unevenly. Arms, legs, and torsos don't have the same proportions in either strength or length as they did last week, so coordination can be unbalanced and ranges of motion can be seriously compromised. Strokes may fall apart or become inconsistent. A swimmer's best stroke may change overnight. Also, various psychological changes are affecting swimming and everything else, and some children become emotional. Interests change and priorities are reordered. Sometimes interest in the opposite sex overwhelms even their interest in swimming and schoolwork. All of these changes can cause athletic performances to stagnate, and it can be a highly frustrating time for all involved. Fortunately, it usually doesn't last long, and the swimmer emerges from the chrysalis as a beautiful butterfly.

In the process of becoming adults, all children go through the same process, but they go through it at different times and rates. Two 12-year-olds on the blocks at a meet might be the same chronological age but five years apart biologically or developmentally. Both early and late developers have their own challenges.

Early developers get bigger and stronger earlier than the others, which means they are more likely to win their races. However, because they can often win without having to work on their technique or train hard, they may not develop a solid work ethic, and their technique may be poor as they bull through the water. From the child's immediate perspective, *not* working hard and *not* working on technique is a rational choice. What he has done has obviously been working since he has been highly successful, so why should he listen to the coach tell him that he needs to work harder or change his stroke? He beats all the other kids who listen to the coach, work harder, and change their strokes!

Then our pragmatist reaches the ages of 13 to 15, and suddenly the other kids who he used to destroy in meets are catching up to him and even passing him. The size and strength advantage that he had relied on has deserted him, and he has no technique or work ethic to fall back on. He is not long for the sport; many early bloomers quit when their easy successes dry up. Coaches can avoid this problem by not allowing the early developers to bask in the temporary limelight, instead training them for their long-run benefit and trying to educate (and their parents) about how they should judge their own performances both in meets and in practices.

The late bloomers are smaller and weaker than the others, so they usually get crushed in swimming meets. If the coach, swimmer, and parent emphasize winning and medals, then there is little chance that this late bloomer will stay in the sport. This, too, is rational. The child thinks, "Why should I keep swimming? I'm obviously lousy, even though I'm working my guts out and doing everything the coach asks." However, if the coach and parents can help the swimmer find enough rewards from swimming—through improvement, meeting personal challenges, or friendships—to stick it out through the lean years, and if the swimmer relies on technique and hard work to overcome the temporary physical deficit, then she is in the driver's seat in a few years. Late bloomers tend to be taller and leaner, and the extra years of technique and endurance development before maturation should lead to higher performance in the end.

Key Issues in Athletic Development

Thus far we have discussed the training program, its parts, and how these parts are implemented for swimmers at varying ages. But no two swimmers are alike, and the complications of real life will always give rise to questions and concerns. Here we discuss some of the recurrent issues that arise from the application of our general training principles.

Early Specialization

There is much argument from researchers and the general public against child athletes specializing too early and thereby stunting their athletic and psychological growth. On the whole this is true, and it is not our intention to turn 10-year-olds into mechanical swimming robots. But it is common in these discussions for all sports to be treated equally. They are not equal, and because of this, the common conclusions cannot be wholly applied to swimming.

Swimming is a peculiar animal. Many of the requisite skills of land sports transfer from one to another. The American triad of football, baseball, and basketball, for example, share many skills, especially at the lower and middle levels of performance. Usually kids who are good at one are good at them all. But when you suspend a person sideways in a liquid, everything changes. Without the usual leverage from pushing off solid ground, technique and subtlety count for more than brute force. Also, a sideways body orientation completely changes the sense of balance needed to perform the fundamental movements. Further, in no other sport do we pull down the length of the body, so the fundamental arm movement in swimming is rarely practiced elsewhere. The kicking movements of swimming are also singular to the sport. Swimming is unique, and for that reason, an early start in swimming is highly beneficial for much-needed technical proficiency if one is to reach high levels in the sport. This does not mean that kids should participate in swimming alone but that swimming should be a major part of their physical activity from a young age.

> An early start in swimming is highly beneficial for much-needed technical proficiency.

Participation in Other Sports

Especially with younger kids, it is ideal for swimmers to play other sports. They should be in the backyard playing soccer, riding their bicycles, or throwing around a baseball or football. You want them developing skills, learning to coordinate their bodies, and becoming better athletes, but you don't necessarily want them joining other organized teams. When a swimmer joins a baseball team or a football team, for example, a massive scheduling conflict is created, with opposing coaches protecting their turf and wrestling for the child's time and attention. Further, in most team sport practices, players spend a large part of their time waiting in line for a turn or waiting for the rest of the kids to show up so practice can start. But when kids play ball for an hour in the backyard, they play the whole time, developing fitness and skills the whole time while having fun. Just as important, when kids play in the backyard, they play with their friends. Usually they do not have adults watching their every movement and trying to control everything. Kids make the rules and adjudicate any conflicts that arise, so they get to exercise some responsibility and leadership in the bargain.

Kids will be better swimmers later if they become better athletes now, and playing helps them do that. Swimming alone does not necessarily give a young athlete all the physical tools she will need to be a top swimmer later; this is why our daily dryland sessions focus on building flexibility, strength, core stability, shoulder stability, and general athleticism. It is also why much of our dryland work incorporates outside play and games. It is important that children be well-rounded athletically, but they can reach that goal in a more beneficial and less conflict-ridden way than is usually supposed.

All this being said, if swimmers are to reach national levels of performance or higher, eventually they need to decide that they are swimmers and concentrate on swimming. Biological necessity dictates that this time is earlier for girls than for boys. By 12, girls must be doing serious training; for boys, they must do so by 14. However, they should still be playing ball in the backyard even as they narrow their focus to swimming.

Burnout and Levels of Interest

Burnout is overrated. Swimmers don't burn out because they come to practice regularly, because they are working hard, or because they are swimming fast. Instead, kids lose motivation and interest when they put a lot of time into an activity but don't seem to get any rewards. Well-designed programs that keep kids improving are the best method to lessen the burnout problem. When swimmers are improving their times, improving their skills, and getting stronger and fitter, they will be motivated to swim.

> Kids lose motivation and interest when they put a lot of time into an activity but don't seem to get any rewards.

More children bore themselves out of sports than burn out. It is common for a swimmer (and parent) to refuse on principle to commit to swimming, usually from the parents not wanting their child to burn out by committing to swimming.

To that end, the swimmer doesn't come to practice much or work hard when he does show up. He makes little or no progress, falls behind his peers, never gets excited about swimming, and gradually loses interest in the sport. When a swimmer like this quits, it is never a surprise. You will have seen the warning signs for a long time and will have lost many arguments trying to get him to see the probable consequences of his choices. Without consistent attendance and hard work, swimmers aren't going to be improving consistently in practices or meets, and without those two key improvements, they aren't going to be having fun. Coaches should expend every effort to teach the team ethos of hard work, commitment, improvement, and excellence and the fun and satisfaction that derive from these. Even so, the message is not always heeded.

A third common occasion for burnout occurs with girls of a certain age, usually 15 or 16. The amount and intensity of work that got a swimmer satisfactory results when she was 12 years old and built like a pencil will not suffice when she has the body of a young woman. Improvements are smaller, and they take a lot more work and commitment to come by. Once again, it is a coach's responsibility to tweak the training program as needed (by adding more strength work for the girls to overcome the strength deficit that puberty brings) and to educate the swimmers and parents about this common situation.

Putting Swimming in Its Proper Place

When I was 14, I quit soccer for swimming. I had reached the point where I couldn't do both sports at the level I wanted to, and too many conflicts existed between practices, meets, and tournaments. I didn't burn out on soccer; I simply preferred one activity to another. U.S. Soccer, which had just lost one player from its rolls, may have decried my desertion, but I saw it as a choice—swimming meant more to me than soccer did, my dreams of being the next Johan Cruyff notwithstanding. A child quitting one activity—even swimming—to do something else that he likes better and has more potential at may be the best thing for that child.

Coaches need to look at each swimmer and try to act in her best long-term interest. Sometimes swimming needs to take a secondary position or be out of the picture entirely.

For example, several of my swimmers have been even more talented musically than athletically. It would have been wrong to pressure them to focus their energies on swimming when it was clear that their true talents lay in making music. If I had been an unprincipled but effective rhetorician, I might have won the battle, but I would have lost the war and perhaps prevented a gifted musician from making a Carnegie Hall debut and turning the music world on its ear.

Girls and Boys

Through the 10-and-under years, the two sexes are similar in size and strength and training responses. But at the ages of 11 and 12, we begin to see both physiological and psychological divergences that widen as children age. For this reason, some teams have separate training groups for girls and boys starting with these ages.

It is commonly understood that the United States has a so-called boys problem, both in the pool and in society. Boys are falling behind girls and dropping out of sport and school. In swimming, girls and boys train together every day, and the effects of girls' earlier maturation plays a large part in so many boys quitting between the ages of 11 and 14. A boy who is small for his age and not going to be winning races any time soon can become embarrassed and frustrated about being dwarfed by most of the girls his age needs some extraordinary incentives to keep swimming. A close-knit group of boys can help immensely, and coaches can do much to create esprit de corps among the boys. Boys need to feel tough, to feel free to compete and trash talk, and to know that their animal spirits are appreciated and will not be squelched. Although we do not have a separate boys group, with our 11 to 14s we do something for boys only almost every day, whether it be having separate boys' and girls' lanes for practice, having the boys run around the lake together before they get in and swim, doing medicine balls for dryland training when the girls are doing abdominal work, or dropping and giving 10 push-ups between sets just for fun.

Late Starts and Missed Steps

If every step in the developmental training progression is important, then starting late and missing steps puts a swimmer at a disadvantage, and the later the start, the greater the disadvantage. This may offend our egalitarian ethic, but the majority of late starters will have a much lower performance ceiling than those who began the program early. The lack of technical skills shows in swimmers who missed the early technical focus, and the lack of aerobic capacity shows in the level and consistency of training for those who missed the early aerobic focus. It is frustrating for swimmer, coach, and parent to see a swimmer who wants to be great but is held back by a poor foundation. (This is a strong argument for parents getting their children involved in the best program they can from the beginning so that each step is well founded.)

However, it is possible to be successful without following the traditional progression. Even some Olympians have gotten late starts. The whole of the talent profile matters, and an athlete can make up for deficits in some areas with superior qualities in others. Further, missing a critical period for technique does not mean swimmers cannot improve their technique, though it does mean that they must do a lot more technical work to get the same benefit. Similarly, if they have missed the aerobic development period, they must do a lot more aerobic work to get the same results. Late-starting swimmers with high aspirations need to be more than usually driven and hard working to make up the deficit they began with.

A few other factors affect late-starting swimmers. The more active and athletic they have been before getting serious about swimming, the better the prognosis, and the particular events the swimmer is targeting matters—a big and strong late starter will likely be more successful in the sprints than in the distance events. Finally, regardless of whether or not a swimmer reaches a national level, there is more to swimming and its benefits than winning an Olympic gold medal or racing at senior nationals. Everyone at every level can benefit.

> Late-starting swimmers with high aspirations need to be more than usually driven and hard working to make up the deficit they began with.

Fitting late-starting swimmers into a developmental progression that assumes an eight-and-under start can be challenging. Ideally, a program would have a separate training group for late starters so that swimmers of similar ages with similar needs could train together, but this is feasible only in a large program with lots of lane space and no staffing issues. The goal is to catch up as well as possible, combining technical and aerobic development and adding strength and speed components. In a small club, the late-starting swimmer will probably be training with younger swimmers at the same performance level. She must be mentally prepared to get walloped by younger kids for a while. The content of her training will be off somewhat as she progresses since she will be doing training that is aimed at younger swimmers' developmental needs, but this work can be supplemented with more aerobic, strength, and technique work.

Meeting Individual Needs in Training Groups

There are many ways to divide swimmers into training groups, depending on the priorities of the club. Swimmers can be grouped by age, ability, sex, training performance, meet performance, or a mixture of these. There is no one right way, but the guiding principle should be that swimmers are given what they need developmentally.

Larger clubs with lots of swimmers, lots of lane space, and large coaching staffs can have training groups that are more homogenous and targeted to specific needs. Smaller clubs that are more pressed for space and staffing usually have more broadly based training groups with wider ranges of age and ability. But even in the latter situation, having separate lanes that target more individual needs is possible, though admittedly difficult for one coach to administer. For example, a training group that takes up four lanes might be doing four different practices, somewhat resembling a circus.

Fast-Tracking Swimmers

A coach or a program should never be an obstacle in the way of a swimmer getting faster. The common method of treating everyone in a group equally by giving everyone the same practice—the same sets, send-offs, and expectations—benefits only a few and offers no incentive for swimmers to strive higher. In any training group, some swimmers will be faster than others. Some will choose to come to practice more, train harder, set higher goals, and (usually) race faster. These swimmers must be rewarded for these choices and given challenging practices that will help them reach their goals. For the fastest swimmers, those who have outgrown their peer group athletically, coaches may have to accommodate their needs by having one lane with only a few people while the rest of the lanes are more densely populated. They could also have different practices for each lane, keep some swimmers later each day for more work, or promote some swimmers to a higher-level training group more quickly than normal.

> The common method of treating everyone in a group equally benefits only a few and offers no incentive for swimmers to strive higher.

When considering this latter option, several factors and potential problems are involved. Moving up means training every day with older kids and a different peer group with different interests. We do not necessarily want a 12-year-old listening to the locker-room talk of most high school students. Physiologically, advanced training groups will be doing training appropriate to older, more mature swimmers. A younger swimmer training with older swimmers may be skipping developmental steps she needs. Even if she is fast, a young swimmer still needs certain kinds and amounts of training at certain times in her biological development; skipping these steps can have ruinous consequences to a talented swimmer's development. For these reasons, accelerated move-ups need to be handled carefully and wisely.

Move-Ups in the Training Progression

Swimmers should move through the program as they age and develop. Unfortunately, move-ups can be contentious because often parents think that their children should be moving up training groups more quickly than the coaches think they should. As previously noted, the distinct training groups have different kinds, volumes, and speeds of training and different expected levels of commitment to swimming; all of these qualities are developmentally determined.

Decisions regarding group promotions should always be in the hands of the coaches. Coaches know the training groups and their demands, they know the swimmers and their daily performances and attitudes, and putting these two together, they know where swimmers would best fit in the program. A coach's aim is to put swimmers where they belong physiologically, psychologically, and developmentally. Swimmers show which groups they belong in not by what they say, but by what they do every day in practice. Their day-to-day practice performance is much more important than their race results in determining where they fit best. When considering promoting a swimmer from one group to the next in the team progression, three factors are most important:

1. The swimmer is leading her current group.
2. The swimmer is consistently training in the lower tier of the higher group across the board, not just in one favorite stroke. The principle here is simple: A swimmer will not fit in with a higher group if she cannot train at its paces.
3. The swimmer has the commitment level of the higher group. Again, the principle is simple: A swimmer will not keep up with the progress of a group if she does not come to practice as much, work as hard, or go to the team meets.

Other factors that weigh in the decision for group placement are the swimmer's age, psychological maturity, physiological needs, competitive maturity, independence and self-reliance, leadership abilities, coachability, and willingness to be held accountable for training and racing. Also, coaches should ensure that the swimmer's parents understand and accept the demands of the higher group placement. It is common and problematic that a swimmer wants to come to practice but his parents will not or cannot take him.

At the time of group promotion decisions, sometimes a swimmer will be on the bubble, her performance and commitment straddling two groups. In this case, it is best to err on the side of caution: When in doubt, stay put. It is much easier to promote someone midseason than to demote him when it becomes obvious he can't handle the work and doesn't yet fit into the higher-level group. Demotions always ruffle feathers of swimmers and parents; promotions rarely do. I can safely say that all of my previous mistakes regarding promotions occurred when I prematurely moved a swimmer to a higher group under pressure from a parent. Doing what is convenient is not the same as doing what is best.

Double Practices

Some programs schedule doubles (two practices per day), and some do not. There are valid arguments to the contrary; for example, the extra sleep will benefit the swimmers more than the extra training. Busy families should not be burdened with the extra trips to the pool because injuries might result from the added stress. After debating the issues, we have decided that properly implemented doubles are a valuable part of the training progression. They allow more focused work on swimmers' individual needs; they allow more time in the water to develop feel, and when the stresses of the training week are allocated intelligently, kids get much better and still stay healthy.

During the school year, only a few of our more advanced 13- to 14-year-olds swim doubles. But summers allow for more water time as well as more recovery time. We take advantage of this coincidence to bump up the volume for swimmers aged 11 and older. Evening practices are as usual, but we offer morning practices several days per week that focus on developing stroke technique. Throughout the year, we have the following general schedule:

- Fast-track 11- to 12-year-olds swim no doubles during the school year and one to two per week during the summer.
- For fast-track 13- to 14-year-olds, we use the following schedule:
  - Fast-track 13-year-old girls swim one to two doubles per week during the school year and two to three per week in the summer.
  - Fast-track 14-year-old girls swim two doubles per week during the school year and three to four per week in the summer.
  - Fast-track 13-year-old boys swim no doubles during the school year and one to two per week in the summer.
  - Fast-track 14-year-old boys swim one to two doubles per week during the school year and two to three per week in the summer.

CHAPTER 3

Creating an Environment of Excellence

Coaches determine the kinds of teams and swimmers they will have by the psychological environments they create. Most often this is done haphazardly and in reaction, with coaches sending mixed messages with predictable results. The adage that good teams are good for a reason and bad teams are bad for a reason certainly applies here. Those reasons are not the presence and absence of talent but rather whether the available talent gets developed. A sound and consistent psychological environment where excellence is expected and both coaches and swimmers are held to the highest standards is like a brisk wind in the sails of talent, helping to discover the talent in the first place and forwarding its development once found. An environment where mediocrity is tolerated or even fostered, on the other hand, is like the doldrums to talent. No sailboat, no matter how sleek, moves fast without wind.

Coaches need to consciously try to instill certain values, beliefs, and attitudes, all of which can be boiled down to excellence at the highest levels without compromise. In a thousand ways every day, coaches are trying to create a certain type of swimmer. Excellent swimmers are tough; they are the embodiments of the Finnish ideal of *sisu*, a determination to overcome any obstacle or adversity. They are self-reliant, not depending on the coach or their parents to do everything for them or make all the decisions. They are competitive and love to race, eager to take on anyone, anytime, anywhere. They have extremely high expectations of themselves and of those around them. They are committed to their swimming. They pay attention; they have a laser-beam focus on what they are doing in practice. They have a sense of craftsmanship, precision, and attention to detail. They continually strive for improvement. They are confident in their abilities, and they show that relaxed confidence under the pressure of important competitions.

For most kids, these traits do not come naturally; they must be cultivated, expected, practiced, encouraged, practiced some more, demanded, and made second nature. Swimmers who do cultivate these virtues will be fast and fun to coach. Coaches can rely on chance, or they can actively work to cultivate these traits.

Culture and Character Building

Conscious culture and character building are one big task with three facets. First, and often overlooked, is making use of the physical environment, the pool area itself, to motivate the athletes. Second is controlling the cognitive environment. This involves explicit parent and swimmer education, mostly written but also including team meetings or parent meetings, where you consciously teach and they consciously learn. Last is creating the training environment and its psychology, which includes consciously fabricated customs, the organization of practices and how that affects swimmers' behaviors, and the coach's style. Swimmers get one consistent message from a hundred directions—in everything they see, read, and hear—from the first day they walk onto a pool deck until the last day they leave one.

Physical Environment

The physical environment can greatly affect the psychology of swimmers; it tells them what kind of team they are, and it makes public the standards that the team holds. If possible, coaches should consider the walls of the pool to be an important part of the program. Decorating the walls can be an effective way to create a team culture. Of course, a coach has more or less control over the physical environment depending on who owns the pool and what kind of pool it is. For example, many outdoor pools have few and inhospitable walls, or the pool owner may frown on adornments. It may be the case that you must make use of portable whiteboards instead of permanent bulletin boards, or that you must send the desired information through the team's Web site or e-mails to members, or that instead of being posted on the walls, relevant postings are put as hard copies in each family's mailbox at the pool. The point is that all coaches and teams have some way of using the physical environment to their advantage—it just takes more imagination in some settings than others. Ideally, anyone walking on your deck should be immediately bombarded with the idea that this is a place where champions train.

> Ideally, anyone walking on your deck should be immediately bombarded with the idea that this is a place where champions train.

The walls serve three motivational purposes. First, quotations highlight the attitudes you are trying to instill in your swimmers. Sometimes swimmers give more heed to a message when it comes from an exotic source. They will readily ignore a coach whom they see every day but take to heart the same words when they come from John Wooden or Winston Churchill. Second, you can post meet qualifying times in order to set standards, challenge swimmers to reach ever higher, and define *fast* for your program. Third, you can use the walls to recognize excellence. Public recognition of excellence is crucial. We need to give recognition where deserved. Kids must know that high performance, and the work that leads to it, will be noticed, valued, and praised to the skies. The less recognition that excellence receives from the public in the form of media coverage, the more recognition it must receive at the pool. The fact that these postings are public and permanent is important: Every swimmer sees these things every day at practice.

There is no end to the things you can post on the walls to motivate your swimmers. You can use readily available tools or formulate your own. The simple plan is to decide what is important to your program, find a way to measure those things, make a game or contest that encourages the behaviors you want from your swimmers, and then post the results publicly. Swimmers who are competitive will eat this up. It is also important, though cumbersome and time consuming, to be consistent and timely about updating the scores or standings. Swimmers lose interest if they work hard to improve but then get no credit for their improvement.

We put a premium on improving daily in practice, training well, performing in competition, and being exceptional in all strokes and distance events. We have chosen our strategies accordingly, a selection of which are discussed later in this section. Teams with other values or goals can easily adjust these games accordingly.

Words of Wisdom

An important section of the walls is covered with hundreds of quotations, words of wisdom from great achievers in numerous disciplines (art and literature, science, business, war and statesmanship, and various sports), serving as a recipe book for success at the highest levels: the way of a champion. We use these every day for individual attitude adjustments and for quotes of the day posted on the whiteboard. Also, frequently during stretching the kids can walk around and find one or two quotations that are especially meaningful to them at that moment.

Standards

This section consists of many lists, including USA Swimming's motivational time standards and the qualifying standards from meets the team will attend, which range from local invitationals to state and regional championships to junior and senior national championships to the Olympic trials. We also have a section of second swim standards, which are estimates of the times it will take to make the A- or B-finals at important meets (based on studying the previous year's results and assuming a slight improvement) so that swimmers will set goals not just to get to the meet but to do well there. There are standards to motivate everyone, no matter the level, and kids will often pore over the lists after practice.

IMX Special Forces

USA Swimming's Individual Medley Xtreme (IMX) Challenge program encourages swimmers to be strong in all four strokes and individual medley. We devote an important section of the wall to IMX rankings because these are key to age group development. Thus, the IMX program dovetails with our program goals and philosophy. USA Swimming's supercomputers do the heavy lifting here; they compile every swim from every registered swimmer, then convert the times to scores for a select group of events. Each swimmer's scores are totaled, updated with each best time, and then ranked against similarly aged swimmers by team, state, region, and across the nation. This is similar to an old-style swimming pentathlon but with running scoring and a quarter of a million competitors.

We post IMX rankings by age group after each meet. Swimmers can see how they compare not only with their teammates but also with swimmers of the same sex and age from across the country. Using a performance gradation that I came up with after analyzing my swimmers' scores, we reward swimmers for achieving levels ranging from diamond and platinum at the top to iron and tin at the entry level. We also keep team IMX records and post an honor roll of swimmers who rank in the top 10 and top 100 in the country and the top 5 in the state for each season.

Super Sets

For particularly brilliant sets (a whole set, not just a single repeat or two), swimmers get their names, the sets, and their repeat times put on a note card and posted on the wall. Usually the coach judges, but swimmers can nominate themselves or their teammates and make a case by putting the facts down on a card. If the coach agrees, their card goes up. The Super Sets wall section recognizes and encourages hard, consistent training.

Kaizen List

Kaizen is Japanese for "continual improvement." In the real world, no swimmer can have a super set every day, but she can still improve every day. For each practice, encourage swimmers to do something better than they have ever done before by having them set a *kaizen* focus. They practice with a serious intention. All swimmers who meet their goals put their names and accomplishments on a list as they leave the pool after practice. When the sheet is full of accomplished goals, post it on the wall.

> Encourage swimmers to do something better than they have ever done before.

Road to the Top

This section of the wall honors meet performance. The road consists of columns of standards proceeding from slowest to fastest, from the entry level of USA Swimming times on the far left (A times, AA times, AAA times, and AAAA times) through national top 10 times, Far Western or Zone Champs qualifier, Sectional or YMCA National qualifier, Grand Prix qualifier, junior national qualifier then medalist, national qualifier then medalist, and finally national champion on the far right. Each time a swimmer achieves a new standard at a meet, we place a small placard with the swimmer's name and event under that standard. The more swimmers who reach a performance level, the more placards are placed under that heading. Each season, swimmers are encouraged to travel as far along the road as they can in as many events as possible. As the bulk of the swimmers improve, the center of gravity shifts to the right. Swimmers can see themselves and their team improve as the placards accumulate.

Honor Clubs

This section of the wall represents an honor roll derived from the Road to the Top wall section. Primary clubs we've used include a AAAA Club, a National Top 10 Club, Senior and Junior National Qualifiers and Medalists, and a Distance Club (with swimmers reaching the AAA level or higher in the distance events). We have one sheet for each season. The goal is to have as many swimmers as possible at each of these levels and more each season. Whenever swimmers notch a club-worthy performance, they are made members of the club with their name and event listed. We laminate these sheets and place them near the pace clock so that the kids see them often. The message is clear: The team is getting better; others training beside you have reached a high level of performance doing what you're doing, and you can reach that high level as well. High performance becomes normal and part of the culture.

Team Records and Rankings

This section includes both short-course and long-course team records, and it is updated after every meet with new records highlighted. Once again, the aim is to show the team that it is getting faster and to publicly acknowledge those swimmers who are setting the bar higher for the rest of the team. It also includes a team top 10 ranking for the current season, updated after each meet so that swimmers can see where they stand in their age group.

Cognitive Environment

The second facet in a program of creating excellence is the cognitive environment. This is more explicitly pedagogical than the first; the aim is for the coach to teach and the swimmers and parents to learn. The message here should interlock with that taught by the pool and the swimmers' surroundings; namely, what kind of a team we are, what the team goals are, and so on. This part of the program has five parts: program philosophy, team policies, newsletters, parent meetings, and team meetings.

Program Philosophy

Every program has a philosophy. It can either be conscious and focused or random and haphazard. A well-thought-out philosophy helps define the program for the coach, swimmers, parents, and potential swimmers and parents. Everyone knows what to expect. Making your philosophy explicit is an effective way of ensuring a good fit between families and your program. In our program, a key document contains the credo (see page 46), a two-page distillation of the philosophy of *arete*.

> Making your philosophy explicit is an effective way of ensuring a good fit between families and your program.

Families who buy into the program, who know what you are like, who know what you believe and what you expect, and who wholeheartedly approve are going to be happy. They are much more likely to appreciate what you are trying to do and how you are doing it when things get tough. Families who don't fit usually joined a team based on what they saw on the surface; they didn't know what was underneath because the coach didn't tell them. The square peg needs to know that you are a round hole. Understanding the philosophy of a program is much more important to a family's happiness than details such as how many times the 12-year-olds train each week.

Team Policies

Every team should have policies that explain, among other matters, expected practice and meet attendance; who chooses meets and which events kids compete in; and training-group composition, emphases, and move-ups. These and other parts of the program should be aligned and consistent with the team philosophy, and they should be collected in a team handbook that is available to every family.

Newsletters

Newsletters are a crucial means to get your message across to swimmers and even more so to parents. The less they know about how excellent programs do things, the more important frequent, substantial newsletters are to building momentum in the right direction. Newsletters serve two main purposes:

1. **To educate about the process of becoming excellent.** Most parents assume it is smooth sailing from novice to national: Join a good team and success is assured. Few understand the developmental process and its implications for training, and few understand the increasing demands on their children as they work toward the summit. Unless they were born into a national-level program, parents simply don't know how excellent clubs operate or how excellent swimmers think and behave. The problem is usually one of ignorance, not ill will. Most are willing to be educated, so coaches must educate them. It is up to us to give them good information, or they will get their information, possibly faulty, from someone else.

2. **To recognize and praise excellent achievement and high performance.** Coaches determine and, by implication, teach parents and swimmers about what *fast* is and what level of performance is high enough to merit public praise or to get a swimmer's name on the wall. This function is similar to and complements the wall postings discussed previously.

Parent Meetings

Newsletters are necessary, but coaches cannot assume that everyone is reading them. Parent meetings are more effective because, once people are in the room, you have a captive audience and can reasonably assume that they are hearing your message. Further, you give the audience the opportunity to ask questions, and you can gauge the mood of the group and discern their concerns by watching them as you talk. What kind of meetings you run and how frequently you run them depends on the particular team and its needs.

Team Meetings

A couple of times in my coaching career I have taken over a team or a training group that had grown used to a coach who was different from me in every way. It was immediately apparent that the training and technical programs I had planned for my swimmers would not work without giving them a crash course in the psychology of excellence, so every day I set aside 10 to 15 minutes to talk with them about various aspects of the way of a champion, often elaborating on a great quotation or a section of the credo. These talks worked. The mental gains we made easily compensated for the dryland or water training time we lost, reinforcing the idea that once you teach swimmers how to think, the hardest part of coaching is done; because their behavior follows from their thoughts, beliefs, and attitudes. I have made these short philosophy talks a regular part of the weekly training program ever since.

> Once you teach swimmers how to think, the hardest part of coaching is done, because their behavior follows from their thoughts, beliefs, and attitudes.

Training Environment

The third facet of culture and character building is the daily training environment viewed in its psychological aspects. This sphere is the most important because it is ubiquitous rather than occasional, and it can be particularly effective because it becomes so normal that it is like the ticking of a clock that you rarely notice. This is the implicit or invisible mental training program. Kids are learning how to think and behave without realizing it; they are unconsciously becoming socialized into the coach-created culture of the group.

Team Customs

One of the important ways the ideal swimmer is created during daily practice is by the coach-created customs of a team. *Normal* is what you say it is; as a coach you determine how things are done, what you expect of the kids (from which they learn what to expect from themselves), what they can expect from you, what is rewarded or punished, and what is praised or criticized. The standards and expectations are clear, and the message that the swimmers and parents get is consistent. A few customary behaviors may include the following:

- Come to practice.
- Come to practice prepared, with equipment in working order.
- Don't stop during warm-up.
- Do all turns and finishes legally and fast.
- Start repeats exactly on time and quickly.
- Get times on every repeat and set goals for each repeat.
- Never swim ugly.

- Don't whine, complain, or make excuses.
- Focus most on technique when tired.
- Always finish sets fast.
- And finally, as the glue holding all these parts together, do things right all the time (or do them over).

With this excellent behavior the norm, you end up with swimmers who are well disciplined and who have earned the confidence borne of disciplined behavior. These swimmers train like champions, and they know it. A corollary to this normal way of doing things is that the older swimmers are expected to model a certain standard of behavior and uphold a certain culture. Remind them frequently that the younger kids look to the older ones to decide how they are supposed to behave, so they had better behave well.

Competitive Atmosphere

A second method for creating the ideal is to organize training lanes so that competition is highly encouraged. Set training intervals to stretch every swimmer, particularly the better and harder-working swimmers. When at all possible, try to have at least two lanes per training interval and place swimmers in lanes so that kids of similar speeds will be racing. Move kids from lane to lane during a set to create competitive matchups, and challenge them to race one another continually. Finally, do all of the short repeat swims side by side, match sprinting and keeping score.

Coaching Roles

Coaches create the swimmers they want to coach through their coaching personalities or styles. No two coaches are identical, but they all must use what they have and fill certain necessary roles. First, the coach must be a soothsayer, seeing how good her kids can be, taking what she sees before her and extrapolating to what the swimmers can become. This requires having experience with fast swimmers in the past and watching their development from year to year, and it requires forward thinking.

To convince his swimmers of his vision of the future, the coach must be a rhetorician. Somehow he must convince them to believe in his picture of their future, getting them to believe that they can be good and to commit to the coach's program so that it comes about. To do this, he must know his kids, and he must know what to say and when to say it to get the action he wants. Obviously, the more success you've had as a coach and the better your swimmers have done, the more believable your vision will be in the swimmers' eyes. But even the best coach has to find a way to reach the swimmers and have them grab his vision for them. That vision has to be not only believable but also desirable.

Next, the coach must be to some extent a statistician. That means knowing all the kids' best times, goal times, and daily repeat times; it's important to constantly

A coach must know her swimmers well in order to lead, encourage, and inspire them to reach their full potential.

challenge them to swim faster, split better, and swim more efficiently by suggesting means to do so. I always have three or four stopwatches running, in addition to one or two pace clocks, and I am continually encouraging, pleading, and nagging them to swim faster and faster, constantly referring practice times to meet and goal times and splits.

In trying to control the psychological environment of practice, coaches should recognize the importance of the little things. A well-placed word, seemingly offhand, can make a world of difference to a young swimmer. On our team, each swimmer leaves the pool after practice with a handshake and a "Good night, champion" from me, no matter how good or how bad the practice for that swimmer. Your swimmers should know that your relationship is deeper than their performance that day and deeper than your judgment of their effort. They should know that their worth is beyond the value of that particular practice and beyond their momentary ranking, and you want them to know that each of them is a champion on a team of champions.

> They should know that their worth is beyond the value of that particular practice and beyond their momentary ranking.

Culture and Goal Setting

Elite athletes are goal-setting machines, and the habit of continual goal setting is a primary reason they climb the ladder to the elite level. An important part of creating an environment of excellence is encouraging continual goal setting. Too often, goals are thought of as big intentions for the end of the season. But for goals to nurture future high performers, they have to be everywhere all the time. Goal setting means having a point or purpose that you are trying to accomplish in everything you do.

Purposes of Goals

Swimming can be a grind—swimmers come to practice every day; they are expected to work harder than they want to; they are tired all the time, and they do not have the free time that most kids do. But goals give swimmers a reason to do the program. They represent something meaningful to a swimmer that she wants to accomplish.

- **Goals give focus.** Most kids' minds are unfocused and highly scattered. Goals get their attention and keep it focused on a target, giving them something to think about and a purpose for training.

- **Goals make decisions easier.** Goals supply higher principles upon which to base thousands of decisions swimmers make every day about what to eat, how to use their limited time, how to attack certain sets in practice, and so on. Thus, goals make life simpler. Swimmers don't have to stress about little things because those decisions are already made by the direction they are heading in.

- **Goals generate self-respect and respect for others.** We become worthy by striving after worthy goals. We value and respect ourselves much more when we know we are attempting something great, working hard and conscientiously, rather than merely skating by and doing the bare minimum. We value our teammates more when we know they are attempting something great, working hard and conscientiously. The atmosphere created when everyone in the pool is aiming high is one of support, respect, and achievement. High goals are contagious.

- **Goals provide a way to evaluate what swimmers have done.** If swimmers never knew their times or could never compare their results with competitors, they would never know how they did. They would never know they fell short and needed to work harder or that they did well and should be pleased with their performance. They would never be able to see the baby steps of accomplishment that make for long-term success. They would be shooting their arrows into the darkness, never knowing whether or not the arrows hit the target.

- **Goals help swimmers maintain a good attitude.** Too many swimmers see training as a chore, and they see meets, especially championship meets, as pressure-filled, frightening experiences. Goals can help swimmers overcome this problem by rearranging their thinking about training and racing. Goals make swimming a game. They make fast swimming and high achievement challenging and energizing, not frightening and anxiety ridden. Continual goal setting and goal reaching builds confidence as swimmers see themselves getting better in a hundred ways every day. Occasionally falling short and trying again builds resilience and determination, and it lets kids see that failure is temporary, more irritating than overwhelming.

> Continual goal setting and goal reaching builds confidence as swimmers see themselves getting better.

■ **Goals liberate.** Most swimmers have no idea how fast they really are, because they only scratch the surface of their potential. When goals are continually being set and accomplished, the bar of self-expectation keeps getting raised—kids start to see just how fast they can become. Suddenly the seemingly overwhelming accomplishments such as making nationals or making the Olympic team get put into perspective and seem possible.

Coach's Role

In order for goals to be motivating, they must belong to the swimmers and be important to them. But coaches play crucial roles in helping swimmers choose and achieve good goals.

1. **Coaches know swimmers' capabilities.** Most young swimmers have no idea how fast they can be; they usually assume they aren't as capable as they really are. The coach teaches high expectations and high standards, acting as a sort of quality-control expert. When swimmers aim higher, they achieve higher.

2. **Coaches understand normal progress.** Because young swimmers do not know what a normal rate of progress is, they do not know how fast they can expect to improve if they work hard.

3. **Coaches have perspective.** Young swimmers have little experience in the swimming world, so they have little perspective. They don't know the various levels of achievement or what it takes to reach them, so they don't know how high they can climb. They will not aim to climb Mount Everest if they do not know that it exists.

4. **Coaches help swimmers attain goals.** Stating a goal without attaching meaning to it is easy. The coach can help the athlete take the goal and give it meaning with the splits along the way and the particular practice habits and performances that will lead to the goal time. The coach also continually reminds the swimmer of what is needed to reach the goal.

Types of Goals

There are several types of swimming goals. *Long-range goals* refer to the level the swimmer wants to attain by the time he leaves high school or college. They are far off in the future. *Season goals* are the swimmer's intentions for the season-ending championships. *Short-range goals* are benchmarks, steps along the way to the season goals, usually races at the various minor meets. Meeting short-range goals lets the swimmer know that he is on target for his season goals; falling short tells him that he has some adjusting to do. Finally, there are *daily goals* in practice. These are simple but immediate: to improve repeat times on certain sets, to pace swims more precisely, to sprint faster going out, to be faster and longer off the walls, to fix technical trouble spots, and so on.

Because swimming is a time-dominated sport, most goals will be time goals. However, skill goals are important as well. Any facet of swimming that can be improved can be a source for goal setting. Swimmers should try to swim not only faster but better—with better technique, fewer strokes per length, and more beautifully. The better the technique, the more time goals swimmers reach.

Long-range goals are necessary but not sufficient. Most swimmers have big things they want to accomplish: winning an Olympic gold medal, swimming at nationals, making USA Swimming's National Age Group Top 10, and so on. These provide the basic direction and excitement for the journey. But when swimmers don't feel good or they hurt or they just don't want to work today, goals far off in the future do not motivate them to act in accordance with them. Effective goals must be immediate, staring the swimmer in the face.

> Continually setting goals and trying to reach them creates interest, excitement, and meaning to every minute of practice.

For this reason, daily goals are the most important of all. Continually setting goals and trying to reach them creates interest, excitement, and meaning to every minute of practice. Every set, swimmers should be thinking, "what can I do in this set to help me reach my big goals and how can I use this set to help me to get better?" Swimmers need to have goals every single time they push off the wall. They should not wait for the coach to spoon-feed them goals; instead, they should take responsibility for their own improvement.

Using Goals in Daily Training

Most clubs and coaches have goal-setting sessions with both age-group and senior swimmers. The point of these sessions is for swimmers to think about where they are right now, where they want to go, and how they're going to get there. Swimmers usually fill out worksheets for five or six of their best events, listing their current best times, goal times at the major meet or meets, and splits necessary to reach the goals.

Some clubs have their swimmers make their goals public so that they are accountable to the group for what they say they are going to achieve. I don't do this anymore. Too many age-group swimmers undershot their goals to the point that most of them had achieved their season goals by the second meet. They had no idea how much they could expect to improve, so the numbers on the goal sheets were meaningless. Now, rather than have a meeting once a season to talk about season-ending goals, we frequently discuss their intentions (i.e., goals) from meet to meet as the season progresses, usually informally before, during, or after practice.

Focus on making goals real and on what swimmers have to do to reach their goals. For instance, a 1:57.5 in the 200 free means swimming 28.0 for the first 50, then 30.0 for the next two 50s, then 29.5 coming home. In practice, a swimmer might not be able to swim the whole race distance at goal time, but if she cannot even swim her goal paces on 50s, then she won't be reaching her goal at the meet. Continually connect what swimmers do in practice to what they want or should be able to do in a race and vice versa. Break down the final time to its parts, such as splits, walls, dives, stroke counts, and stroke rates, and work to improve these parts. By improving every day, swimmers make goals happen.

Finally, even more than the big goals for the season, take the little goals seriously. For every set, encourage or even require your swimmers to set goals for sets, for rounds of a set, and for individual repeats. These goals are based on previous practice history and future racing goals.

Honesty

Many swimmers talk about big goals, but far fewer are willing to do the work to reach those goals. Swimmers must realize that, the more activities that gobble their time, energies, and interests, the worse they will do in each of them. We can't do everything, and if we try, something has to give. This is a matter of priorities. When violin, soccer, babysitting, and going to the mall with friends conflict with swimming, or when swimming consistently loses in the competition for time and energy (especially when just this once becomes just about all the time), then swimmers need to reevaluate. They must be honest about their commitment to swimming and set their goals accordingly because setting a goal without making a commitment to achieving it is worthless. Although I am in favor of well-rounded students, much that passes for being well rounded is simply a disguise for mediocrity and lack of commitment. Excellence in any field takes dedication and focus, choosing one thing rather than many.

Most people emphasize the sacrifice that it takes to be an excellent swimmer. They see sacrifice as a losing proposition, stressing what they have to give up in order to be good. The excellent person reverses that thinking: He concentrates on what he is getting by giving up things that aren't as important to him. In the long run, the satisfaction, self-confidence, sense of accomplishment, and firm friendships that a committed swimmer gains will far outweigh any momentary pleasures he foregoes.

Attention to Detail

A necessary condition for the goal process is for swimmers to pay attention to their results so they can use those results to set new goals for the future. Paying attention means getting their time on every repeat so they know how fast they swam and can compare it with their goal for that repeat. It means counting their strokes each length so they know how efficient their technique was and can compare it with their goal. It means paying attention to high elbows or stroke tempos, again so they can compare them with their goals. If they never pay attention to their results, their goals have no purpose and cannot help them improve. Further, if

> Sweating the small stuff is the only way to make the big stuff (dreams and goals) come true.

swimmers are not leaving at the proper time but rather a little early or a little late, then the time on the pace clock means nothing. To get their times properly, they must leave when they are supposed to, note when they finish, and know how to add and subtract correctly and quickly. Sweating the small stuff is the only way to make the big stuff (dreams and goals) come true.

Swimmers as Dreamers

If swimmers are going to dream, they should dream big. They will never get anywhere in swimming or in any endeavor if they settle for mediocrity. All great achievements started with dreams of greatness. These dreams were probably considered unrealistic, foolish, and hopelessly nonsensical by the dreamer's friends, family, and acquaintances—until the dreams were made to come true; at which point everyone jumped on the bandwagon, wanted to be the athlete's best friend, and claimed "I knew it all along." This is one more reason for swimmers to spend time around other people who are striving for greatness and who will support them in their dreams.

Simple Recipe for Success

Have a dream.
Set a goal.
Get to work.

Swimming Against the Current

Coaches who are interested in building world-class swimming programs must realize that we are paddling against the current, and unless we take extraordinary measures, our swimmers will fall into the general morass of mediocrity. In a society addicted to fast food, cheap imported goods, grade inflation, quick-fix weight-loss fads, and a pill for every problem, there will not be much traffic on the long, arduous road to world-class performance. The message kids are getting from their friends, schoolmates, and society does not encourage excellence or the habits and behaviors that lead to it. They are constantly encouraged to be like everybody else, to conform to the mean. Teenagers, who are at a critical period in forming their characters, are especially exposed and susceptible to this message. Striving for excellence and admitting it is usually criticized as being elitist and unbalanced.

Therefore, if we want fast swimmers, we need to create an oasis where it's acceptable to be different—a place where excellence is valued, admired, encouraged, expected, rewarded, and emulated. We need to protect excellence. We have to take into account the messages our swimmers are getting from elsewhere and ensure that the rewards we offer our kids for buying into our program and for succeeding in it are more valuable than any competing rewards.

We are aiming to create a certain kind of swimmer and culture. Everything about the program encourages some behaviors and discourages others, and those behaviors form a swimmer's character and the team's culture. We are creating an ethos of excellence, an expectation of success, a universal striving for high achievement. We are consciously attempting to create a culture in which excellence can flourish and where national- and international-level performance will be the standard.

The Credo

This is the credo—Latin for "I believe"—in its current incarnation for my team, the York Y, in York, Pennsylvania. This is the most important piece of paper detailing what our program is about. Underlying its affirmations is the philosophy of *arete*, what I understand athletic, intellectual, and spiritual excellence to be. The affirmations serve as the attitudes that I am trying to teach my swimmers every day. I wrote the credo 15 years ago for a summer league team I was coaching in Utah, and it has been with me ever since. It is posted on our pool walls and on our team Web site, and each swimmer gets a new copy periodically to put up on the family refrigerator.

FIGURE 3.1

The Credo

YORK Y EXCELLENCE

We are committed to excellence. We have a burning desire to succeed.

We believe that excellence is only achieved through commitment, self-discipline, and hard work. There is no easy road to excellence.

We believe that excellence is a way of life. Swimming is one aspect of a life well and beautifully lived.

We have high expectations of ourselves and of those around us.

We can do anything we set our minds to.

We believe in our own capabilities. We refuse to limit ourselves by thinking small.

We are not normal, or average, or mediocre, and we will not pretend to be.

We rise above the crowd. We are not afraid to distinguish ourselves.

We never settle for mediocrity.

We are never satisfied. We know it can always be done just a little better. We are in quest of perfection.

We are improving every day, getting fitter, stronger, faster, tougher, smarter, and better.

We enjoy our excellence, working hard, testing ourselves, improving, and excelling. We push the envelope daily.

We become worthy by striving after high and worthy goals.

YORK Y PRIDE

We are proud to be members of the York Y Swim Team.

We all work to make York Y a team we can be proud of.

(continued)

FIGURE 3.1 *(continued)*

Each swimmer is responsible for the success of the team.

Each swimmer is responsible for the reputation of the team, so we carry ourselves with dignity, knowing our behavior and our words reflect on our teammates.

We treat one another the way we wish to be treated—with respect.

We behave like ladies and gentlemen.

We don't whine when we lose, and we don't gloat when we win. We embody quiet confidence.

We are confident because we have done everything right, we have done more than was asked, and we are physically and mentally stronger than the rest. We are York Y.

YORK Y UNITY

We support our own and our teammates' excellence.

We encourage positive peer pressure: We help our teammates to be their best.

Every swimmer on this team is important and has a role to play in helping the team reach its goals.

We respect one another. We value one another. We look for the good in one another.

We know that teams only succeed when their members pull for and care for one another.

Champions hang around champions.

YORK Y RESPONSIBILITY

We set a good example for others to follow.

We make no excuses.

We take responsibility for our actions. We don't look for someone else to blame.

We make things happen. We are in control of our destinies.

We don't hope for miracles. We create them by hard work.

We leave nothing to chance.

YORK Y PERSISTENCE AND DEDICATION

We are in for the long haul. We don't look for quick fixes or instant gratification. We know there is no substitute for hard work.

Success is determined by thousands of daily decisions to excel.

Anyone can set goals; we are special because we are willing to work to achieve our goals.

We make our daily decisions guided by our long-term swimming goals.

We embody consistent persistence. We finish what we start.

YORK Y COURAGE

We relish challenges.

We see opportunities everywhere. And we take advantage of them.

We know that succeeding means taking risks. We are not afraid of losing, because we learn volumes from every loss.

We value the worthy opponent above all others; he alone pushes us to our limits and shows us our weaknesses. He brings out our best and helps us become better.

PART II

Assessing and Refining Stroke Technique

CHAPTER 4

Recognizing What to Teach

Good technique is an important part of competitive performance. Looking at the big picture of the training program, technique is one corner of the elite triad with physiology and mental qualities the others. On the one hand, if a swimmer has poor technique and spends a lot of energy going nowhere, it's going to be difficult to compete, even if she has the biggest engine around. On the other hand, being efficient but slow doesn't help much. A common coach's assessment is, "He's a pretty swimmer; he's just not fast."

The criterion skill—the aim of our work—is not slow and perfect stroke drills but good technique at race speeds when the body is stressed and fatigued. Good technique is necessary but not sufficient. You can't just do technique work, even with young kids. You need to condition the racing stroke, and improvements in fitness and technique must go hand in hand. The goal is not just pretty swimmers but swimmers who are beautiful, fit, and mentally tough.

Defining Good Technique

Good technique means efficient swimming: When a swimmer pulls, the body moves forward, and when she kicks, the same result is observed. She is rewarded for her efforts. Bad technique means that the swimmer expends a lot of energy for not much benefit. This is the Macbeth stroke, full of sound and fury, accomplishing nothing—lots of splash, going nowhere. With good technique, swimmers can move at the same speed with less effort, or they can expend the same amount of effort and move at a faster speed.

The distinguishing mark of most great athletes is not power, size, or strength but the ability to use what they have most efficiently. Watch Michael Phelps, Natalie Coughlin, Ryan Lochte, or Ian Thorpe swim. Most champion swimmers are models for great technique, not brute strength. They seem so smooth, effortless, controlled, and graceful. They never seem to be moving nearly as fast as they actually are, and they never seem to be trying hard, even when moving at world-record pace. They are relaxed and easy, even at top speed. Swimmers who are good technicians possess the following qualities:

- **Sensitivity.** Beautiful swimmers have the ability to feel subtle pressure changes on the propelling surfaces of their bodies. They are alert to the feel of fluctuations of momentum, leverage or the lack of it, and when it is time to pull, how to pull, how hard, and in what direction.

- **Attention.** Being able to feel pressure changes is one thing, but if swimmers are thinking about what's for dinner and not about their technique, that ability doesn't help them much. Good technicians are constantly paying attention to their bodies in the water. They read the signals that their bodies are sending.

- **Relaxation.** Beautiful swimmers relax whatever muscles are not actively propelling the body forward, especially when at top speed, fatigued, and under stress.

- **Flexibility.** Good range of motion in the joints is crucial to staying relaxed and to maintaining good technique when fatigued.

- **Coordination.** Swimmers must have a good feel for which muscles and how much muscle to use at any speed, how the body parts work together most efficiently, and how to adjust under changing situations.

- **Attitude.** Swimmers must be coachable; they must be willing to try something different and to do it repetitively until it's habitual, even if it doesn't feel comfortable or fast at first.

- **Fitness.** Slow prettiness is useless. Racing puts huge physical demands on the athlete, and he needs to be strong and fit enough for his technique to handle those demands over the course of a race and an entire meet with several races.

Using Swimming Models

No two snowflakes are exactly alike, and no two swimmers' bodies are exactly alike in bone length and proportions, muscle strength and proportions, flexibility, and so on. It is reasonable to expect that no two swimmers can swim exactly alike—a stroke that optimizes one swimmer's conformation would not do so for another. As each swimmer grows, her body changes drastically in all the parameters just mentioned and more, so a stroke perfect for a swimmer when she is 10 will not be perfect for her when she is 16. Swimmers are unique, and each swimmer changes.

> No two swimmers can swim exactly alike.

But every human body attempting to move fast through the water has to obey certain biomechanical and hydrodynamic rules. Age-group coaches watch enough slow and ugly swimming to realize that some ways of swimming just do not work. On the other hand, watching the Olympics on television shows that some ways of swimming work quite well.

I have found that teaching young swimmers proper technique is most effective using models. A model is someone who exemplifies skills that lead to fast swimming. Models give living targets to aim at when working with young swimmers. I came to my models by a process that was time consuming but worth it. I began with this goal: to find out what makes swimmers fast. I did not begin knowing the answers; instead, I let the answers come to me. It made sense to look to the top of the pyramid to find models. World champions are assumed to be swimming correctly, almost perfectly; they have found an effective accommodation of the rules to their bodies. Although no two international-class swimmers look exactly the same, the difference between two elite swimmers is negligible compared to the difference between an elite swimmer and a mediocre age-grouper. The fastest swimmers share 99.9 percent of their technique DNA. On the road to international success, survival of the fittest has weeded out most inefficiencies.

I watched a lot of fast swimming, in person and on video, trying to see what the best swimmers do, how their strokes are constructed, and where their speed comes from. What do the top swimmers have in common technically, and what differentiates those at the summit from those just below? Then I watched a range of age-groupers, from very fast to very slow, trying to see what they do. What do the fastest age-groupers have in common with the world's best swimmers? What distinguishes fast young swimmers from slow young swimmers? By extensive comparison, I tried to discover the keys to swimming speed. After compiling a short list of fundamental stroke points for each stroke (what I call the *stroke catechism*; see chapters 5, 6, and 7), I chose a few models for each stroke, top swimmers who seemed the most beautiful and efficient in the water.

Applying stroke models to real kids requires prudence. Have your swimmers watch a lot of stroke video so that they get a sense of the whole stroke, its parts, and how they fit together. Using the catechism and its stroke cues as goals to aim for, swimmers practice each stroke in the water, trying to come closer and closer to the models as they practice. You may not be able to get every 9-year-old looking like Kirsty Coventry, but they will look a lot better than if you had simply let them swim laps and perpetuate their original inefficiencies. Still, it is important to realize that a model is not a Procrustean bed, and you must try to fit the individual body to the stroke. Using models, try to find what works best for each swimmer. Be open to alternatives that are outside the model but may be even better than it.

Common Competitive Stroke Principles

Each of the four competitive swimming strokes has its own rules and list of fundamentals (see chapters 6 and 7). However, there are general principles of good technique that are common to all the strokes.

Cleanliness

Even at race speeds, elite swimmers look a lot simpler and less complicated than a typical age-group swimmer. There is nothing extra—the stroke is stripped down to the basics. They have controlled front ends, with soft entries instead of crash landings; there is a notable lack of splash, and they are not creating large waves that retard progress. Movement is smooth and accelerating. It looks easy.

Directness

Elite swimmers' strokes are a work of art. Nothing could be added or subtracted, with every part furthering the main purpose of speed. Every movement is necessary. No body parts are thrown out of the way, no body parts sway or wiggle the wrong way, and there are no stops or pauses that don't belong. Most young swimmers include a variety of pauses, stops, jerks, and movements that don't belong and that detract from the goal of moving forward fast.

Momentum

Simply put, momentum means forward speed, and you want as much as you can get. For a swimmer, maximizing momentum has three parts. First, swimmers aim to increase the propulsive forces by having a strong and effective pull and kick. Second, they aim to decrease drag by streamlining movement so that the body slips easily through the water. Finally, they aim to keep the momentum constant, a straight line rather than a roller coaster. The game in swimming is first to create momentum and then to maintain it as much as possible.

> Momentum means forward speed, and you want as much as you can get.

Increase Propulsion

Good technique in swimming is more difficult to cultivate than in, say, running. When you run, you know that when you push off the ground, the ground is going to stay there and your body is going to leap forward. Further, the harder you push, the faster you run. This is not necessarily the case for a swimmer in the water. Water slips around the hand and arm if the swimmer doesn't pull just right, and the situation gets worse if she tries to overpower the water. Great subtlety is called for. The swimmer must lock onto the water with the hand and forearm—the high-elbow position—getting as much traction on the water as possible before pulling backward. Similarly, flexible ankles press against the water whereas typical ankles just crash against it. Swimming fast isn't so much a matter of how fast the swimmer turns over but how well.

The front end of the stroke is crucial—no front end, no pull. If a swimmer doesn't have traction on the water out front, he is never going to get it later. This requires patience and feel. The swimmer must first get the arm and body into a position of leverage so that the pull can be effective—with a body roll and press in free and back and with sculling motions in fly and breast. Only when the swimmer has set up the pull correctly and locked onto the water does he apply strong backward pressure. Most age-group swimmers turn over faster than they can control; they ram their arms into the water and rip backward. They never actually grab hold of any water, so their arms move quickly but their bodies stay in one place.

Swimmers need to get that leverage as far in front of them as they can, aiming for the longest effective pull. They should reach forward, grab hold, begin patiently, and then accelerate throughout a long pull. This builds the most momentum with the longest impulse and takes advantage of the strong trunk muscles throughout the pull.

In free, back, and fly, where drag forces (as opposed to lift) are primarily responsible for moving a swimmer forward, the palm of the hand should face backward, blade squared. I like the fingers pointing down to the bottom on free and fly (fingers down, elbows up with good wrists). The fingers suddenly changing the direction that they are pointing usually indicates a loss of pressure or traction on the water—the swimmer is letting go of the water and slipping. Associated with that loss of traction is usually a problem in another part of the body (e.g., head lifting or a broken kick).

Finish the accelerated pull with a flowing exit. Force is better maintained (joint health as well) by rounding the finish than by stopping the hand abruptly to change direction. Also, the recovery begins ballistically, borrowing momentum already created during the pull so the swimmer does not stop his arm and have to lift it up to recover, which stresses the shoulders and causes the legs to sway.

Decrease Drag

Poor swimmers stop as much as they go, creating almost as much resistance as propulsion. It's like Jeff Gordon trying to race with the brakes on. The power and strength are there, and a lot of effort is expended, but the body's alignment in the water does not allow any of this to be translated into forward movement. This is the definition of inefficiency.

The swimmer's goal is to reduce frontal resistance by streamlining the body. This is crucial. Lance Armstrong and company devoted thousands of hours and spent millions of dollars to achieve minute reductions in wind resistance when Armstrong raced, yet the wind resistance in cycling is insignificant compared with the resistance that must be overcome in swimming. Visualize the swimming body from the point of view of the water. The more smoothly the water can get around the body parts and the fewer abrupt blockages, the better. Ideally, people would be like dolphins or sea lions, whose smooth body contours present few impediments that slow the oncoming flow of water, but alas, we pay the price for opposable thumbs. Our arms and legs, though problematic from a hydrodynamic point of view, are all we have, so we must make some accommodations to our humanity. The aim is to put the body in a position to decrease drag while still enabling the arms to pull and the legs to kick powerfully.

In trying to understand this challenge, we can borrow the ideas of roll, pitch, and yaw from boats. Swimmers experience yaw when their legs sway side to side horizontally in freestyle or backstroke; it is always bad. Roll is the body rotating side to side on its long axis in freestyle or backstroke. Roll is good up to a point; the optimal amount of roll enables the swimmer to catch hold of the water efficiently and brings in the strong core muscles to strengthen the pull. Pitch is a tipping from front to back on the body's short axis, as in butterfly and breaststroke. Pitch is also good up to a point, but the greater the pitch, the greater the impediment to forward movement because the body becomes shaped like a snowplow. As a general rule, the more the body is oriented like a snowplow in the water, the slower it moves; the more it's like a horizontal sharpened pencil, the faster. Second, the more swimmers bounce up and down or sway side to side, the slower they will go; the smoother and more direct the stroke, the faster they will go. Add a powerful engine to a smooth, horizontal sharpened pencil, and you get a speedy swimmer.

Keep Momentum Constant

Constancy of momentum is key. When swimmers are not applying propulsive force, they are slowing down. Pauses or stops in a stroke—periods in the stroke cycle when the body slows down noticeably—cost speed and energy. This situation is similar to city driving, which entails much stopping and going; you are continually putting on the brakes and having to overcome inertia at each stoplight, and this slower driving takes much more energy than faster but more constant freeway driving. Likewise, stop-and-go swimming takes a lot more energy than a stroke that maintains momentum and has as close to constant propulsion as possible. Economical technique maintains momentum and speed. Though counterintuitive, it is easier to swim fast than slow.

> Economical technique maintains momentum and speed.

Eliminate the gap between propulsive phases as much as possible. Each stroke is a physics problem with its own physical, biomechanical, and hydrodynamic rules that result in challenges. With proper technique, constant propulsion is almost possible in the alternating strokes; freestyle will be faster than backstroke because of biomechanical advantages. The situation in the symmetrical strokes is less ideal. The butterfly pull creates massive momentum, but the simultaneous recovery of the arms and legs creates massive deceleration. The goal is to minimize deceleration during the recovery with horizontal streamlining. Breaststroke is the most challenging of all because the pull is truncated and indirect, and the kick backward is powerful, but the recovery kills speed.

Harmony of Stroke Rhythm

One of the key points in good stroke technique is the idea of stroke rhythm. A good rhythm looks easy and smooth, even at race speeds. Elite athletes are graceful and beautiful when practicing their craft. This beauty is the product of bodily integrity, which means the parts of an athlete's body are working together as a whole rather than against each other as disparate parts. The pull, the kick, and the body roll or pitch all work together on the same timing, contributing to forward speed. Note that this is different from having a technically perfect pull, the strongest kick, or even the greatest aerobic capacity ever recorded. Good rhythm means harmony, the parts fitting and working together optimally.

Having a taut body with good connection between limbs and core helps create rhythm by bringing the strong trunk muscles to bear on propulsion. A lack of connection means a soggy, sloppy body with a lot of frame flex: The hand and arm move fast, but the body just sits there. Good connection means the arms, torso, and legs work together for good rhythm.

An analogy from medicine and drug interactions illustrates the idea of rhythm. Some drugs neutralize each other when they are taken together and have no effect. This is called *antagonism*. In this situation, $1 + 1 = 0$. Other drugs multiply the effects of each other, sometimes in a small way, sometimes in a large way. Now we have *synergism*, where $1 + 1 = 5$, and *potentiation*, where $1 + 1 = 10$.

Transferring this idea to swimming, the torso and limbs of a poor swimmer counteract each other. The swimmer's body seems to be at war with itself. No movements are smooth and graceful, there is a lot of splashing and violence, and everything looks like a struggle. This is antagonism (arms + legs + torso = zero, or close to it). At the level of nationally ranked age-groupers, we see synergism (arms + legs + torso = 5). The level of athlete is high, the stroke rhythm is good, the body parts are working together, and the strokes are smooth and fast. Sometimes a swimmer comes along whose strokes are practically perfect and whose movements are surpassingly beautiful, smooth, and fast. This is potentiation (arms + legs + torso = 10). These are athletes such as Ian Thorpe, Roland Matthes, Michael Phelps, Kosuke Kitajima, Matt Biondi, Krisztina Egerszegi, Inge de Bruijn, Mark Spitz, Tracy Caulkins, and Natalie Coughlin.

Challenges to Good Technique

There is nothing like working on technique with age-groupers to frustrate and smack you in the face with an overwhelming sense of your own ignorance. What are they doing? Why can't they do this right? How can that possibly feel good? Why don't they do what you tell them to? Don't they ever listen? Why does that look so goofy? Can't he tell that he's not going anywhere? Age-groupers were created to teach coaches humility.

Coaches' Challenges

Coaches often create more problems than they solve by sending mixed messages or giving contradictory goals. A few common examples are demanding fast swimming and low stroke counts before a swimmer can do both at the same time; talking about technique before a set, then continually harping on times during the set; or following up a slow technique set where stroke perfection is demanded with a sprint set where the only thing that matters is the time on the stopwatch. These are effective means of coaching a stroke change right out of a swimmer.

Further, coaches often inadvertently create inefficient strokes by the kinds of training they give their swimmers. Every length they swim, swimmers' bodies are learning something, responding and adapting to the work and stresses. Certain kinds of sets create certain types of strokes. Survival strokes are created by frequent long sets with intervals so tight that the swimmers are struggling just to make the sendoffs. Short, choppy, power-oriented strokes are created by overemphasizing high-speed sprinting sets. Pretty strokes that wilt under stress are created by miles of slow stroke drills. There is a place in the training program for many kinds of sets, but they must be used with prudence and with attention to their technical consequences.

A coach's differing expectations for different kinds of sets also implicitly encourage swimmers to compartmentalize their strokes, using different strokes for different purposes and occasions. For instance, a swimmer will have one freestyle that she uses when she races, another that she uses when doing long aerobic sets in practice, another that she uses when doing slow stroke work, and a separate power stroke for sprinting.

When coaches ignore the stroke faults that we see in practice, we end up with inefficient swimmers. Telling a swimmer something once doesn't mean the coach has done his job. Because most swimmers' attentions spans are embarrassingly short, they have to be reminded over and over. This tries a coach's patience as well as his ability to keep tabs on what every swimmer in a group is doing and what each needs to be reminded of, in what ways, and how often.

> Taking technique seriously means being willing to devote time and sacrifice yardage to building and maintaining good technique.

Often coaches talk about the importance of technique but don't mean it. Taking technique seriously means being willing to devote time and sacrifice yardage to building and maintaining good technique. It means constantly reinforcing good technique in daily training. It means obsessing in practice not just about times but also about how those times are achieved. Swimmers see through the pretense and know what is important to you.

Finally, just because a coach is teaching certain stroke points doesn't necessarily mean that the swimmers are following your directions. Watching age-groupers underwater is the most striking way to see the difference between what you're teaching and what they're doing. To discover what isn't working and what needs to change in your coaching, look for patterns of mistakes—your training and teaching created those trouble spots. A few times in the past, I discovered that things weren't as I thought they were, and it was too late to change before the championships.

Swimmers' Challenges

Making stroke changes is difficult. Coach Gennadi Touretski has said that it took about 100,000 meters of focused swimming for Olympic champion Alex Popov to make a minor change in his freestyle. Alex Popov was extraordinarily motivated, coachable, attentive, and sensitive, especially compared with the average age-grouper.

Knowledge (or lack thereof) usually isn't the problem. If you explain things adequately and keep it simple, swimmers will understand what you want them to do. Ability (or lack thereof) usually isn't the problem either. Swimmers can do the skills, as is immediately obvious when they are threatened with repeating a set if they don't swim correctly. The real challenge in coaching is keeping young swimmers focused until good skills become habitual and then continually reinforcing and polishing those good habits. Many barriers stand in the way of positive change.

■ **Difficulty.** It is hard to form a new habit, especially when the old habit is natural and automatic. Change requires thinking about the change all the time and practicing it over and over until it is just as natural and automatic as the previous habit. Swimmers must think about skills they had done unthinkingly, and most kids aren't good at focusing for longer than two seconds. This is especially true for young swimmers who love splashing each other and for chatty swimmers who simply must discuss the day's events while you are trying to explain the intricacies of the freestyle pull.

■ **Discomfort.** Changes are also hard to make because they often hurt. Different ways of swimming a stroke use different muscles and muscle patterns, and often swimmers will complain after trying a new stroke that they hurt in strange places. This is to be expected; the new muscle-use patterns are not very strong. A coach will see this new discomfort as a good thing, a sign that something is changing for the better. The swimmer, on the other hand, will not see sore muscles as a positive, and he will be inclined to resist swimming in a way that hurts and is more tiring.

■ **Lack of trust.** True coachability is rare. It is the rare swimmer who trusts that a new stroke that feels unnatural and makes her slower (at least initially) is for the best. The more success a swimmer has had with a bad stroke, the less likely she is to want to change. This makes some sense; if it ain't broke, don't fix it. This attitude is common with young swimmers who are bigger and stronger than their peers and who win because of their size and strength.

■ **Ignorance.** Most swimmers have no clue what they are actually doing when they swim. One of the fundamental roles of a coach is to teach swimmers to feel what they are doing and to learn to read the signals their bodies are sending about what is working and what is not.

■ **Complexity.** Change is hard because the one little stroke point you want to change is part of a larger, multipart whole; each part of which has accommodated its functioning to all the other parts as they currently are, even if they are theoretically inefficient. A change in one part affects all the others. We coaches on deck see the one small part we want fixed and assume that changing it is simple. To the swimmer, however, the change is not so simple.

■ **Competitiveness.** Sometimes even great virtues can work against an athlete. Competitiveness is a virtue in an athlete, and coaches try to instill it in all their athletes. But often the most competitive kids are the least willing to slow down and focus on their strokes—they might lose the repeat or swim too slowly! A coach must walk a fine line, getting the swimmer to correctly define winning (swimming fast but not at the expense of good form) without turning a raging lion into a demure house cat.

■ **Lack of confidence.** Most swimmers don't like to do things they aren't good at. However well intended, lectures aimed at convincing them that their weak areas are precisely those where they can see the most striking improvement often fall on deaf ears.

Swimmers need a strong motive to change their strokes since the barriers in the way of positive change are high. Kids are strongly wedded to their comfort zones, and stroke changes entail getting knocked out of those comfort zones for long periods of time. Sometimes it takes a while to find an effective motive to change, and sometimes it takes failure—they discover that they can't succeed unless they change.

CHAPTER 5

Teaching Technique Effectively

What do you want to see when you watch your kids swim? You should look for strokes that work and that are efficient. Some basic talent markers include the following:

- **Smoothness and ease, especially at speed.** The swimmer is moving fast but doesn't seem to be trying.

- **Good distance per stroke.** Each stroke moves the swimmer forward exceptionally well.

- **Good rate control.** The swimmer gets faster well, maintaining a smooth stroke rhythm and a long stroke as the stroke rate increases.

What do you not want to see? Ugly and inefficient strokes that obey the law of diminishing returns, a large increase in effort only slightly increasing speed. When you are watching from the pool deck, certain looks should set off warning bells in your head:

- Swimmers whose movements are jerky or bouncing, or whose bodies sway side to side (back and free especially) or climb up or dive down (breast and fly)

- Swimmers who are obviously working hard but are taking a lot of strokes and going nowhere

- Swimmers whose strokes are *heavily geared* (a term from rowing), meaning they are heavy looking, labored, and do not allow the swimmer to accelerate or increase tempo

- Swimmers who have completely different strokes when they move from practices to meets

Whenever you hear those warning bells, you should immediately wonder, what exactly is causing this swimmer's problem? Is it his conformation? A strength imbalance? Lack of flexibility? Lack of coordination? The phase of his biological development and all its consequences? Fatigue? Inattention? Could the underlying problem be the way you teach the stroke or the way you train it? Has the stress of practice overwhelmed the swimmer's ability to maintain proper stroke mechanics? There are many possible reasons for a swimmer's inefficiency, and a coach can more likely find a solution to the problem if she looks at the swimmer and the situation comprehensively in trying to pinpoint its cause.

Think About Technique Constantly

In order for age-group swimmers to have good technique, it's got to be important to the coach for his swimmers to have good technique. It takes a lot of work to bring this about—work that only happens if the end result is truly valued. Nothing is easier than talking about how important good technique is without taking the necessary steps to bring it about. Beautiful swimming must be an obsession.

> Nothing is easier than talking about how important good technique is without taking the necessary steps to bring it about.

There are three main sources of technical knowledge for the swimming coach. The most important of these is the swimmers in the water. Learn from your swimmers. Watch carefully what your kids are doing in the water, how their strokes adapt to the kind of sets you give them, how their strokes change when you don't say anything, and how they change when you do. Coaching by walking around, or watching strokes from many perspectives, is helpful. Becoming a two-year-old again, continually asking *why* and never being satisfied with easy answers, is also helpful—and so is being willing to take responsibility for the problems you see.

When watching, be alert for patterns. When you see patterns—psychological, physiological, tactical, or technical—common to many swimmers in a group, it means that the teaching and training are having a common effect on the swimmers. Swimmers' strokes are constantly changing as their bodies (and technique) respond and adapt to the training and the instruction. As soon as I start feeling pretty good about how my swimmers look, I'll be jolted by one swimmer, then another, and then hordes developing the same bad pattern. The immediate question in my mind is, how did I create this? The next is, how do I get us back on course?

Individual patterns are also instructive. When a swimmer shows a pattern of stroke problems spanning several strokes, it points to something in that swimmer's conformation, flexibilities, coordination, or peculiar pattern of muscular strengths and weaknesses. Figuring out what causes her to swim the way she does offers a window of insight into what tactics of stroke correction may be most effective with that swimmer.

The second important source of knowledge about technique is swimming video. This is much easier to find than it used to be, and watching swimming videos into the early hours of the morning is great fun. Race video of elite-level swimming is best, especially when watched with the question in mind, what makes these swimmers so fast? Unlike life on the pool deck, you can play and replay video at various speeds, watching for new things each time. Race video is preferred to stroke technique video—with the latter you rarely know what speeds the athlete is swimming at, and the athlete is conscientiously and artificially focusing on technique. You want to watch athletes in the wild, going in for the kill, not athletes in a laboratory experiment where conditions are perfect and antiseptic. That said, one benefit of technique videos is the multitude of underwater vantages they provide. Swimmers are like icebergs—much of what is important is hidden from view to a coach on the deck or to a camera in the stands, and it is difficult to find underwater video from important races.

Studying video of your own age-groupers is less aesthetically pleasing but just as important as studying the atypical Michael Phelps. By watching the best in action, it is easy to be lulled into thinking that fast, beautiful swimming is normal and easy; watching mediocre age-groupers, you realize how difficult it really is. You can learn a lot about what not to do by watching slow swimmers. Comparing the charactcristics of slower swimmers with those of faster swimmers, you can discover what is responsible for the difference in the quality of movement. Be forewarned that the first time you watch your own age-groupers underwater, you will be mortified and shocked. They are doing so much more wrong than you ever realized, and they aren't doing what you've been teaching them to do.

A third fruitful source of ideas is elsewhere: adopting ideas from other sports and disciplines. I have learned a lot about swimming stroke technique from sculling and rowing, kayaking, speed skating, cross-country skiing, and more. Also, a good book on motor learning is worth its weight in gold. Leavening your mind with ideas from a variety of perspectives knocks you out of your comfort zone and enables breakthrough thinking.

No matter how much we think about technique or how much we think we know about it, there is always more to learn. My best thinking about strokes has been born of confusion, being dissatisfied with how my kids were swimming and unsure about exactly what my models were doing to swim so fast. Feeling constantly dissatisfied about one's knowledge is a fruitful though uncomfortable condition. Coaches whose thoughts about technique remain static are probably not as smart as they think they are. There is always a better way, and coaches should be aiming to find it. Meditating on a mountaintop usually helps.

Suggestions for Teaching Technique

Creating beautiful swimmers is difficult. Think of the myth of Sisyphus. His punishment from the gods was to push a boulder up a steep hill for eternity. Every time he almost reached the top, the boulder rolled back down to the bottom, and he had to start all over again. I have been frustrated many times when, after spending hours every day emphasizing good technique, I did not see good strokes at meets. I have been frustrated just as many times when, after spending hours doing all the right stroke drills and refining them to perfection, we looked the same as we always did when we switched to full stroke.

The harsh reality was that I was doing something wrong. Either we weren't working on the right things, or I wasn't teaching and training properly so that the right things would show up when needed. It was back to square one, trying to figure out how to do things better. The following suggestions are offered as lessons learned from many years of mistakes. They lay no claim to perfection or completeness.

Work on Technique All the Time

If technique is important to you, then you must emphasize technique all the time under all sorts of physiological conditions. You cannot relegate it to the occasional technique set or concentrate it in the first two weeks of the season. You must talk about good technique, emphasize it, and demand it all the time through a range of speeds. Not every set is designed for technical improvement, but every set can be done with an eye to technique.

Look to the Whole Body

In swimming, three facts complicate the creation of beautiful strokes. First, we are dealing with a body suspended sideways in a liquid, so Newton's third law applies in overdrive—every action causes an equal and opposite reaction. Second, all the swimming strokes use all the parts of the body. Third, each of the swimming strokes is a continuous skill, meaning that one part or skill flows directly into the next with no breaks. Put these three facts together and we have the *principle of accommodation*: All the parts or skills of a stroke are always wedded to one another, and the action of one part of the body will always affect the other parts.

As a result, a swimmer never has only one stroke problem; instead, he has one problem at one end and at least one more related problem somewhere else. For instance, if a freestyler lifts his head to breathe, that movement will be counteracted by a problem with the leading arm, a problem with the alignment of the legs, and a problem with the recovering arm. Each of these parts of the body has reacted to and accommodated the lifting of the head so that they work together. Even an awful stroke works in a twisted sort of way. Age-group swimmers' strokes are a series of accommodations to mistakes, and little of the expended energy moves the body forward.

For these reasons, stroke improvements are complicated, particularly for the swimmer who has to make the changes. It is not nearly so simple as just fixing x or y. Although it may be easy for the coach to single out a particular skill for improvement, a swimmer cannot easily separate a particular skill from the stroke or stroke drill she is practicing. The one skill is embedded in a whole with many parts that are all connected, and to change one thing, the swimmer must change everything. For this reason, coaches should not expect their suggestions to take the first time. Frequently revisit the same lesson. Expect glacial as opposed to revolutionary change. Slow, gradual, and continual technical improvement—in tandem with continual and gradual physiological improvements—should be the goal.

> Coaches should not expect their suggestions to take the first time. Frequently revisit the same lesson.

There is, however, a silver lining. The interconnectedness of swimming makes life more difficult for the swimmer trying to be perfect technically, but in a way it makes life easier for the coach trying to make improvements. Because problems are never solitary but occur in pairs or more, there are numerous avenues to solving any stroke problem. If starting from the hands doesn't work, for example, then try fixing the problem from the kick.

Keep Things Simple

Swimming strokes are complicated. In order to understand these complex wholes and to be able to explain them to children and adolescents, it is helpful to formulate a set of fundamental stroke points for each stroke. We call this the *stroke catechism*. This catechism breaks each complex stroke into its simple parts. Each part is easily understood, remembered, and performed. We work on these fundamentals in the context of the whole stroke so that stroke rhythm is intact. Note that the catechism is just the skeleton; the flesh is put on in the early season and then intermittently throughout the season when we watch video together, go over each stroke thoroughly, discuss the principles of good and bad strokes, and explain each stroke point in detail. Each point is a cue that is quickly communicated from coach to swimmer and from swimmer to swimmer in the same words every time so that there is no misunderstanding.

The catechism is a work in progress. It will evolve slowly, being added to or subtracted from based on what you see the kids doing in the water and how that compares with the ideal stroke in your head. If a stroke point doesn't work, meaning that it results in unexpected stroke problems (unwanted accommodations in other parts of the body), if the swimmers don't seem to understand it well, or if you notice that after a while you are not using it much, simply throw it out and put something better in its place.

Focus on the Fundamentals

It is better to have a small number of fundamental stroke points for each stroke than to have so many that they confuse the swimmers. Think through each stroke and determine your priorities for what you think is important and what is irrelevant. Don't get too precise or fancy. Kids' bodies are constantly changing in various ways. As swimmers get fitter and faster, their ideal strokes and their physical abilities to maintain those ideal strokes will change accordingly. Additionally, growth spurts change the body's proportions, so a stroke that is perfect today won't be perfect six months from now. Give swimmers a general goal and let them find a way to reach it within the range of their current abilities and strengths.

Keep Them Moving

The most important variable in learning is the amount and quality of practice. The more quality repeats that an athlete swims, the more his body will learn the lessons of good technique and the fitter his body will be, so he will be able to maintain good technique longer and at faster paces. When we practice, we don't sit around; an hour of practice is filled with an hour of practicing.

> The more quality repeats that an athlete swims, the more his body will learn the lessons of good technique.

Assume that most children have short attention spans, and assume that we want to keep their heart rates up to improve fitness. Don't overburden them with 10 minutes of complicated instruction that they aren't going to listen to, that they probably cannot understand, and that they will need another warm-up to recover from. Instead, make stroke instructions short and sweet, and confine most of them to the intervals between repeats, not to the beginning of sets. Use the cue words from the catechism; they convey a lot of meaning in a few words. Frequent, short reminders sprinkled throughout a set are better than one long speech at the beginning.

Swim Full Stroke

Stroke drills are the time-tested, proven method of teaching stroke technique. In many programs, swimmers do as much drilling as swimming. Most coaches employ stroke drills frequently and have abiding faith in them to improve technique. The unexamined assumption is that drills work. But I disagree with the widespread reliance on stroke drills to improve stroke technique because drills are not an efficient means to the desired end, and they do not follow principles of motor learning. There are much better ways to work on technique—ways that use practice time more efficiently and that result in prettier strokes that are more functional for racing.

The following pitfalls of stroke drills detail why swimming full stroke is more effective than performing stroke drills:

- **Stroke drills take too much time for too few results.** I have always believed in the primacy of good technique in swimming. Over the years I have experimented with myriad ways of teaching and training technique. I even used to be a true believer in the efficacy of stroke drills. My teams would spend hours trying to do drills perfectly, mastering each step in a drill progression before moving to the next. My swimmers improved their stroke drills, yet when we returned to full stroke nothing had changed, and they didn't look the way I wanted them to when they raced. I was trying to do everything right, but it wasn't working. Further, each drill helped one aspect of the stroke but hurt others, so a second drill was necessary to cure the ills created by the first; the negative effects of the second drill had to be counteracted by a third drill, and so on. All this took time, and our practice time was limited. We spent too much effort improving strokes indirectly. Why not just cut to the chase and work on the strokes?

- **Little learning transfer occurs from stroke drills to the full stroke.** I am against relying on stroke drills because they conflict with principles of motor learning. There is little transfer of learning from the stroke drills to the full stroke. Transfer is small for beginners just learning a skill, but the more developed the skill, the less transfer there is. Motor skills and motor patterns (complicated combinations of these skills) are specific.

- **Stroke drills teach swimmers' bodies the wrong lessons.** Coaches usually assign a stroke drill to focus on one particular aspect of a stroke as part practice. It is no such thing. Rather, it is a different whole practice. As discussed, swimming strokes are continuous, with each part or skill connected to the others and embedded in a specific whole with a specific rhythm. The whole and the rhythm of the full stroke are completely different from the whole and rhythm of the stroke drill. When coaches have their swimmers perform drills, the swimmers' bodies are learning the complete lesson of the stroke drill, not just the portions coaches want them to retain for the full stroke. Coaches may be able to intellectually separate that one desired part from the drill, but the swimmers' bodies cannot. There is more interference between competing motor patterns—the stroke drill and the full stroke—than there is transfer of desired skills.

■ **We are much better off working on a desired skill when it is embedded in its proper context: the full stroke.** A high-elbow recovery is just as easy to work on when doing freestyle as when doing the catch-up stroke drill, so why confuse the issue? The desired stroke change is going to have to accommodate the myriad parts and rhythm of the full stroke anyway, so getting right to the point is easier and more direct for both swimmer and coach.

■ **Most stroke drills destroy the desired stroke rhythm.** Stroke rhythm is key to good stroke technique and to swimming fast with good technique. Good rhythm means harmony, the parts of the body working together to form the look of a stroke. This harmony is very specific. Most stroke drills destroy the desired stroke rhythm, making them harmful rather than helpful to our aim of creating beautiful and fast strokes. As one example, the popular catch-up drill (also known as *touch and pull*) emphasizes strong kicking and a patient front end, both of which are good things. But it also teaches late torso roll and static body position. The drill completely perverts the proper relation and timing of the pull to the body roll and of one arm pull to the other as practiced when swimming freestyle.

For these reasons, I gradually changed my mind and my program. Over the last few years, we have done almost no drills for freestyle and backstroke, and we have done very few for butterfly and breaststroke. We still do a lot of work on technique, because swimming is a technique-limited sport, but almost all of our specific technique time is spent swimming full stroke, with continually varying technical emphases and continually varying paces (see the Putting Principles into Practice section on page 72). The swimmers look better in the water both when training and when racing, and our time is better spent.

You do not have to eliminate stroke drills entirely. They can be useful in certain situations and with certain swimmers. First, a few stroke drills that retain the stroke rhythm of the full stroke can be used occasionally. (You will find some examples in chapter 7.) Second, because the energy requirements to do butterfly and breaststroke correctly at race tempos are so high, swimmers cannot do much training without their strokes falling apart. Certain drills allow swimmers to retain the desired stroke rhythm and to train longer and faster in these strokes.

Third, for younger swimmers the criterion skill is not race-speed perfection but control and adaptability of technique. Swimmers aged 10 and under should do many drills in all strokes. They need to learn as many movement patterns, stroke rhythms, and kicking and breathing patterns as possible so that they amass an arsenal of movements, allowing them more control and coordination down the road. The more movements swimmers learn and master early, the more control they will have over their chosen movements later on. This is also the rationale for doing a wide variety of dryland exercises and for encouraging kids to play other sports for fun. A 10-year-old who is athletic with good coordination, agility, balance, speed, endurance, and general body control will be a better swimmer.

> The more movements swimmers learn and master early, the more control they will have over their chosen movements later on.

Work on Technique Under Stress

At most programs, technique work is done easily and at slow speeds. It is true that skills are best learned initially at slow speeds and with little physical and mental stress. However, it is also true that the body is good at figuring out how much strength is required for any action and at activating only those motor units from the whole of a muscle to do the job. I call this the *principle of motor prudence*. It is why we don't pull the door handle off when we open a door and why we don't grind our pen into the paper when we write. If we primarily work on technical perfection during easy, slow swimming, then we only recruit a small proportion of the total motor units of the muscles involved in swimming. In other words, we are only teaching a small part of the muscles the correct stroke.

This is problematic because the criterion skill, once again, is good technique at race pace under stress and when fatigued. The intensities and stresses of racing will quickly overwhelm the small amounts of the whole muscles that we have taught to swim well with slow and easy stroke work. This is why so many swimmers who look beautiful when doing stroke work turn ugly almost immediately when they race.

To counter this problem, start the learning process at slow speeds and low intensities, but quickly work to harder, faster swimming with the focus on technical improvements and the desired stroke rhythm. Descending series, in which swimmers get faster as sets progress, teach the swimmer control over a range of speeds. Adding resistance increases the proportion of muscle used in technical work. When used intelligently and carefully, parachutes, paddles, and stretch cords increase strength endurance and teach muscles to swim more beautifully with the desired motor patterns.

Help Swimmers Help Themselves

Swimmers who wait for their coaches to do everything for them remain immature no matter their age. An important part of the coach's charge is to teach swimmers to grow up as athletes. Coaches create mature swimmers by helping them pay attention, helping them become aware of what their bodies are doing when they swim, and helping them take responsibility for their improvement.

Teach Attention

A swimmer may be a motor genius, but if she's focused on other things, her talent is for naught. The only way for a swimmer to correct an ingrained stroke fault is to pay close attention to every stroke that she swims. But most swimmers' minds are wandering from start to finish of practice, and kids who don't pay attention can't make stroke changes.

Coaches can help swimmers build habits of paying attention by carefully guiding their attention. The longer you ask them to swim with a single focus, the less they pay attention to it. You must keep their minds occupied by continually changing the technique focus as they swim—variety adds interest and makes them think. You can increase their motivation to stay focused by reminding them of how much they will improve when they make these stroke changes and fix past mistakes.

Finally, you should continually ask them leading questions: What are you doing with your left hand on your pull? Are your knees breaking the surface on your backstroke kick? Is that a six-beat kick? Guide their attention to ensure that they are heading in the same direction you are.

Teach Awareness

A swimmer who cannot feel the difference between an efficient pull pattern and an inefficient one is not likely to get very fast, yet most swimmers have no idea what they are doing when they swim. Further, many swimmers are completely reliant on the coach to tell them what they are doing correctly and incorrectly. They do not even attempt to think (or feel) for themselves.

Coaches can help their swimmers become more aware of their bodies as they move through the water. Emphasize feel. Tell them how you want them to feel when they swim, and let them figure out how to do it. Teach kids to feel their own errors and excellences by paying attention to the signals their bodies are sending them, such as the feel of water pressure against certain parts of their bodies, the feel of that pressure as it changes throughout a pull, or the sound of the water as they swim smoothly or as they thrash. Alert them to warning signs of bad technique, such as feeling their legs sway as they recover their arms on freestyle or seeing their hands enter the water on butterfly. Their bodies are providing crucial information about what they are doing, but swimmers have to pay attention to that information for it to be valuable.

Another tactic is to force swimmers to feel their stroke in new ways. We are fighting the comfort zone of ingrained motor patterns, when kids are so deep in a rut that they are dead to what swimming feels like. Sometimes even a small change, such as requiring that a swimmer breathe every third stroke on freestyle instead of only to her favorite side, is enough to force her out of the usual rut, allowing her to feel the stroke in a new way and opening up the possibility that she can make a desired change. Sometimes stronger medicine is called for, a change big enough to raze the network of accommodations that has been formed and then create a new stroke. For instance, have a swimmer breathe to the side on butterfly (instead of the traditional forward breathing) or recover with straight arms on freestyle (instead of the traditional high-elbow recovery). Often this new stroke will be much closer to the model, or goal stroke, than the stubbornly flawed stroke from before.

Ask questions instead of simply giving the answers. If a coach is constantly telling the swimmers what they're doing wrong and exactly how to fix the problems, the swimmers never learn anything, and the coach must keep micromanaging with each successive stroke problem. Let swimmers work through their stroke problems. Steer them to think about what they're actually doing.

> Let swimmers work through their stroke problems. Steer them to think about what they're actually doing.

Teach Responsibility

Many swimmers will not think about their technique or try to swim correctly until the coach explicitly points out something for them to work on or is standing right over them. No matter how closely a coach pays attention, he can only watch any one swimmer for a small portion of any practice. If a swimmer only works on efficiency for a small portion of any practice, her strokes will not improve much. To counteract this problem, coaches must emphasize daily that swimmers become active participants in their own technical improvement. The message should be, "I don't make you better. You make you better. I can give you the tools, but you must finish the job." This is part of the bigger idea of taking personal responsibility for their swimming and helping themselves get better.

Structure Practice for Effective Learning

How you construct a training set matters. For this section, we assume a distinction between learning and perfecting a motor skill, which requires variety, and conditioning a skill already learned, which requires repetition. Sets with different aims are constructed differently. To be most effective, sets aimed at learning or technical improvement should use the following principles.

Random Is More Effective Than Blocked Practice for Learning

Two ways to structure training sets are blocked and random practice. *Blocked practice* is repeating a skill again and again before moving on to next one. Swimmers can focus on one skill, refining and perfecting it. This is the most common method of performing stroke work. *Random practice*, on the other hand, varies the skill practiced from repeat to repeat so that the swimmer can never dial in on one skill. With each repeat, his motor memory has to start over, generating a new movement solution to the problem before him: the motor pattern (what to do) with its associated parameters (e.g., how hard, how fast). His body gets practice at figuring out what is needed and how to do it; it learns how to think in the moment. Present performance of skills is not as polished or precise as with blocked practice.

Set Shorthand

The shorthand coaches use for describing training sets can vary and is usually abbreviated. In most programs, FR is freestyle, BK is backstroke, FL is butterfly, and BR is breaststroke. To avoid confusion, let's look at some common forms of set abbreviations.

- ▶ 20 × 50 FR @ :50—This means 20 repeats of 50 meters leaving every 50 seconds.
- ▶ 20 × 50 FR @ :10R—This means 20 repeats of 50 meters with a rest interval of 10 seconds.
- ▶ 20 × 50 @ :50 desc. 1 to 5 or 4 × (5 × 50 @ :50 desc. 1 to 5)—Both of these mean 20 repeats of 50 meters in which swimmers descend (get faster) from the first repeat to the fifth. On the next five repeats, they start at the speed of the first repeat and then descend again. The process of descending continues on every five repeats until the swimmers reach 20.

But we must distinguish between learning and performance. Learning is what is retained tomorrow, not what is performed today. If having swimmers look pretty right now is the priority, then blocked practice—repeating a skill over and over—is best. If the goal is learning and technical improvement, then random practice, with its continual variety of skills, is preferred. Having to make continual adjustments is a key to learning motor skills.

A simple form of a random practice set for swimming would be 20 × 50 FR @ :50, varying the stroke focus each repeat, cycling through the cues of the stroke catechism for instance. A more complex form, which requires that swimmers are familiar with the focal points for all four strokes, would be 20 × 50 @ :50, changing both the stroke and the stroke focus with each repeat. For optimal learning, the bigger the change in skills from one repeat to the next, the better—change both stroke and focus.

Variable Is More Effective Than Constant Practice for Learning

Constant practice means repeating a skill at the same load or stress again and again, such as swimming 20 × 50 FR @ :50, holding :30 with a perfect stroke. Similar to blocked practice, the athlete quickly figures out the movement solution and repeats it with a high degree of precision. *Variable practice* is repeating a skill but continually varying the loads or stresses so that the parameters individualizing the movement pattern are changing with every repeat. In swimming, a number of variables can be manipulated to vary the stress, including tempo (stroke rate), times (intensity), strokes per length, and resistance. Similar to random practice, the athlete is continually challenged to think on the fly, coming up with new movement solutions for each repeat. The stroke must respond to a range of stresses, speeds, levels of fatigue, and so on, as it must in a race. Variable practice teaches control and adaptability, both necessary for learning and improvement.

A simple example of variable practice would be four rounds of 5 × 50 FR @ :50, with controlled descending from :33 to :28 on each round, trying to retain the same motor pattern as speed increases. Another example would be 20 × 50 FR @ :50, holding a steady pace but varying the stroke count (number of strokes per length).

Combine Random and Variable Practice for Optimal Learning

In the optimal blend of these two kinds of practice, just about everything would be changing with every repeat: stroke, stroke emphasis, tempo, time, stroke count, rest interval, breathing patterns, perhaps equipment, kick rhythms, and so on. Swimmers are making continual adjustments—their motor brains are having to think all the time. It is challenging to plan a training set with such variety, and it is often frustrating to watch one since the swimmers' level of performance is not nearly as high as with blocked or constant practice. It is paradoxical that the most learning is taking place when practice looks the most chaotic and the least learning is taking place when practice looks the most perfect. The coach must be strong enough to resist the desire for immediate gratification.

> The most learning is taking place when practice looks the most chaotic and the least learning is taking place when practice looks the most perfect.

Putting Principles Into Practice

There are innumerable ways to bring these principles to life; coaches are limited only by their imaginations. The essence is to vary the demands on the swimmer, give her changing targets to aim at and forcing her body to respond to continual motor challenges. The demands will probably be minimal when a group begins this type of program. But as swimmers become more skilled and have better control over their bodies, the training sets should increase in complexity so that the swimmers are always kept on the edge of their abilities. Following are three of the many technique development sets we include in our training program.

Neuromuscular Games

Neuromuscular games direct swimmers' attention to one aspect of the stroke and ask them to alternate ways of performing it. As a simple instance, on a freestyle set swimmers can alternate one repeat with straight-arm recovery and one with high-elbow (traditional) recovery. Further, they can alternate between a six-beat kick and a two-beat kick, between catch-up timing and oppositional timing, or between breathing to one side only and bilateral breathing. In any of these cases, the swimmers alternate between two very different ways of performing a skill, maintaining precise control over aspects of the skill that they usually perform unthinkingly and sloppily, and gaining a new awareness of what they are doing in the water. Once the swimmers reach a certain point of control, we begin manipulating two variables at once. For instance, they might swim down with straight-arm recovery and six-beat kick, come back with high-elbow recovery and two-beat kick, and so on. The point is to have the swimmers think about each length, because the focus is changing continually. Freestyle seems to have more obvious variables than other strokes (for instance, there is only one right way to recover in back), but a creative coach can think up hundreds of variations on this theme.

Rainbow Focus, Pass It On

The rainbow focus uses a long set of short repeats on short rest, say 25s or 50s with 10 seconds of rest, and we change the stroke focus every repeat or two. As the leading group of swimmers finishes each repeat, the coach calls out the next stroke focus using the cues from the stroke catechism, such as "Double explosion out the back!" on butterfly. Before the leaders begin the next repeat, they yell out the focus to the swimmers in the second group as they come to the wall, who then yell the focus to the third group, and so on. In passing along the stroke focus, they must use the cue words and nothing but the cue words. They are not allowed to add their personality to the focus because it results in confusion for those down the line.

There are several advantages to this format. Having each swimmer shout the focus aloud to the next swimmer helps reinforce in his mind what he is to think about, so attention improves dramatically. It also keeps things moving. The coach does not have to wait for all of the swimmers to finish before announcing the stroke focus, so groups can do short-rest aerobic sets and achieve both fitness and technical improvements. Throughout the season, these sets get more complicated and demanding as we change strokes, paces, breathing patterns, and stroke counts.

Stroke-Count Games and Progressions

Usually when swimmers fatigue, their strokes get short and choppy. This seems to be the natural and unconscious reaction to discomfort. With stroke-count games, we control the number of strokes per length and we have the swimmers aim at precise goals. In this way, we counteract the natural shortening and make the swimmers conscious of keeping their strokes long and efficient under stress. There are so many variations here that it would be pointless to try to list them all, but a simple example would be two rounds of 5 × 100 breaststroke, short course. On each round, complete the following repeats:

- Repeat 1: 100 meters at 8 strokes per length (S/L)
- Repeat 2: 75 meters at 8 S/L, 25 meters at 7 S/L
- Repeat 3: 50 meters at 8 S/L, 50 meters at 7 S/L
- Repeat 4: 25 meters at 8 S/L, 75 meters at 7 S/L
- Repeat 5: 100 meters at 7 S/L

The second round is swum faster than the first. This is a challenging type of set; the difficulty increases as each round progresses, particularly if speeds are maintained as the number of strokes decreases. Swimmers must focus on their technique and their streamlining every length. Coaches must ensure that good stroke rhythm is maintained as swimmers get longer and more tired.

Fitness and Efficiency Work Together

Technique is important, but it isn't everything. A swimmer's ability to maintain efficient stroke mechanics is limited by her fitness or physiology. There will come a breaking point, whether in practice or in a race, where the intensity or duration overwhelms her ability to swim with the desired mechanics. A major aim of training is to move that breaking point so that the improved physiological capacities enable the swimmer to swim farther, faster, and prettier. Every day in practice, coaches must have one eye on physiology and the other on stroke technique, always remembering the criterion skill: good technique under the stress of racing.

Often, sets will be constructed with physiological gains in mind. Unlike specific technique sets which are aimed at learning or perfecting strokes, these sets focus on conditioning the skills already acquired, which takes repetition as opposed to variety. An important means of conditioning the racing stroke is descending sets, or training the stroke through a range of speeds with an eye toward technique, especially as fatigue hits. For training fly and breast, short rest sets alternating freestyle with stroke repeats are also useful for maintaining good technique under stress. Training is discussed further in upcoming chapters, particularly in chapter 9.

CHAPTER 6

Improving Freestyle and Backstroke

When done well, swimming looks easy. But in reality, swimming is complicated. There is a lot that has to happen just right and at just the right times. All the body parts are working at the same time, the body is suspended sideways in a liquid while everything is happening, and the muscles are getting fatigued—so each movement becomes progressively harder. The best way to teach and work on perfecting the strokes is to simplify them to their fundamentals, the most important stroke points. Each movement is simple to perform—a child does not have to be a motor genius to keep his head steady or to recover with elbows high in freestyle, for example. Each fundamental can be focused on and practiced one at a time while a swimmer performs the full stroke. The challenge, of course, is to keep the swimmers constantly thinking about and practicing these fundamentals until they become good habits and to train swimmers so that they can maintain the fundamentals when fatigued.

Chapters 6 and 7 discuss the fundamentals for the individual strokes, using the stroke catechism as the skeleton. These chapters also assume the common fundamentals discussed in chapter 4: cleanliness, directness, creating and maintaining momentum, keeping the momentum as constant as possible, and harmony of stroke rhythm. Each stroke fundamental is discussed in detail and followed by a list of one or more common problems with this part of the stroke. You can put these principles into practice every day in the workout, and you can fix problems implicitly by having swimmers focus on doing the right things—the stroke fundamentals of the catechism—and not by pointing out the various things swimmers are doing wrong. In other words, you say "Do this!" rather than "Don't do that!"

For each stroke, you will find cues from the catechism. Each cue, or stroke point, is short, simple, easily communicated, and easily understood. During practice, you can simply state the stroke point and in a few words convey a wealth of information about what you want swimmers to do. Because the swimming stroke is a continuous action, the separate fundamentals blend into one another. Doing one well leads to doing the next well; performing one poorly leads to performing the next poorly.

Freestyle Stroke Catechism

Freestyle is the fastest competitive stroke, the stroke with more events than any other, and the stroke that forms the base of training for most programs. Most obviously, freestyle is an oppositional stroke performed on the stomach, with alternating arm pulls and alternating flutter kicks. These stroke basics determine the particular challenges of going fast in freestyle, finding what will work and what will not.

BODY LONG AND TAUT

You want swimmers to have a long, horizontal, streamlined body, and you want to see a connection between the strong trunk muscles and the pulling and kicking motions. Swimming with ankle buoys—placing the pull buoy between the ankles instead of the thighs—develops this fundamental. This gives swimmers horizontal high points at the chest (caused by the lungs) and the ankles (caused by the buoy), and they must try to maintain a perfectly horizontal body line by keeping the torso and legs straight and true.

Common Stroke Faults

Soggy-spaghetti or wiggle-worm bodies destroy the streamlining of the body. A slack core provides no foundation for the pull and the kick to connect to and does not bring the strong trunk muscles into play.

HEAD STEADY AND LEVEL

When swimmers are not breathing, their heads should be still and quiet. They should be looking straight down underneath them, with the back of the neck unwrinkled. The head should be an extension of the long body line. A still head acts as a stable center around which the rest of the stroke moves.

Common Stroke Faults

Many swimmers often lift up, throw, duck, or bury their heads in conjunction with breathing. Unnecessary head motion is a leading cause of stroke inefficiencies in all other parts of the body. It is amazing how swimmers will almost immediately smooth out their strokes and fix many seemingly unrelated stroke problems simply by keeping their heads still.

ONE-GOGGLE BREATHING

When a swimmer breathes, her head should be horizontal, and only one goggle, one nostril, half the mouth, and half the chin should be visible from the deck (see figure 6.1). Everything else should be underwater. To accomplish this, swimmers should breathe by moving their heads with the shoulder roll, not independently so that the breathing action fits into the body rhythm already established. Swimmers breathe on the stretch—while the lead arm is reaching forward, the pulling arm is finishing the stroke, and the body is stretching to its greatest extent.

FIGURE 6.1   **Head movement is minimal when the swimmer breathes.**

Common Stroke Faults

Turning the head radically to breathe so that anyone on the deck can see the swimmer's opposite ear (similar to the girl in *The Exorcist*) has a negative effect on the pull. Some swimmers breathe late, initiating the breathing motion when the pull is half finished, or they move their heads on a completely different rhythm from that of the rest of the body parts. These head problems radiate to the rest of the body.

ROLL AND REACH TO THE CATCH

Coaches generally refer to the beginning of the pull, when the swimmer first grabs hold of the water, as the *catch*. We want swimmers to get traction on the water as far in front of them as they can by extending the shoulder and shoulder blade as the body begins to roll on its side as shown in figure 6.2. The goal is the longest effective pull. This fundamental also helps align the pull and the body roll in the same rhythm.

Common Stroke Faults

Swimmers who are in a hurry often pull too soon, before their bodies are rolled onto the side and their arms are repositioned to pull effectively. When the catch is too short and quick, the resultant pull is too short and biomechanically unsound.

FIGURE 6.2   **The swimmer rolls and reaches for the longest effective pull.**

WRIST, ROTATE, AND RESISTANCE

This stroke cue defines the three Rs of the catch: Cock the wrist, rotate the elbow, and feel resistance (see figure 6.3). (Note that this is a reworking of the traditional high-elbow pull.) Because the pull is the prime mover of swimming, this is arguably the most fundamental of all the stroke fundamentals. After rolling and reaching, swimmers press down with the fingertips, thus cocking the wrist, and then rotate the elbow out and around (medially) so that the forearm goes nearly vertical (see figure 6.4) while the upper arm remains nearly horizontal and near the surface. Then and only then they press backward with the first hard pressure of the pull. Swimmers should feel resistance—pressure and purchase—on the palm, the inside of the forearm, and the inside of the upper arm as they pull. They must be patient and set up the segments of the arm before the pull begins so that it can begin well; after all, well begun is half done. No pull means no speed, no matter how straight and true the body line or how steady the head.

FIGURE 6.3   Proper position for the catch.

Common Stroke Faults

Most swimmers are too impatient to set up the pull effectively, especially when they race. When they ram their arms into the water like a pile driver and rip backward, they push water in the wrong directions. When they begin their pulls with the hand and elbow on a level or nearly level plane, the arm slips through the water and the body goes nowhere. When they attempt to pull with straight arms, the lack of strength makes their elbows drop and their strokes collapse halfway through the pull.

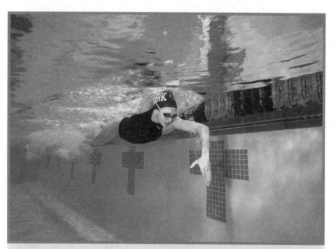

FIGURE 6.4   At the beginning of the pull, the forearm should have a nearly vertical orientation.

ROLL THROUGH THE PULL, SLOW TO FAST

Swimmers should aim to catch the water out front when the torso is facing one way and to finish the pull when it is facing the other way. As they pull, the body rolls around its long axis. The arm pull and body roll work in the same rhythm. The body roll makes the arm recovery easier (and easier on the shoulder joints), gives length to the stroke, increases the power of the pull (because the arms don't bear the entire burden), gives the pull greater leverage, permits easier breathing, and reduces drag when the timing is correct. The hand and arm should accelerate gradually but constantly throughout the pull: Start now, finish fast.

Common Stroke Faults

When a swimmer's head, arms, kick, and body roll all work on different rhythms, one effort counteracts another. When swimmers roll too far onto each side, the usual results are a wide scissor kick and a dropped-elbow pull instead of the desired six-beat kick and high-elbow pull. When they pull with no acceleration out the back end, they appear to be moving in slow motion and there is no power at the finish of the stroke. When they accelerate badly by dropping the elbow and sliding out the back in order to move their hands quickly, the body stays put despite the quick hands.

ON YOUR SIDE, ELBOW HIGH

Swimmers should finish the pull on the side and recover the arm by lifting the elbow instead of throwing the arm from the shoulder. The recovery arm is kept close to the body (see figure 6.5), relaxed and effortless. The recovery should look easy from the pool deck and feel easy when performed. This sort of recovery is also much easier on the shoulders, keeps the body in its long line, and leads to consistent entry positions and thus consistent catch points.

FIGURE 6.5   **The recovery arm should be close to the body and relaxed.**

Common Stroke Faults

Swimmers often display wild, throwing, jerking recoveries, which may be coupled with breathing problems (head lifting, throwing, and ducking), crossing over the midline at the head entry, wide sideways sculling at the front of the pull, and swaying sideways with the hips and legs. In this situation you can see the equal and opposite reactions of swimming—one problem causes several others.

STRONG AND STEADY SIX-BEAT

A six-beat kick means a swimmer flutter-kicks six times during a stroke cycle. Since each freestyle stroke cycle contains two arm pulls—usually termed *two strokes*—there are three kicks per pull or stroke. A consistent, balanced six-beat kick provides a good foundation for a consistent, balanced freestyle. It gives control to the whole stroke and enables a swimmer to be patient at the front end of the arm stroke so that the pull is set up well. A steady six-beat kick is more easily learned when a swimmer is young and will consider as normal a coach's request or command to six-beat kick all the time. The six-beat rhythm is easily practiced by having the swimmers count their kicks when they swim freestyle (or backstroke), three kicks per pull, counting "one, two, three" repetitively.

The beat should be strong and steady, like a metronome. Through this simple exercise, almost all swimmers can quickly add the six-beat rhythm to their repertoire. All swimmers, even female distance aces (who usually swim with a two-beat kick), should be able to do a good six-beat kick to come home strong and have an extra gear when racing.

FIGURE 6.6 **Proper technique for a six-beat kick shown underwater.**

The technique of the kick is as important as its rhythm. Coaches must teach proper kicking technique because it does not come naturally to most swimmers. Many awful kickers aren't lazy; they are just trying to kick with inefficient, energy-sapping technique. Ideally, the kick is fairly small, within the shadow of the body's streamline. The leg stays straight on the upbeat (recovery), but the knee must bend at the beginning of the downbeat to produce a powerful snap (see figures 6.6 and 6.7). In other words, swimmers should not kick with straight legs, as is often taught. They should use all these joints—hips, knees, and ankles—to produce fast speed.

Common Stroke Faults

Kicking oddities, such as hitches in the timing, crossed ankles, or wide scissoring of the legs, are always tied to problems elsewhere. For example, whenever the ankles smash together, there is a slip sideways in the pull as the swimmer loses traction on the water. Again, swimmers who splay their legs in a wide scissor have rolled too far onto the side and are trying to regain their balance.

FIGURE 6.7 **Proper technique for a six-beat kick shown from above the surface.**

STRAIGHT FORWARD, STRAIGHT BACKWARD

This stroke cue exemplifies the principle of directness. The pull is straight backward down the midline with as little lateral (side-to-side) movement as possible. The recovery arm moves straight forward, close to the body, with as little lateral sway as possible. The palm faces backward and the fingertips point downward throughout both the pull and recovery.

Common Stroke Faults

Swimmers who swing their recovery arms wide or whose pulls include side-to-side sculling require accommodations in other body parts. Soon, little of their effort is propelling the body forward and much is counteracting incorrect actions.

BALANCE LEFT TO RIGHT

Every stroke taken should be identical and efficient, left arm or right arm, regardless of what side a swimmer is breathing to. Michael Phelps and many other elite male swimmers gallop or lope when they swim freestyle because they almost always breathe to one side only. When they breathe to the right, for instance, their left arm pull is shorter and deeper with less effective high-elbow positioning. When watching these swimmers underwater, you can see that one arm pull is much stronger and more efficient than the other. I have a difficult time believing that this is a good thing, even if they are swimming fast. Two efficient pulls should result in faster swimming than one efficient and one not.

To create stroking that is as even as possible, we swim many freestyle sets with a *balance focus:* The swimmers alternate a length or a repeat breathing every third arm pull, then one breathing every left arm pull only, then one breathing every right only, then one breathing every fifth arm pull. By varying the breathing patterns, swimmers become comfortable breathing on either side, and they learn to feel subtle differences in their stroke patterns and rhythms. All strokes should feel identical, and swimmers are to be alert to changes, particularly ones caused by poor head position and breathing mechanics.

Common Stroke Faults

Most swimmers have uneven, unbalanced strokes. Strokes taken while breathing are often much less efficient and powerful than nonbreathing strokes.

Freestyle Summary

Sometimes we use a shortened version of this freestyle catechism that includes four stroke points, one focus emphasizing the pull, one the kick, one the breath, and one the recovery, so that the major bases are covered. During a training set, swimmers focus on one stroke point during each repeat, cycling through the four, ensuring that they are swimming with technique in mind all the time. The freestyle summary is as follows:

- ▶ Wrist, rotate, resistance
- ▶ Strong and steady six-beat
- ▶ One-goggle breathing
- ▶ On your side, elbow high

Backstroke Stroke Catechism

The fundamentals of backstroke and those of freestyle share many similarities. Both strokes are swum horizontally in the water with the body rolling on its long axis, both are asymmetrical with alternate arm stroking and alternate leg kicking, and in both, the arm pull is down the length of the body. In backstroke, however, the head is more easily controlled and does not lead to as many problems as in freestyle, and freestyle is faster because of biomechanical advantages.

HEAD STEADY

Swimmers should never move the head. There is no reason to look around, especially for the wall at a turn or finish. The head should be the center of stillness and permanence, the axis that the shoulders and hips roll around. An easy breathing and stroking rhythm is created by breathing in as one arm recovers and breathing out as the other recovers.

Common Stroke Faults

If swimmers wag, wiggle, or bob their heads, their shoulders and hips are pulled out of line. This hurts their streamlining and increases drag or resistance. Also, when swimmers quickly inhale and exhale with every recovery, they pant instead of breathe.

LEGS UP, STRONG AND STEADY SIX-BEAT

Swimmers should keep their bodies as horizontal and streamlined as possible, with the hips and the flutter kick close to the surface (see figure 6.8). A small and steady flutter kick helps maintain stroke control and horizontal body position. The kick should boil the water rather than splash, and the knees should stay just at the water's surface. The kick should sound like a metronome.

FIGURE 6.8　**Proper six-beat kick technique.**

Common Stroke Faults

Some swimmers' kicks are deep and heavy, losing the horizontal body position and creating more resistance than propulsion. As in freestyle, an irregular kick—replete with pauses, stops, ankles crashing together, knees bicycling well above the surface, or legs splayed wide—is a drag problem in itself and is symptomatic of stroke problems in other parts of the body.

AGGRESSIVE SHOULDER AND PINKY IN

FIGURE 6.9　**The hand, arm, shoulder, and hip roll at the same time.**

Most coaches teach a pinky-first hand entry directly ahead of the shoulder. Even more important, however, swimmers should not just set the hand into the water but should roll the hand, arm, shoulder, and hip into the water at the same time (see figure 6.9). Thus, the entry happens with the whole side of the body, not just one finger, and the entry ends at the proper catch depth, not stopping at the surface. The entry and the drive downward to the catch should be clean, quick, strong, and one motion.

Common Stroke Faults

Most young swimmers perform the hand entry and start the arm pull while still flat on their backs. It is difficult to recover from this flawed beginning. Their arms and torsos are working on different rhythms, and they are too impatient to roll down to the proper catch depth. Instead, the hand rests on the surface (usually overreaching behind the head as opposed to directly in line with the shoulder) and immediately pushes sideways. As a result, the swimmers gain no purchase on the water, they put pressure in the wrong direction, and their legs sway out of line.

WRIST, ROTATE, AND RESISTANCE

A good catch is crucial to a good pull. The backstroke catch is directly analogous to the freestyle catch. When the swimmer has aggressively rolled to the catch depth, with the hand about 8 inches (20 cm) below the surface, the arm must be repositioned to pull backward (see figure 6.10). Swimmers should press with the fingertips to cock the wrist, rotate the elbow to orient the forearm, then press backward toward the feet with the hand, forearm, and inside of the upper arm as shown in figure 6.11. In the old days there was a lot of up-and-down motion in the backstroke pull, but not anymore. Most top backstrokers swim with direct, almost horizontal arm pulls. Most importantly, we want swimmers to pull backstroke beside them, not underneath or behind them; the angles on the shoulder joint should be easy, not extreme.

FIGURE 6.10 **The swimmer repositions the arm for an effective pull backwards.**

Common Stroke Faults

Watching young swimmers, one would think that a backstroke catch is nearly impossible to do well. Most swimmers rush the entry and catch, never getting good traction or purchase on the water. Others drop the elbow and slide their hands and arms to the finish, like a kayak paddle turned sideways slipping through a stroke. Alternatively, they pull with straight arms in a semicircle, directing the water sideways most of the time and causing their legs to sway back and forth.

FIGURE 6.11 **The elbow bends 90 degrees halfway through the pull.**

ENGAGE AND SQUEEZE THE LATS

FIGURE 6.12 **Halfway through the pull, the swimmer keeps the elbow high (pointed toward the bottom) and uses the lats to press backward with the hand and forearm.**

The latissimus dorsi muscles of the back are much stronger than the arms. We strengthen the pull by engaging the lats to do much of the work. Swimmers pull by keeping the elbow high and squeezing the lats. (Since the swimmers are on their backs, maintaining a high elbow means keeping the elbow pointed down toward the bottom. See figure 6.12.) They hang onto the water with the hand and forearm, and they keep pressing all the way to the back of the stroke, accelerating all the while. This allows the greatest impulse: force applied for the longest distance.

Common Stroke Faults

When the muscles of the body core are not strong or the torso is not maintained straight and true during the swimming stroke, there is little connection between the arms and torso, and the swimmer overpowers the pull by doing all the work with the arms.

AGGRESSIVE HIP AND THUMB OUT

Just as we want swimmers to enter the water with the side of the body, we want them to exit the water with the side of the body. They should finish pushing, then simultaneously roll the hip, shoulder, and hand—thumb first—vertically into the recovery. The finish of the pull (see figure 6.13) and start of the recovery is fast and flowing, and it takes almost no effort.

FIGURE 6.13 **Proper positioning for the pull finish.**

Common Stroke Faults

Swimmers who finish very deep must slowly extract their arms from the water, similar to pulling an arm out of wet cement. This kills any momentum the pull has created, and it takes a lot of effort. Swimmers who slide out the back half of the stroke by rolling their hips before the pull has concluded will lose pressure on the water and power at the finish of the pull.

EASY AND RELAXED RECOVERY

The recovery arm should swing straight, relaxed, and vertical (see figure 6.14). At the end of the recovery, the hand should enter directly over the shoulder. The shoulder should be out of the water through much of the recovery so that the recovery arm doesn't plow through the water. The recovery should look and feel easy.

Common Stroke Faults

When a swimmer's recovery arm swings sideways off the hip instead of vertically, it causes the legs to sway sideways. This reveals a deeper problem with the arm pull.

FIGURE 6.14 **Proper recovery arm position.**

CHAPTER 7

Improving Butterfly and Breaststroke

Butterfly and breaststroke are so misunderstood. Butterfly has a bad reputation among most swimmers as being difficult. They complain about having to race or train fly, and when they are allowed to choose their own races at meets, they avoid it. Training and racing fly should not be causes for complaint but for celebration. Swimmers have the choice of using a racing stroke or a survival stroke. Racing stroke is forward and fast; survival stroke is vertical and slow. Most age-groupers think butterfly is difficult because they swim survival stroke in practice all the time and in races as soon as they get tired. Survival stroke is indeed difficult, exhausting, inefficient, and ugly. No wonder they fear it.

With breaststroke, the thinking is, either you are or you aren't a breaststroker. If you weren't born a breaststroker, then you won't be fast. There is nothing you can do to change the situation; therefore, there is little point in working hard at the stroke. There does seem to be a bigger gap between the top breaststrokers and everyone else, and it is probably the case that genetic gifts, such as leg ranges of motion, play a bigger part in breaststroke success than in other strokes. But it is also true that much of the gap can be made up with flexibility development and training.

Coaches and swimmers can overcome these prejudices by thinking correctly about the strokes. With butterfly, train and race with the racing stroke and expect fast swimming. The butterfly stroke is like a greyhound who will never be happy cooped up in a tiny dog run. To be enjoyed properly, butterfly must be raced. For breaststroke, the training program should try to overcome the biggest disadvantage of swimmers who are, to use a phrase from coach Jon Urbanchek, man-made breaststrokers, and that is a lack of crucial flexibilities. Encourage swimmers to swim well and swim fast, no matter the stroke.

Butterfly Stroke Catechism

Fast butterflyers are fast for a reason: They have the engine (physiology), the efficiency (good technique), and the mentality (race). Slow flyers have none of these. If Michael Phelps swam fly like your typical age-grouper, he wouldn't be Michael Phelps. As with the other strokes, the whole stroke is broken into its fundamental stroke points or cues, and these solve the most common stroke mistakes made by age-groupers. Before we discuss the catechism, though, a few notes on butterfly timing are in order.

The relationship of movements of the arms, legs, and torso is precisely coordinated. There are four parts to the pull and, given two kicks per arm cycle, four parts to the kick. They fit together as follows:

1. The first kick begins its downbeat as the hands enter the water and begin to reach forward and reposition for the pull.
2. The recovery or upbeat of the kick occurs as the hands pull diagonally in toward the navel.
3. The downbeat of the second kick occurs as the hands push directly backward at the end of the pull.
4. The upbeat of the kick occurs as the arms are recovering out of the water.

Swimmers who are out of phase have problems swimming fast, and their strokes are characterized by stops, jerks, and generally violent movements. Swimmers whose body parts are working in harmony are beautiful to watch.

Butterfly presents an interesting physics problem: The pull and kick are tremendously strong, but the swimmer slows down radically during the arm recovery since there is nothing pushing her forward. In fact, the opposite occurs: The legs are recovering by pressing up, which pulls the hips down, and the arms are recovering by swinging forward, which pulls the body backward. The body will decelerate no matter what, so it is important that the swimmer does nothing to worsen the situation by neglecting the kick at the end of the pull or by keeping the head up too long or too high during the recovery. Both moves cause the hips to drop and stop the swimmer almost dead in the water. The physics of butterfly demands a streamlined body position at this critical moment.

SOFT ENTRY, BUNS UP

The entry of the hands should be light, quick, and soft so that the momentum flows forward. The hands are set in at shoulder width and near the surface as they initiate pressure against the water. The hips should be high (buns up; see figure 7.1) and the body position almost level (figure 7.2) as the hands enter. There is no dead time at the front end of the stroke, and the body is positioned to pull well.

FIGURE 7.1   At the entry of the hands, the hips are high.

Common Stroke Faults

There are many ways to kill momentum at the hand entry. Some swimmers dive with the arms and head deep underwater upon entry so that the pull starts 2 feet (60 cm) below the surface, leading to a series of problems. Some collapse at the front end with heavy pile-driver entries; you can see these swimmers stop dead in the water. Others have a long, passive glide after they enter, gradually slowing to a stop before they pull.

FIGURE 7.2   At the entry of the hands, the body position is almost level.

WRIST, ROTATE, AND RESISTANCE

The faster swimmers can be doing something that produces momentum, the better. Just as in the freestyle and backstroke (see chapter 6), swimmers want to reposition the hands, forearms, and upper arms so that immediately after the entry of the hands, the fingers point down and the elbow is high as shown in figure 7.3. This is the classic high-elbow position, and it produces a pulling orientation that is biomechanically sound and powerful. The swimmer presses in the right directions so that he moves forward fast.

FIGURE 7.3   The swimmer needs a high elbow position soon after the catch.

FIGURE 7.4 With a brief outward sweep, the swimmer catches to begin the arm pull.

In freestyle and backstroke, the body roll helps reposition the arms; in butterfly, a short, outward sweep or scull combined with the pitch of the body does the task (see figure 7.4). Note that the purpose of the short, outsweep or scull is not to support the body, as it does with poor butterflyers, but to reposition the arms for quick backward pressure against the water.

Common Stroke Faults

Many swimmers have a wide, outward sweep instead of a short, quick scull, losing momentum instead of gaining leverage. Others press down on the water to support the body during a breath, wasting the effort that should be propelling the body forward. Some drop the elbows so that the hands and forearms are essentially horizontal; their arms slide through the pull instead of gaining traction, so the pull is ineffective.

FIGURE 7.5 Side view of hands sweeping in.

FIGURE 7.6 The hands nearly touch underneath the chest.

ROUND THE BEND, INTO THE MIDDLE, AND OUT THE BACK

We are aiming for a long, powerful pull that sweeps slightly out then powerfully in and backward, with good traction on the water the entire way and a gradual acceleration of the hands from start to finish. First, swimmers reach forward and scull outward to reposition the hands and forearms and grab hold of the water as the legs are kicking down. Next, they sweep the hands diagonally in and back until the thumbs touch or nearly touch under the chest (see figures 7.5 and 7.6). Then they push straight backward as the second kick snaps downward for maximum forward momentum. Good pressure on hands and forearms throughout the entire pull is crucial. Though it is not necessary for the thumbs to actually touch, swimmers know that, if they do, they are pulling inside and not leaving the pull wide. This is especially important when swimmers get tired and the pull tends to get wider, shorter, slower, and weaker.

Common Stroke Faults

Almost all bad butterflyers have wide and short pulls that become very short and very wide when they get tired. By the end of a race, they are pulling their hands out at the navel.

STAY LOW, DRIVE FORWARD

We want a fly where every stroke is the same, at the same level, and moves the body the same distance forward, whether the swimmer is breathing or not. Swimmers should feel that they are driving the body forward, not up. On the nonbreathing strokes, they should drive the crown of the head directly forward; on the breathing strokes, they should drive the eyebrows forward (not the chin). Here we see one of the most important distinctions between fast and slow butterflyers: Slow flyers use their arms and legs to support their bodies as they lift upward, whereas fast flyers use the water and proper body positioning to support themselves, so they can use energy from the arms and legs to drive forward. This is not a question of effort but of effort correctly or incorrectly applied. Slow flyers can be working just as hard as fast flyers; their work is simply misplaced.

Common Stroke Faults

Most young butterflyers climb high out of the water and then collapse back into it on every breathing stroke. This wastes a lot of energy.

BREATHE EARLY WITH YOUR EYEBROWS

This stroke cue is the corollary to the previous one about staying low and driving forward. Instead of lifting the body or reaching the chin forward to breathe, swimmers should reach forward with

their eyebrows and stay low as shown in figure 7.7. This process begins early in the pull, and the swimmer actually breathes as the pull is exploding backward and the arms begin the recovery. The goal is to have the head and body at the same level on every stroke and to have the body driving forward on every stroke, whether breathing or not. Momentum is a beautiful thing and needs preserving.

FIGURE 7.7 **The swimmer drives forward on the breathing stroke.**

Common Stroke Faults

Breathing too late or too long ruins the body's streamline and stops forward progress. If the swimmer breathes while the arms are recovering, the hips drop and the body goes vertical. If the swimmer keeps the chin reaching forward so long that she can see her hands entering the water in front of her, the body's orientation at the entry of the hands is the opposite of what we want. A stroke started badly never gets better.

ONE UP, ONE DOWN; NO FIRST, NO LAST

In our practices, swimmers are required to breathe every other stroke (one up, one down) and are not allowed to breathe the first or last strokes of a length (no first, no last). Though the best butterflyer in the world breathes every stroke in his races, the typical age-grouper is not Michael Phelps.

For age-groupers, breathing every other stroke is easier and faster. It preserves a horizontal body position and helps keep the stroke driving forward. Often swimmers will complain that breathing one up, one down is too difficult; however, it is only hard if they do not practice it, and swimming forward is much easier and more pleasurable than swimming vertically. Tell your swimmers that once they are world class, they can choose their own breathing pattern.

Common Stroke Faults

Most young swimmers have uneven butterfly strokes. Their nonbreathing strokes are much more efficient, forward, and powerful than their breathing strokes. The more strokes they breathe in a row, the slower they swim and the more vertical their body position. This is especially true at the end of races, when swimmers are tired and their stroke mechanics have deteriorated. Every meet, coaches watch heat after heat of kids going vertical and barely moving as they struggle to finish races. Also, breathing the first stroke off a wall and breathing the last stroke into a wall both mean going up, not forward.

DOUBLE EXPLOSION OUT THE BACK

FIGURE 7.8   **At the start of the double explosion, the knees are bent at about 90 degrees and the hands are close together ready to press backward.**

FIGURE 7.9   **At the end of the double explosion, the body is straight and almost horizontal.**

The goal here is to have a double explosion consisting of a powerful push backward with the hands simultaneously with a powerful kick downward with the feet (see figures 7.8 and 7.9). This combination should launch swimmers' bodies forward so that they feel like they are being shot out of a cannon. If they don't feel this propulsion, the timing is not right. Kicking hard and correctly out the back of the stroke is probably the single most important fundamental of butterfly for young swimmers. It increases momentum and improves the streamlining of the body.

Common Stroke Faults

Most young or tired swimmers do not kick as they finish the pull, leaving the arms to do all the work. Their arms are not strong enough for this, and as a result, the pull is not finished properly and the body goes vertical. Another problem is swimmers pulling their legs up (recovering the legs) as they finish the arm pull, thus aggravating the harmful body position. When swimmers kick after the pull is finished, they destroy stroke rhythm because the body parts are out of phase.

RECOVER WITH A FLING, NOT A LIFT

Swimmers should press from the finish of the pull right into a flinging recovery. They should not slow the hands down and then lift the arms for the recovery. The recovery should be ballistic and effortless, controlled but relaxed as shown in figure 7.10. If it feels hard, swimmers are doing it wrong. The arms should be kept nearly straight and the body alignment flat. From a physicist's point of view, the recovery is the critical moment for maintaining the momentum just produced by the double explosion of the pull and kick. The body is decelerating quickly, so it must be kept horizontal and streamlined to lessen the damage.

FIGURE 7.10 **An easy and relaxed butterfly recovery.**

Common Stroke Faults

The most common problem is a heavy recovery, in which the swimmer lifts the arms out of the water. To uncover the cause of this problem, we have to go back a couple of steps. (Remember, stroke problems are not singular but plural. One problem is tied to several others, and the cumulative effect destroys momentum.) A deep entry leads to a deep pull and a deep finish, creating a big problem when it comes time to breathe and to recover the arms. Swimmers are forced to breathe late and to lift their arms straight up to recover, causing their bodies to go vertical. Lifting the arms out of the water from a dead stop takes a lot of energy. Also, swimmers with very wide pulls also have very short pulls, and when swimmers pull out early, they lift their arms to recover.

WORK ALL FOUR BEATS OF THE KICK

As noted earlier in the chapter, two kicks accompany each stroke cycle. Each kick consists of a downbeat (the power beat or snap) and an upbeat (the recovery beat or press), so there are four beats to a stroke cycle. Kicking up is just as important as kicking down. Though most of the power is created by the quick downbeat, if the swimmer does not then immediately recover or press up, the legs and feet are not in position for the next powerful downbeat, which causes the arms and legs to be out of phase. It is probably the case that the kick at the front end of the stroke, as the hands are entering the water, is done more from the hips and emphasizes body position; the kick at the back end of the stroke, as the hands are finishing the pull, is done more from the knees and emphasizes foot speed.

Common Stroke Faults

When a swimmer has no recovery or a late one, the feet are not positioned correctly to kick the down beat. The legs and arms are out of phase and the body parts work against each other, producing a stroke that is jerky, heavy, tiring, and slow.

Butterfly Triad

Swimmers gain or lose the most time during the final quarter of a race. Most swimmers are falling apart and falling back; a precious few are looking good and forging ahead. Maintaining stroke mechanics and speed when fatigued is key to swimming fast and winning races. We put special emphasis on the last quarter of our fly sets and have a triad of rules that the swimmers must live by:

▶ Breathing pattern: Maintain one up, one down.
▶ Legs: Maintain the powerful kick out the back of the stroke.
▶ Tempo: Maintain the stroke rate.

Age-Group Butterfly Training

Many coaches have succeeded in getting many ways of butterfly training to work, and I have experimented with various methods in the past. My preference is for short and fast butterfly swimming that prepares swimmers to race. It takes a lot of strength to do butterfly well because of the nature of the pull and the velocity changes during the stroke cycle. Few swimmers can hold an efficient stroke for very long at race speeds; most fall quickly into survival stroke, which is ugly and slow.

It is true that a swimmer struggling through long fly sets in practice is not pre-destined to use that same survival stroke in a race, but training one way in order to race another way seems inefficient. For this reason, I do not assign long sets of straight fly. Instead, our butterfly training is fast, pretty, and aerobic, the latter so that it can be sustained. We do swim long sets, most of which are short-rest sets, but we intersperse short, fast butterfly with fly stroke drills or with freestyle swimming. The distances of full-stroke fly are always short. We almost never swim longer than 100 of straight fly; most repeats are 25s and 50s for 12-and-under swimmers up to 100s for 13- to 14-year-olds. But fly is always swum fast and with technique points in mind.

As a common example in our program, we might do a main set of 200s, alternating 25 free and 25 fly, swimming all the fly fast and descending the 200s from start to finish so that the freestyle portion of each repeat is swum faster and faster while the fly portion maintains 200 race pace throughout. We expect swimmers to work down to their best meet time for the 200 fly by the end of the set. Because the fly swimming is all fast, we are training the stroke we want to see when we race, and because this is all short-rest swimming, it is aerobic and sustainable. I call these sets of alternating free and fly *Sarah Dotzels* after the girl who helped invent them (much to her chagrin when I became obsessed with them).

In preparatory sets, before the main aerobic or sprint sets, you might throw in a short technique set with stroke drills. I have argued in chapter 5 for the near abolition of stroke drills; here, given the physical difficulty of holding racing stroke for long periods, I relax my militancy. Here are four basic drills for fly:

■ **One-arm butterfly A-form (1-arm-A).** The arm not used is kept in front, spearing forward, and the swimmer breathes to the side. The body remains flat throughout.

■ **One-arm fly B-form (1-arm-B).** The arm not used is kept by the side, and the swimmer breathes to the front. Again, the body is flat. This form of the drill is more demanding than the A-form.

■ **Single–double A-form (S/D–A).** Alternate a one-arm stroke with a full double-arm stroke of fly; for instance, left arm only, full stroke, right arm only, full stroke. During the one-arm stroke, the arm not used is parked in front, reaching forward. Swimmers breathe to the side during each one-arm stroke.

■ **Single–double B-form (S/D–B).** Again, alternate a one-arm stroke with a full stroke of fly, but this time swimmers breathe to the front during each full stroke.

Our 11-and-over swimmers use, and use sparingly, only the two forms of single–double fly drill. These drills are acceptable because the swimmers can maintain proper stroke rhythm during both. Our 10-and-under swimmers use all four of the drills, since we are more concerned with swimmers at this level learning many motor patterns than with their specializing in racing-stroke patterns.

Use fins as advisedly as you use stroke drills. Fins seriously affect the kick, and a proper kick is critical to good butterfly, both in terms of the technique of the kick and the timing of the kick and pull. On the other hand, fins provide more support from the back end so that swimmers can work on the various pulling or breathing focus points more effectively.

In butterfly work, emphasize the stroke points in the catechism, often employing the rainbow-focus, pass-it-on format discussed in chapter 5 (see page 72). Don't tell swimmers what not to do; rather, ask them to swim with one focus on one repeat, another focus on the next repeat, and so on. Cycle through all the stroke points several times during a set, the swimmers continually thinking about and working on their strokes and swimming fast as they do so.

Coaches are continually faced with the tug-of-war between stroke counts and stroke tempo. It is usually argued that with young swimmers, stroke count—or distance per stroke—is the more important of the two and demands more emphasis in training. Generally, I accept this argument, but with butterfly it does not ring true. Many age-groupers swim fly with a tempo that is too slow because they include pauses, stops, or glides that do not belong. Asking kids to swim at a certain (low) stroke count per length usually leads to even more unnatural elongation of the stroke and to poor stroke rhythm. Focus instead on the stroke fundamentals and on maintaining a fairly quick tempo to produce the kind of stroke you want to see. As the swimmer gets stronger, this natural, efficient stroke lengthens out.

It is the coach's responsibility to help the swimmers build efficient racing strokes and to design sets that train these racing strokes. Butterfly needs to be swum fast but aerobically. To flesh out the skeleton of these training principles, figure 7.11 on page 96 details a butterfly training session for age-group swimmers of varying ages and levels. Note that the difficulty and expectations get higher from age to age; swimming, drilling, and kicking are mixed; swimmers are continually focusing on technique, and we keep the swimmers moving and get a lot done in a practice. It is also important to note that we took a long time to build to this level of sustained intensity.

FIGURE 7.11

Sample Butterfly Days
for Three Levels of Age-Groupers

STRONG 9- to 10-Year-Olds (Total Volume: 4,000 Yards or Meters)

1,200 warm-up (400 IM, 400 fly mix kick and drill, 400 IM)

4 rounds of the following:
   4 × 50 fly drills on :55 (on each round complete one of each fly drill; page 94)
   100 fly kick on back (round 1 on 2:00, round 2 on 1:55, round 3 on 1:50, round 4 on 1:45)

32 × 25 on :30, alternating moderate-pace free and fast fly

6 rounds of 4 × 25 fly on :30 with 1-minute rest between rounds to discuss technique

400 free at moderate pace, long and smooth and pretty

STRONG 11- to 12-Year-Olds (Total Volume: 5,600 Yards or Meters)

1,200 warm-up (400 IM, 400 fly mix kick and drill, 400 IM)

12 × 50 fly drill on :50, alternating S/D–A and S/D–B with rainbow focus (page 72)

24 × 50 on :50, alternating fly drill and fly kick on back (hands down)

40 × 25, alternating free for max distance per stroke (DPS) and fast fly with rainbow focus (page 72)
   First 20 on :25 and last 20 faster on :30

5 rounds of the following with fins:
   4 × 25 fly on :25
   100 free on 1:30, long and smooth

600 free moderate pace, aiming for max DPS and counting strokes

STRONG 13- to 14-Year-Olds (Total Volume: 7,500 Yards or Meters)

2,000 warm-up (400 IM, 4 × 100 fly kick on back, 400 IM, 4 × 100 fly drill, 400 IM)

16 × 50 on :45, alternating fly drill and fly kick on back

4 rounds of the following:
   2 × 50 fly drill on :45
   100 fly kick on back on 1:30
   4 × 25 fly descend on :25

2 rounds of 1,000 in a progressive Sarah Dotzel pyramid:
   25 free, 25 fly, 50 free, 50 fly, 75 free, 75 fly, 100 free, 100 fly, 100 free, 100 fly, 75 free, 75 fly,
      50 free, 50 fly, 25 free, 25 fly
   Round 1 straight through
   Round 2 with 25s on :25, 50s on :45, 75s on 1:05, 100s on 1:25

300 backstroke, long and smooth

4 rounds of the following:
   4 × 25 fly very fast (round 1 on :20, round 2 on :25, round 3 on :30, round 4 on :35)
   100 free for max DPS on 1:30

8 × 50 free on :45, long and smooth

Breaststroke Stroke Catechism

Of all the competitive strokes, breaststroke provides the most variety among world- and national-class swimmers, though over the past several years the trend has been moving away from lifting the shoulders and head high out of the water and toward a flatter, more forward stroke. Just as with butterfly, breaststroke presents special physics problems. This is the slowest stroke for a reason. The double-arm pull, though truncated, is strong, but the recovery of the arms creates resistance that slows the swimmer. The kick is powerful, but again the recovery of the legs creates tremendous resistance that slows the swimmer. The puzzle for the coach and swimmer is to find ways to lessen the resistance and maintain the momentum created by the powerful pull and kick. He who creates that speed and maintains it best wins. Because of the dramatic decelerations, streamlining is key to the stroke, especially at critical moments such as the transition from pull to kick.

Pull

The pull is divided into three parts: the outsweep, which is preparatory and sets up the propulsive part of the pull; the insweeping scull toward the breast, which is the power source of the pull and provides the forward momentum; and the shoot or lunge forward, which is the recovery of the arms to the starting position. Body position, head attitude, and path and speed of the hands and forearms are all crucial factors determining the strength of the pull.

START AND FINISH LONG AND STRAIGHT

Everything begins from a streamlined position near the surface, with the body stretched long, skinny, and taut (see figure 7.12). Swimmers should squeeze the ears with the arms and look down at the pool bottom. This is also the position to revisit at the end of every stroke. How long the swimmer holds this base glide position is determined by the length of the race and the quality of the kick. The longer the race or stronger the kick, the longer a swimmer may glide between strokes.

Common Stroke Faults

When a swimmer's body is configured like a jellyfish—head up with eyes looking forward, body core soggy, arms apart, legs dangling—she is not going anywhere fast.

FIGURE 7.12 **Proper body position for the start and end of each stroke.**

STAY FLAT ON THE OUTSWEEP

Swimmers should keep the head down and the body horizontal on the water's surface as they stretch forward and press outward with their hands and forearms. Hands should be slightly below the surface and should sweep to about 6 to 8 inches (15-20 cm) outside the shoulders.

Common Stroke Faults

Swimmers who lift the head quickly as the hands sweep outward, thus forcing the pull to support the weight of the head and shoulders, change the nature and effectiveness of the pull for the worse.

REACH, GRAB ON, AND POP THE HIPS

Swimmers should feel a stretch through the lat muscles of the upper back as they reach and press outward. As the hands round the corner, transitioning from the outsweep to the insweep, swimmers grab onto the water with their hands and forearms and press their hips forward, thus

engaging the body core (see figure 7.13). The pull is done with the whole body, not just the arms or the hands.

Common Stroke Faults

Swimmers who try to arm the pull, as if the torso did not exist, overwhelm their ability to pull correctly. Also, swimmers who sweep their hands around so far that their insweep begins behind their shoulders have no leverage point and cannot use their torso muscles to help pull the body forward.

FIGURE 7.13 The insweep begins as the swimmer grabs hold of the water.

POWER-SQUEEZE THE ARMS

Swimmers should sweep and squeeze inward with the whole arm, feeling pressure along the length of the arm; the angle of the elbow is almost constant throughout the sweep. The large

muscles of the upper back and chest should be fully engaged during the sweep. As the arms sweep inward, the head and shoulders rise somewhat and the breath is taken (see figure 7.14).

Common Stroke Faults

Many swimmers do not use their whole arms to pull, nor do they try to connect the arm pull to the strong torso muscles. They either rip the elbows into the body while the hands and forearms stay put, or they keep the elbows well wide of the body and slide the hands inside.

FIGURE 7.14 The head and shoulders rise as the arms squeeze inward.

SCRUNCH THE SHOULDERS, SHOOT THE HANDS, AND KEEP THE BACK DRY

The finish of the insweep flows into the recovery of the arms forward. As swimmers finish the insweep and begin moving the hands forward, they should scrunch their shoulders against their necks and get skinny and streamlined, as if they are trying to squeeze through a keyhole (see figure 7.15). The hands do not slow down or stop at the chest; rather, they pick up speed as they shoot or lunge straight forward—not down—into a streamline. If the lunge is indeed straight forward, then the back should be dry or nearly so when the legs kick and the body stretches out to its greatest extent as shown in figure 7.16. The torso, head, and arms should be streamlined. The hips should ride high throughout the entire stroke without rising or falling much.

FIGURE 7.15 **Scrunching for a streamlined recovery of the arms.**

Common Stroke Faults

Swimmers who leave the pull half done—with wide elbows, wide hands, and a snowplow-like body configuration—or who sweep their hands inward but stop them at the chest, tend to stop and drop: Their forward motion ceases and they crash straight down. Swimmers who come up too high on the insweep and breath often dive well below the surface on the recovery, resulting in many problems.

FIGURE 7.16 **The back is dry as the legs begin to kick backward.**

QUIET HEAD

The head should work and move with the shoulders. Violent head movements serve no purpose. As swimmers sweep inward with the hands, they should tilt the head slightly, focusing on a point slightly in front of them, not miles off in the distance. Then the head slowly returns to the neutral position as the hands shoot straight forward on the recovery. Swimmers can practice keeping the head still by swimming with a tennis ball under the chin.

Common Stroke Faults

Jerking the head up for the breath lowers the hips; smashing the head back down after the breath creates resistance and waves. Looking sideways at competitors destroys stroke rhythm.

HANDS MODERATE, FAST, AND SUPERFAST

The hands accelerate from start to finish. The hand speed is moderate and building on the out-sweep, fast and getting faster on the squeeze inward, and superfast on the recovery shooting forward.

Common Stroke Faults

Poor breaststrokers often rip their hands and arms straight back without first setting up the pull and getting traction on the water, or they slow the hands as they approach the chest, ensuring that momentum slows and body position drops.

Kick

The aim with the breaststroke kick is to catch onto and press backward against the water with flared-out feet and shins, all the while maintaining horizontal stream-lining with the rest of the body. This takes specialized ranges of motion of the hip, knee, and ankle. The kick is easy to describe but difficult to do well.

HEELS TO YOUR REAR

On the recovery of the legs, the body should be streamlined at the surface. Keeping the knees fairly still and at about hip width, swimmers draw the heels up toward the rear with the big toes almost touching. The legs and feet should hide in the shadow of the body. Swimmers should not pull the knees up underneath the body or collapse at the hips; instead, they should try to keep a straight line from shoulders through the hips to the knees as the feet recover. Many top breaststrokers keep their shoulder-to-knee line almost straight as they are recovering their feet, but right before they begin kicking backward, they flex their hips to bring the strong hip muscles into play. They gain more in propulsion than they lose in streamlining.

Common Stroke Faults

When swimmers pull the knees up until the shoulder-to-knee line is a right angle, the streamlining of the body is destroyed and massive resistance is created. Pulling the heels up only halfway to the rear, usually because of poor flexibility, makes swimmers lose much of the power and catch of the kick.

FLARE THE FEET

With the heels at the rear and the feet slightly wider than the knees, flare the feet outward so the toes point to the side of the pool (see figure 7.17). The more squared the feet, the more water the swimmer will be catching hold of and pushing back against. From the side view (as shown in figure 7.18), observe the horizontal streamline of the torso and arms and the angle created by the thighs.

Common Stroke Faults

Poor ankle flexibility leads to the foot being positioned incorrectly for a strong push back against the water. Many poor breaststrokers have their feet pointing in the same direction as they kick, so the feet slip through the water instead of pushing against it. Also, the wider the knees, the more difficult it is to position the feet correctly.

FIGURE 7.17 **The feet catching hold of the water and pressing backward from behind.**

FIGURE 7.18 **A streamlined torso as the feet prepare to catch and begin the kick.**

KICK STRAIGHT BACK, SNAP, AND REACH

With the feet wider than the knees and flared out near the rear, the swimmer kicks backward horizontally, feeling the water pressure against the inside of the feet and shins. The kick is finished with a snap of the feet and a reach with the legs, bringing the feet together and streamlining the body as the legs go into glide mode. This snap and reach provides a last little surge forward, and it brings the legs near the surface.

Common Stroke Faults

The wider the knees and the narrower the feet at the beginning of the propulsive phase, the more the kick will be directed straight outward from the body instead of backward.

QUICK FEET

Quiet, streamlined legs are needed through most of the stroke cycle, but when it comes time for the legs to move, they recover, catch, and kick backward quickly. The kick is compact and powerful.

Common Stroke Faults

Slow feet produce a slow kick. Most bad breaststrokers have wide, slow kicks. They push water slowly in the wrong directions.

Timing

The timing of the arms and the legs depends on the style of breaststroke used. With an undulating or butterfly rhythm, there will be a distinct overlap between the pull and the kick (see figure 7.19). With a wave style or flatter style, the hands

will be almost fully recovered and the torso and arms almost horizontally streamlined before the legs begin kicking backward. For any particular swimmer, the coach's eye and the swimmer's feel will tell if the timing is right. We want a graceful stroke in which momentum flows forward constantly, with each propulsive movement piggybacking on the momentum of the previous one. A common mistake is the stroke rhythm that starts and stops repeatedly as the body crashes to a halt after each pull or kick.

FIGURE 7.19 An undulating breaststroker with an overlap between kick and pull.

Age-Group Breaststroke Training

The biggest difference between fast and slow breaststrokers is the strength of the kick. Good breaststrokers can get their legs and feet into positions of biomechanical strength and efficiency whereas poor breaststrokers cannot. The latter may work hard, but they are pushing less water and pushing it in the wrong directions. In individual medley–based programs, every swimmer participates in individual medley, and a poor breaststroke can sink the ship. Thus, age-group coaches can't simply ignore this problem as a senior coach can, in theory at least, when working with an older national-level flyer who can't breaststroke.

Swimmers need fit legs and effective kicks. Breaststroke kicking for man-made breaststrokers is crucial to their development. Coaches must develop the flexibilities and ranges of motion early. To that end, we incorporate a special breaststroke leg stretching routine into our dryland training several times a week (see chapter 9). Further, we do more kicking and kicking-oriented drills with breaststroke than with the other strokes.

As with butterfly training, we use only a few stroke drills, and we use them advisedly. Here the difference between an elite swimmer and an age-grouper is important in determining the content of the training program. An elite senior breaststroker may spend a large percentage of her everyday training swimming breaststroke. For that reason, a myriad of drills might be necessary to vary the stresses and to keep the swimmer's stroke, timing, and attitude fresh. But if we coach young swimmers who train breaststroke only a couple of times each week, we cannot do 15 pulling-oriented drills and 15 kicking-oriented drills if we want to get anything accomplished. We need less French pastry, more meat and potatoes.

However, we use a few drills from time to time. Stroke drills may be a part of a training program, but they cannot substitute for swimming the full stroke fast and with good technique. Using drills occasionally must help coaches and swimmers attain this goal and not become a diversion that gets in the way of the goal. The following drills emphasize body position, perfect technique, power, and proper stroke rhythm:

- **Double-kick (or triple-kick) breaststroke.** This is the traditional one-pull–two-kick or one-pull–three-kick stroke drill. Swimmers should focus on working the legs hard; finishing each kick well; streamlining the torso, head, and arms; and maintaining proper timing between the pull and kick.

- **Two-count pause breaststroke.** This drill emphasizes streamlining and body position. After the kick is completed, the swimmer pauses in a streamline for two counts before beginning the next pull.

- **Breaststroke pull with buoy (or ankle buoy).** Obviously, this drill works the arms for technique and power. Using the buoy between the ankles adds difficulty. Instruct swimmers to keep their bodies straight, taut, and as horizontal as possible while pulling.

- **Dolphin-kick breaststroke pull.** This form of pulling has less resistance, so this drill emphasizes rhythm, tempo, and hand speed.

Earlier we discussed how it seems advisable for butterfly to emphasize stroke tempo rather than distance per stroke. For breaststroke, the opposite is true. The most common mistake among poor breaststrokers is to swim too vertical and too short and quick. Distance per stroke work stretches them out and makes them more horizontal. This should be done at various speeds so that the kids don't just swim long, slow, sloppy strokes. Swimming fast with a long stroke demands a strong pull, a strong kick, and a taut streamline—our goal exactly. Figure 7.20 on page 104 is a sample breaststroke training day for various levels of age-group swimmers. In each practice there is a wide variety of kicking, pulling, drilling, and swimming, with most of the practice concentrating on breaststroke work. Coaches demand solid technique and honest effort throughout.

FIGURE 7.20

Sample Breaststroke Days
for Three Levels of Age-Groupers

STRONG 10 and Unders (Total Volume: 4,900 Yards or Meters)

1,200 warm-up (400 IM, 400 breast mixed kick and swim, 400 IM)

16×50 on 1:00, alternating breast kick and triple kick (one-pull–three-kick) breaststroke drill (see drills on page 103)

18×50 on 1:00, alternating breaststroke pull with buoy drill, dolphin-kick breaststroke pull drill, and breast for max distance per stroke (DPS)

16×25 breast on :30, holding goal stroke per length (S/L) (use moderate pace on 1 to 8, descend on 9 to 12, and descend on 13 to 16)

12×50 breast on 1:00, holding goal S/L (use moderate pace on 1 to 4, descend on 5 to 8, and descend on 9 to 12)

24×25 on :30, alternating moderate pace at goal S/L and fast at goal S/L + 1*

400 back long and smooth, 4 dolphins off each wall

STRONG 11- to 12-Year-Olds (Total Volume: 5,400 Yards or Meters)

1,200 warm-up (400 IM, 400 breast mix kick and swim, 400 IM)

4 rounds of the following:
    100 breast kick (50 for max DPS, 50 for speed) on :10 rest
    100 two-kick–one-pull (50 for max DPS, 50 for speed) on :10 rest

Max DPS set, count S/L and hold goal counts throughout each of the following:
    12×25 breast on :30
    8×25 two-kick–one-pull on :30
    6×50 breast on :55
    4×50 two-kick–one-pull on :55
    4×25 breast fast on :30
    4×25 two-kick–one-pull fast on :30

500 back build with 5 underwater dolphins off each wall

10×100 breast on 1:50 (descend on 1 to 5 and 6 to 10)

200 back, long and smooth

20×25 on :30, alternating moderate free and very fast breast

Warm down

STRONG 13- to 14-Year-Olds (Total Volume: 6,900 Yards or Meters)

2,000 warm-up (400 IM, 400 breast kick build, 400 IM, 8×50 breast on :10 rest at max DPS, 400 IM)

5×300 breast on :15 rest, completing the following for each 300:
    100 kick-oriented drill (double- or triple-kick breaststroke drills)
    100 pull-oriented drill (dolphin-kick breaststroke pull or breaststroke pull with buoy drill)
    100 breast maximum DPS

16×50 on :50, alternating DPS-focus breast and fast breast

16×50 on :45, alternating moderate free and faster breast

16×50 on :50, alternating moderate free and fastest breast

1,000 straight swim, alternating 75 back (long and smooth) and 25 breast sprint

Warm down

---

*Goal + 1 S/L means the goal stroke count per length plus one, so the strokes are slightly shorter but always accompanied by more speed.

CHAPTER 8

Improving Starts, Turns, and Finishes

There is not an age-group swimmer alive who could not improve his times drastically by improving his starts, turns, and finishes—the *details* of swimming. Many close races are won or lost by these details. In short-course swimming in particular, the proportion of each race controlled by these skills is high, especially since many swimmers are exploiting the underwater dolphins off the walls. The shorter the race, the greater the importance of the details.

Most coaches have their swimmers work explicitly on their walls for at least a portion of each week's training. But every swimmer performs a start, turns, and a finish on every single repeat of every practice. How swimmers perform these everyday details is the most important determinant of how they will perform in their races. They have to see that the walls are important before they will take them seriously.

The most important point regarding details is to keep it simple. There are only a few fundamentals to each skill, and none requires a swimmer to be a motor genius to perform it well. Good details require attention more than talent. If swimmers want to have fast turns or fast starts when they race, or if they want to win close races, then they must practice these skills every single time they do them in their daily training. They must make a habit of doing things well. Miracles are not allowed—50,000 slow, sloppy turns in practice result in slow, sloppy turns at meets.

Starts

Even though a swimmer performs only one start each race compared with numerous turns and even more swimming strokes, some practice time set aside for work on starts is well warranted. Even if the starts work is not extensive, swimmers can work on them without even getting on the blocks. Every time they push off the wall, they can practice quick reactions, powerful and streamlined underwater kicks, powerful and horizontal breakout strokes, and so on. It's not exactly the same, but it builds the same habits.

Forward-Dive Starts

There are four kinds of forward starts: the traditional grab start and three variations of the track start, including a leaning-forward track, a full backward track, and a medium backward track (see figures 8.1 to 8.4). I prefer the medium track start, though all four are seen in international competition and I allow swimmers to choose another kind if the medium track does not work for them. Generally, track starts give swimmers more stability on the block, and both of the leaning back track starts allow the swimmer to use the arms to pull against the block for momentum. They also create more impulse, or greater time of force applied against the block. The forward track start is the quickest to the water but the least powerful. The full backward is slowest off the block, and often the back leg is bent to an extreme that compromises the power that the start produces. The medium backward splits the difference—it is quick and powerful.

FIGURE 8.1 **The traditional grab start.**

FIGURE 8.2 **The leaning-forward track start.**

FIGURE 8.3   The full backward track start.

FIGURE 8.4   The medium backward track start.

Similar to the stroke catechism in previous chapters, the start can be broken into its component skills so that coaches can teach and swimmers can understand and perform the skills more effectively.

- **Be cool.** When swimmers are on the block, they should not be looking around. Instead, they need their eyes forward, intent and focused, with the scowl of a champion on their faces. Their body language should shout, "Don't mess with me. I'm here to race my guts out!"

- **Grab and lean back.** Swimmers should curl the toes of the front foot around the block so that it doesn't slip when they push. The back foot should be about one foot-length behind the front foot. They lean back until their weight is toward the back foot and they feel a stretch through their arms and back, like a rubber band ready to snap.

- **Explode.** Swimmers use both their arms and legs to catapult themselves horizontally forward off the block with a straight, streamlined body as shown in figure 8.5. They should neither leap up to the sky nor drop off the block like a rock.

FIGURE 8.5   Horizontal explosion off the block.

FIGURE 8.6   **Streamlined flight, ready for a clean entry.**

- **Streamline.** When swimmers are in the air, their bodies need to be straight, taut, and streamlined, with the head ducked under the arms and the hands either clamped or one on top of the other. Their bodies must be streamlined before hitting the water; if they wait until afterward, it is too late and momentum is lost. The angle of attack should be as horizontal as possible without belly flopping (see figure 8.6). Clean entries, with little splash and the whole body entering through the same hole in the water, are ideal.

- **Use hyperspeed dolphins.** This point applies to freestyle and butterfly starts, where the swimmer kicks underwater dolphins before reaching the surface to swim. Once the swimmer enters the water, he keeps his body straight and still for a split second, then dolphins with short, fast kicks—hyperspeed—to maintain the momentum from the dive and to preserve streamlining. Big, slow dolphins destroy the streamline and are not fast. A respectable distance for underwater dolphins is about 10 meters for 10-and-under swimmers and 12 meters for 11-and-over swimmers.

FIGURE 8.7   **Breakout stroke that drives the body forward.**

- **Break out.** Swimmers should surface as horizontally as they can, surging forward (see figure 8.7) with their first strokes, not up. They should not breathe the first two or more strokes on butterfly and the first several strokes on freestyle. The first few strokes should set the tone for the rest of the length.

Backstroke Starts

Just as with the forward start, there are several kinds of backstroke starts. Three basic types are the traditional start, the newer Japanese start, and the catapult start (see figures 8.8 to 8.10). In the traditional start, the hips are close to the wall and the shoulders close to the block, so the torso is practically vertical and the knees are bent to an extreme. The Japanese start is characterized by the torso angling slightly away from the wall and the head leaning back; this is the quickest of the starts. In the catapult start, the hips are away from the wall, the knees are bent only to about 90 degrees, and the shoulders lean in close to the hands, so the torso is angled into the wall.

FIGURE 8.8   **The traditional start.**

FIGURE 8.9   **The Japanese start.**

FIGURE 8.10   **The catapult start.**

I prefer the catapult start, in particular with age-groupers, because the pressure of the feet is directed horizontally into the wall, resulting in fewer slips off the wall. Also, this start provides a powerful explosion off the block, combining a catapulting of the torso backward (the hips acting as the fulcrum) and a springing of the legs. On the other kinds of backstroke starts, the knees are bent to such an extreme that swimmers often get stuck and cannot extend the legs quickly. With the traditional start, the torso is vertical and all the weight is directed downward, increasing the chances that the feet will slip.

With the prevalence of sticky touch pads that the toes can reliably grip onto, it is much easier to do a fast and effective backstroke start than it used to be. Even so, backstroke starts are difficult for age-group swimmers to master because their legs are not nearly as powerful as the senior swimmers', the swimmers are blind to the water behind them, and most teams spend little time practicing the technical fundamentals of it.

As with forward starts, backstroke starts can be broken into a small number of skills. Practicing these skills helps swimmers become proficient and comfortable, and a little goes a long way. The positioning on the blocks is important for leverage and power; we will often hold swimmers in the take-your-marks position to ensure that hands, feet, hips, shoulders, and heads are set correctly before we let them go. Practicing backstroke starts with the touch pads helps swimmers get the traction on the wall that they will get when they race.

- **Plant your feet, toes dry.** Thanks to recent rule changes, swimmers can keep their toes above the surface of the water, but not curled over the lip of the gutter. The toes should be dry, with the feet as high as they are allowed to be. That way, the swimmer will apply pressure horizontally into the wall, aiding stability and power.

- **Load the spring with hips away.** On the command, "Take your marks," the shoulders come in toward the block and the hips move away, with the knees bent at a right angle and the rear at the surface. The swimmer does not have to push her body up to get out of the water, so she does not plow through the water on the start. The horizontal pressure into the wall moves the body horizontally backward, not up.

- **Use the triple.** Swimmers explode off the block horizontally backward with the hands first, then the head, and finally the legs. The torso is catapulted away from the wall. This three-part movement should happen seamlessly, smoothly, and powerfully.

FIGURE 8.11   **Streamlined flight with arched back for clean entry.**

- **Arch and streamline.** Swimmers should try to enter the water cleanly with the whole body entering through one hole, just as when doing a forward dive. Arching the back helps get the hips out of the water and allows a cleaner flight (see figure 8.11). As soon as the head enters, the chin is pulled to the chest so the swimmer doesn't dive to the bottom.

- **Use hyperspeed.** Underwater dolphins should be small, tight, quick, and powerful so that the body maintains its streamlined posture. Just before the swimmer surfaces and begins to swim, he transitions from dolphins to flutter kicks.

- **Break out.** Swimmers should surface horizontally with full forward momentum. The first two breakout strokes must be powerful and should set the rhythm for the rest of the length.

Relay Starts

There are several ways of doing relay starts, some fancier than others. The two basic kinds are those where the swimmer steps forward with one or both feet as she swings her arms and those where the swimmers stands with both feet at the front of the block as she swings her arms with a double-arm backstroke action. (see figures 8.12 and 8.13). I prefer standing swing starts because they are effective, simple, easy to teach, easy to learn, less prone to swimmer miscalculation and disqualifications, and as fast as any others.

FIGURE 8.12 **Halfway through the backward arm swing on a standing swing start.**

FIGURE 8.13 **Exploding off the block.**

It is important to teach swimmers that the responsibility for a good start is shared—the swimmer coming in and the swimmer on the blocks both have crucial jobs. The finish must be fast, consistent, and reliable, and the start must be timed perfectly off this finish. If done well, a relay start gives about a 0.7-second advantage over a flat start. Ideally, we want a nail-to-nail relay start, as shown in figure 8.14, where the finishing swimmer is fully stretched out and touching the wall with her fingernails while the swimmer on the block is fully stretched out and touching the block only with her toenails. Figure 8.15 shows an ineffective, slow relay start.

FIGURE 8.14 **A nail-to-nail relay start.**

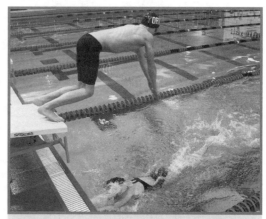

FIGURE 8.15 **An ineffective, slow relay start.**

In teaching swimmers to time the start correctly, an effective rule of thumb is to have the swimmer on the block begin her arm swing when the incoming swimmer begins her last arm recovery. With this as a starting point, work to make the timing more precise. We use a relay-start scoring system to practice timing. In this game, each start is scored from 0 to 5. The number signifies the number of tenths of a second the start diverged from perfection—the higher the number, the worse the start. A score of 0 means a perfect nail-to-nail start, and a 5 means the swimmer on the block stayed put while the incoming swimmer finished, got out, toweled off, and started cheering for the relay. Perfection is an admirable goal, but in local meets a perfect start will probably get a team disqualified for a false start. In practice we aim for a score of 1 to ensure a fast but safe start.

Working on Starts

When we work on starts, we use an assembly-line format to have the swimmers practice as many focused starts in a given amount of time as possible. Coaches keep their comments to a minimum by focusing on the fundamentals. You may say a word or two to a swimmer walking by on the way to the blocks, but skip the extended discussions. Watch for patterns of mistakes. When you note several swimmers doing something you don't like, gather the group quickly, tell them what you want to see, and send them back to working on being perfect. Give them things to think about, have them try different ways of doing things, and have them compare the results. They get a feel for the skills by practicing them. As with stroke technique work, focus more on what to do rather than what not to do. With a little guidance, swimmers can work out most problems for themselves.

One method of giving the coach numerous sets of eyes is to enlist the senior swimmers to help coach younger swimmers. In our program we combine seniors and juniors for a portion of Friday afternoon workouts, and during this time we focus on details. Seniors are responsible for modeling the correct execution of skills and for teaching and coaching the junior swimmers in their lane. Coaches may add a few general comments to the entire group now and then, but mostly they watch as the older kids coach the younger kids.

To work on relay starts, combine the assembly line format with the relay start scoring game. As soon as the swimmer surfaces after a start, the coach calls out the score for the dive. With this immediate feedback, the swimmer can correlate the timing with the score and recalibrate for the next start. Another helpful relay format is to focus on one stroke for a period of time. For instance, for 15 minutes every incoming swimmer does backstroke. The outgoing swimmers can do whatever stroke they wish, but everybody gets practice starting off backstroke finishes and getting into a comfortable rhythm doing so. Then we may spend the next 15 minutes starting off an incoming flyer. This format has the added bonus of giving everyone work on both starts and finishes.

Turns

At every meet, turns determine the outcome of some races. Some swimmers get consistently crushed on turns, and others gain a clear advantage. For the most part, meet performances are created in daily practice; turn problems in meets are really turn problems in practice. Habits created every day are almost impossible to change once a month, so swimmers must practice the way they want to race.

Both technique and mentality are important. Good turns are simple, with only a few fundamentals; whereas poor turns are often artificially complicated, with the swimmer adding things that don't belong and that take up time. Doing turns correctly matters. But the biggest difference between swimmers with fast turns and those with slow ones is not technique but attitude. Fast turners see walls as a place to pick up speed and gain an advantage, not as a place to rest. They go into attack mode whenever they approach a wall. Slow turners never have a sense of urgency, so their turns are lazy and powerless.

The two basic kinds of turns are flip turns and open turns. But no matter the kind, it is helpful to think of the turn as having three parts: the approach, the turn on the wall, and the send-away.

1. **Approach.** Most swimmers wait until the last stroke of a length to set up their turn, but this is too late. A good turn begins five to seven meters from the wall. Swimmers need to prepare for the turn, gauge their strokes in order to reach the wall on a full stroke with maximum speed, and accelerate into the wall. If the approach is bad, with the swimmer either gliding in or jamming the last stroke, the turn will be slow and the swimmer will lose ground, even if it is technically sound.

2. **Turn on the wall.** Obviously, flip turns and open turns are completely different. But with all turns, the goal is to get on and off the wall as quickly as possible. To work on this quickness for the fly and breast, time swimmers from the moment their hands touch the wall to the moment their feet leave it. For the free and back, time them from when the feet leave the water on the somersault until the feet leave the wall on the push-off. Have swimmers work to bring their times down.

3. **Send-away.** Here we distinguish between the breaststroke send-away, which consists of the underwater pullout sequence, and the send-away for all the other turns, which consists of underwater dolphins until the breakout strokes. But generally, we want a straight, taut, streamlined body exploding off the wall. On the breakout strokes, we want the swimmers moving through the surface horizontally forward, not straight up.

Flip Turns

Freestyle and backstroke are the two variations of flip turns. Done correctly, they speed up a swimmer while allowing a brief respite from swimming, thus explaining why short-course times are faster than long-course times for the same events.

Freestyle Approach

Unless swimmers take a lot of momentum into the wall, they will not take much off of it. The approach is crucial to maintaining speed; any hitches, pauses, or stops are deadly against good competitors. The turn should be seamless and fast.

- **Use attack mode.** Swimmers need to attack the wall; this is an attitude as much as a technique. They should not breathe the last two strokes into the wall.

- **Keep your eyes on the cross.** Swimmers should keep their eyes on the cross on the end of the pool for precision. Many coaches prefer to have their swimmers focus on the *T* on the pool bottom. But given the differences in water depth and clarity from pool to pool, swimmers can time their turns more precisely by focusing on the wall. The slight loss in streamlining is made up for by the improved timing.

- **Gauge for a full stroke.** Fast in, fast out. Gliding in or chopping the last stroke into the wall kills momentum just when swimmers want to be moving full speed ahead. Instead, they should gauge their strokes into the wall from several strokes out so that they can finish with a strong, full stroke with hands at their sides. Any necessary adjustments in stroke length are spread out over several strokes rather than concentrated on the last one.

Freestyle Turn on the Wall

For a flip turn, the turn on the wall consists of somersaulting and planting the feet on it for the push-off. Quickness is crucial.

FIGURE 8.16 **Beginning the quad.**

FIGURE 8.17 **A swimmer planting on the wall with a nearly straight line from hips to fingertips.**

- **Do the quad.** For a fast somersault, four things need to happen quickly all once: Duck the chin, dolphin-kick powerfully, tuck at the middle, and back-scull with both hands toward the face (see figure 8.16). The quad gets the feet over and on the wall quickly. The body should be a small spinning ball in a tuck position, not a layout.

- **Plant and go.** The legs flip straight over on the somersault, and the feet plant on the wall with the toes pointing upward. On the wall, it's one touch and go. There is no twisting and turning on it, and there is no waiting to turn over onto the stomach before pushing off. Instead, swimmers get off the wall as fast as they can and worry about twisting after they push off (see figure 8.17). They should not add any extra motions that take time and slow them down.

Freestyle Send-Away

The send-away takes the speed from the somersault and adds the power of the push-off and the underwater kicking. Underwater dolphin kicking is an important weapon in the arsenal of most top swimmers.

■ **Explode.** The push off the wall is powerful, with a straight back and taut body— no sogginess.

■ **Streamline.** The head is tucked tight against the upper arms, the elbows are squeezed tight, and the hands are placed one on the other. The swimmer resembles a skinny sharpened pencil coming off the wall (see figure 8.18).

FIGURE 8.18 **A swimmer streamlining off the wall.**

■ **Use hyperspeed.** Small, powerful, quick dolphins, working both beats of each kick, are more powerful and streamlined than big, slow dolphins. Every kick from first to last must be powerful. One common mistake is for swimmers to start strong but get progressively weaker until they are almost motionless by the last kick. Underwater

FIGURE 8.19 **A swimmer performing dolphins off the wall with perfect streamlining.**

dolphins on the send-away (see figure 8.19) are becoming important even with age-groupers, especially in short-course yards racing. Age-groupers must practice this skill.

■ **Break out.** For most swimmers, the first two breakout strokes are wimpy giveaways. This wastes an opportunity to carry the speed from the push-off and underwater dolphins into the swimming. After a freestyle turn, swimmers should always pull with the bottom arm first (this may not be the arm whose hand is on the bottom), and they should make the breakout strokes long, strong, and powerful, causing the body to surge forward and setting a good rhythm for the length. Never breathe the first two strokes (or more, for short races) since effort and momentum are wasted by climbing upward to breathe.

Backstroke Approach

Being blind to the upcoming wall unnerves many swimmers, whose tentative backstroke walls cause them to lose a lot of time to their competitors. Aggressiveness walls can cover a multitude of swimming sins.

- **Know what you can and cannot do.** Knowing the rules is essential for the backstroke approach. A swimmer may turn onto his stomach the last stroke of each length (except for the last length—the swimmer must finish the race on his back). The turn must be continuous. Even if he is farther away from the wall than he wanted to be, he may not stop the last pull once it is started, and he may not glide or kick after the last pull is completed. The swimmer must flow seamlessly from the pull into the somersault.

- **Use attack mode.** Accelerate into the wall, picking up the tempo the last couple of strokes.

- **Know your count.** It is distressing how many swimmers do not know their stroke count from the flags to the wall on backstroke. This is fundamental, and it is absolutely necessary for a fast turn. Just as fundamental is consistently swimming fast to the wall so that swimmers take the same number of strokes every time. If they approach sometimes slowly and sometimes quickly, their counts will not be consistent, and they will always be guessing where they are. When they know where the wall is, they can swim in quickly with no looking around, no chopping strokes, and no breaking rhythm.

Backstroke Turn on the Wall

Because the swimmers perform the actual turn starting from on the stomach, the fundamentals of the freestyle turn apply. The only real differences are that the last stroke or two are even more important for speed into the wall, and the swimmer stays on her back coming off the wall.

- **Roll, reach, pull, snap.** Swimmers must increase momentum into the wall. Gliding into the wall is illegal, slow, and common. Half-stroking into the wall puts on the brakes and kills momentum. Instead, the last stroke should be a long one with a stretch. That way, the pull performed while on the stomach is strong and powers the swimmer into the turn.

- **Do the quad.** This is the same four motions as in the freestyle somersault: Duck the chin, dolphin hard, tuck at the middle, and back-scull with the hands. When these motions are simultaneous, the somersault is quick.

Backstroke Send-Away

Using the speed and aggressiveness of the turn on the wall, the swimmer powers into the send-away, leaving the wall on his back and making sure to surface by the 15-meter mark.

- **Explode.** This is similar to freestyle but easier, since the swimmer hits the wall on her back and gets to stay on it. There is one touch and go with a powerful push off the wall, back straight and body taut.

- **Streamline, hyperspeed kick, and break out.** The body is straight and taut, the head is ducked under the arms, and the hands are one on top of the other. Underwater dolphins should be small, tight, quick, and powerful so that the body maintains its streamlined posture. Just before the swimmer surfaces and begins to swim, he transitions from dolphins to flutter kicks. The breakout is horizontal with full forward momentum. Even in age-group competition, underwater dolphin kicks have become necessary in order to be competitive. It is a good policy to do at least four dolphins off every wall every time, and when doing four becomes comfortable and normal, increase to five, then six, and so on.

Open Turns

There are five variations of open turns, four of which are similar: breast to breast, fly to fly, and the individual medley transition turns of fly to back and breast to free. The fifth kind, the back-to-breast individual medley transition turn, is performed differently and discussed separately.

General Open-Turn Approach

For these open turns, the swimmer is coming into the wall doing either fly or breast, and judging the wall correctly is more challenging than on flip turns.

- **Gauge for a full stroke.** Swimmers should start preparing for the wall from several strokes away. It is better to adjust the last several strokes slightly than to adjust the last stroke drastically. Gliding or short-stroking into the wall kills speed.

- **Touch with two hands.** The two hands touch simultaneously every time. Even though the rules do not stipulate it, it is safest to touch at the surface with the hands level. If swimmers get lazy and touch with one hand in practice, chances are good that they will do the same thing in a race and get disqualified. Keep things simple and practice the way you want to race: legally and fast.

Open Turn on the Wall   Whether coming in doing breaststroke or butterfly, the turn on the wall is the same. Quickness and simplicity are key; slow turns usually include actions that don't belong and that take time to perform.

- **Pull away.** Never grab onto the gutter. Touching at the surface, the first hand barely touches the wall and then pulls away immediately along with the shoulder (see figure 8.20). The second hand stays put, pressing against the wall. This combination of pulling away and pressing puts the swimmer on her side.

FIGURE 8.20   **The first hand pulls away while the wall hand moves to press.**

FIGURE 8.21 Pivoting with nothing touching the wall.

▪ **Pivot and drop.** After the swimmer has pulled away with the first hand, arm, and shoulder, and while the second hand is still lightly pressing into the wall, the knees pull up quickly and tightly. As the knees drive to the chest, the second hand leaves the wall, so for a split second the body is pivoting and nothing is touching the wall (see figure 8.21). The second hand tucks behind the ear on its way to meet the first hand in a streamline. The feet plant on the wall with the toes pointing to the side of the pool, and the swimmer pushes off the wall on his side. Turning onto the stomach before pushing off, though common with younger swimmers, wastes time. Simply ensure that the shoulders are past the vertical and the body is more on the front than on the back. (Note that the opposite is true for the fly-to-back individual medley transition turn, where the body must be slightly more on the back than the front.)

▪ **Turn on a line.** Swimmers should never grab onto the gutter and lift the body up, nor should they duck the head deep under water before the push-off. The head goes in and out of the wall on a line.

Open-Turn Send-Away There are two variations of the send-away. On butterfly, backstroke, and freestyle push-offs, swimmers leave the wall with underwater dolphins. On breaststroke push-offs, swimmers leave the wall and perform the breaststroke underwater pullout sequence. Either way, good send-aways mean speed. Follow these points for the dolphin send-away:

▪ **Explode.** When the feet are planted to push off the wall, the body should be a straight line from the rear to the fingertips. It is a taut body that will be immediately streamlined. The push-off is powerful and explosive.

▪ **Streamline, use hyperspeed, and break out.** The body is straight and taut, the head is ducked under the arms, and the hands are one on top of the other. Underwater dolphins should be small, tight, quick, and powerful so that the body maintains its streamlined posture. The breakout is horizontal, with full forward momentum. Smooth transitions are crucial, first between the initial glide and the underwater dolphins and then between the dolphins and the swimming. Driving forward with the breakout strokes is crucial for any stroke. Further, for freestyle, swimmers should not breathe the first two strokes off the wall, and for butterfly, they should not breathe the first stroke of a length.

For the breaststroke send-away, the underwater pullout sequence is used (It is also used in the back-to-breast individual medley transition turn; see page 120). Underwater pullouts are the great equalizer of breaststroke races. Even poor breaststrokers who streamline well, have a strong butterfly pull and kick, and can fake a single compact breaststroke kick can compete on the walls with the fastest swimmers, and they will have eight or nine fewer meters to swim.

The rules are important here. While underwater, swimmers are allowed one pull past the hips (essentially a butterfly pull), one dolphin kick that is taken after the pull has begun, and one breaststroke kick. Before the underwater pull is taken, the shoulders and hips must be horizontal. Many swimmers are disqualified because they rush to pull before they have flattened out to horizontal. Also, the swimmer's head must break the surface before the arms begin the insweep of the second pull. Here again, swimmers are disqualified for staying too deep and starting their second pull while still submerged.

- **Explode.** When the feet are planted to push off the wall, the body should be a straight line from the rear to the fingertips; it is a taut body that will be immediately streamlined. The push-off is powerful and explosive.

- **Glide.** The swimmer holds a tight streamline for a count of two.

- **Power pull and dolphin.** Swimmers take one strong butterfly pull and one short, quick dolphin kick. Some top swimmers dolphin at the beginning of the pull, and others dolphin at the end of the pull. The jury is still out on which is more effective. More important is how the kick is performed. The dolphin kick should be small, fast, and powerful, sending the body forward. At its completion, the body should be straight, streamlined, and horizontal (see figure 8.22). Most swimmers do this wrong; they do a big, slow, undulating dolphin, finishing the kick with the body in a jackknife position instead of a straight line.

FIGURE 8.22 **Streamlining after the breaststroke power pull and dolphin kick.**

- **Glide again.** If the swimmer pulled and dolphin-kicked effectively, she may now glide, with a perfect horizontal streamline, for a count of one.

- **Sneak both recoveries.** Hands and feet recover simultaneously. The swimmer sneaks the hands up close to the body and sneaks the heels to the rear while keeping the knees still. The hands have twice as far to travel as the feet, so the feet will recover first and be positioned to kick.

- **Kick into the breakout.** The swimmer kicks backward while reaching with the hands to a full stretch forward and driving into the first stroke at the surface. Swimmers can establish their stroke rhythm immediately by making the breakout stroke powerful and forward. Most swimmers follow a sloppy underwater pullout with a weak breakout, and it takes them several strokes before they are in rhythm.

Back-to-Breast Approach

The backstroke-to-breaststroke transition is the turn where the most time is won or lost of any turns in the repertoire. Doing it correctly and quickly means gaining on nearly everyone you race against. The two most common ways of performing this transition turn are the traditional open turn and the crossover flip turn. Almost no age-group swimmers do the crossover. Even at the national level, while many swimmers do the crossover in the 200 individual medley, few do it in the 400 individual medley. Generally, the crossover turn is quicker off the wall, but the push-off is not as powerful, so the two turns even out in the end. Further, unless the crossover is done precisely, the likelihood of a disqualification is fairly high. The crossover is much harder to teach and perform. For these reasons, teach the open turn to your age-group swimmers and save the crossover for the seniors.

Back-to-Breast Turn   The keys to this turn are simplicity and aggressiveness. A correct approach is both. Being blind to the upcoming wall unnerves many swimmers, whose tentative approaches cause them to slow drastically.

■ **Know your count and attack.** Swimmers must know their stroke count from flags to wall and swim in as fast as they can without hesitation. Unless they know exactly where the wall is, their turn is doomed.

■ **Touch on the side.** Swimmers finish their last stroke with the body rolled on its side, head steady, and the top arm on the hip. They touch the wall at gutter level with the bottom arm (see figure 8.23). The biggest mistake kids make on this transition turn is touching the wall while on their backs with their shoulders flat; it is impossible to do a fast turn from this starting point. The second biggest mistake is turning their heads and looking for the wall as they approach; this often results in rolling their shoulders past the vertical for an instant disqualification.

FIGURE 8.23   On the touch, the body is on its side with the touching hand at the surface and the top arm on the hip.

Back-to-Breast Turn on the Wall   The great challenge with the actual turn is to make it as simple as possible, with few movements required. Most swimmers make this turn complicated and, as a result, slow. The body remains on its side throughout the turn.

■ **Leave the side arm.** As swimmers touch the wall, they leave the top arm that is by their side in place.

- **Knees up quick.** The knees pull up to the chest while the side arm stays in place, the hand of the touch arm should press into the wall, and the body remains on its side (see figure 8.24).

- **Touch-arm to streamline.** Just before the feet hit the wall, the touch arm leaves and spears behind the ear to a streamline with the other arm. The body stays on its side (but past the vertical, of course) as the legs push off

FIGURE 8.24 **Knees pulling to the chest.**

the wall. You may find that most swimmers are astonished when you teach them this turn. What had been so difficult and complicated is suddenly simple and fast.

Back-to-Breast Send-Away   Here we have a normal breaststroke underwater pullout sequence in all its parts.

- **Explode.** When the feet are planted to push off the wall, the body should be a straight, taut line from the rear to the fingertips. The push-off is powerful and explosive.

- **Underwater pullout sequence.** The swimmer glides in a tight streamline for two counts, then takes the long, strong butterfly pull and the associated short, quick dolphin kick. After this speed boost, the swimmer glides again in a perfect horizontal streamline for about one count. The hands and feet sneak their recoveries simultaneously, and then the kick pushes backward as the swimmer reaches the hands forward to begin the breakout stroke. Rhythm is established from that strong, forward breakout.

Finishes

Every day in practice and every month at meets, swimmers lose races they should have won by letting up at the very end, gliding into the wall with legs dragging and head up, or letting someone else spear their hands to the wall first. This is especially frustrating because doing things right would not have taken any extra effort, only extra focus. Every bad finish is a mental mistake caused by a swimmer not planning out the finish beforehand.

If you want swimmers to finish well and win touch-outs at meets, then expect them to finish correctly every time they finish a repeat in training. You must convince swimmers how important good finishes can be to winning races; a swimmer who does not see the point will not do what you ask. When approaching the end of any race, swimmers should pretend they are finishing an Olympic final and race accordingly. They should race anyone close to them, even if the other swimmers are unaware of the race. Finishing fast must be a habit.

FIGURE 8.25 A butterfly finish on a full stroke with head down and body nearly horizontal.

Good finishes require a killer attitude, and they require focus—the only thing in life that matters right now is getting your hand on the wall first. Swimmers must gauge their strokes so they finish on a full stroke (see figure 8.25), neither gliding in nor short-stroking. They should kick like crazy into every finish. They should punch the wall with the fingertips about 4 inches (10 cm) below the surface, and never grab onto the gutter. On free and fly, it is ideal to not breathe the last 10 meters or so into the finish, since every breath slows the swimmer down and takes her concentration off the target. On backstroke, the last arm into the wall should not be a long, languid recovery but a spear and lunge with the head thrown back and the legs dolphin-kicking for all they are worth (but making sure not to take the whole body underwater, which is illegal). On breaststroke, swimmers should drive the body forward and lunge to the wall; too many swimmers get short and vertical as they overtempo the finishes.

Underwater Dolphins

Given how important fast walls are for fast racing, training underwater dolphins is essential. However, coaches can become frustrated when they set aside practice time for underwater dolphin work only to have swimmers completely ignore dolphins as soon as the special work ends. The challenge is getting kids to work on dolphins all the time and not compartmentalize underwater dolphins as something they do well a few times a week and then ignore.

Part of the problem arises from coaches expecting more from the swimmers than they can reasonably do. In a perfect world, every swimmer would kick seven or eight powerful dolphins off every wall in every practice. But no matter what coaches would like, swimmers cannot be great all the time. Perfect walls are simply too stressful to do every time, especially on extended aerobic sets. And if the coach asks for eight dolphins in a situation where the swimmers simply cannot do eight, they will often do zero. The result is a frustrated coach and swimmers with sloppy walls.

Even if swimmers cannot be great all of the time, they can be great sometimes—in properly constructed sets that transfer to racing—and very good the rest of the time. With attention, they can gradually improve both their good and great performances as the season progresses. It is important to teach, establish, and enforce a group standard for normal walls, including the minimum number and quality of underwater dolphins that will be expected. A useful principle is to start small and progress with baby steps. A few dolphins done well are better than several dolphins done poorly, so begin by asking for only three dolphins off the walls. Increase the expectations only when a swimmer consistently and comfortably does things right and shows she is ready to move on.

With normal walls as a foundation, we sprinkle some *super walls* training throughout each week. Super walls are racing walls. The underwater dolphins are deeper than normal to avoid the turbulence at or near the surface, longer than normal with six to eight dolphins instead of three or four, and faster than normal at racing intensity with more power from the core of the body.

Gradually increase the repeat distances and the speed of the repeats where super walls are expected so that the swimmers learn to practice great walls under something approximating racing stresses. Be sure to increase the amount of super walls work as you approach the target or championship meet. The aim is to have swimmers associate going fast with doing super walls in practice and to associate racing with doing super walls at meets.

PART III

Training and Preparing Swimmers

CHAPTER 9

Training Age-Group Swimmers

Pretty swimmers who think like champions still need to be fit. This chapter discusses how to train swimmers for fitness—what might be thought of as building the engine. Because the three sides of the triad for long-term development interconnect, the chapter touches briefly on psychology and technique. In other words, fitness includes attitude and technique.

There are as many training programs as there are coaches. Whatever the program, there are too many things to do in the little time allotted, and you must make choices. These choices should follow from the philosophy of the program and from your experience and knowledge of developmental physiology, biology, psychology, and technique. Choices have consequences. What you emphasize or neglect will show in what your swimmers do well and what they do not. At any swim meet, look for patterns among a team's swimmers and you will be able to determine what they emphasize in daily practice. Some teams obviously do a lot more freestyle than anything else. Other teams obviously sprint most of the time because their swimmers are nonexistent in the longer events. No matter how good the coach or the program, every program will have weaknesses. You cannot emphasize everything, so you need to pick your spots and realize that by being strong in some areas, you will be weaker in others. Coaches need to decide what they think is more important and apportion training time accordingly.

From one season to the next, the list of priorities will probably change slightly as a coach interprets the results of the previous season and figures out what needs improving. At the end of every season, I always have a list of things we did not do to my satisfaction and an even longer list of things to do differently in the coming season. I have never done the same program for two seasons. In the words of Aussie coaching legend Percy Cerutty, "To be satisfied is to be finished."

Basic Training Principles for Age-Groupers

Every exercise physiology book has a list of training principles. These lists can be short and fundamental, or they can be long and complicated. I try to keep things clean and simple, so my list is a short one. Each of the following principles is tailored to young swimmers.

Adaptation

Swimming seems simple: Train, recover, and come back stronger tomorrow. Train a bit faster. Recover, and come back stronger the next day. Repeat. Swimmers improve because training hard and conscientiously causes certain metabolic, physiological, neuromuscular, and psychological changes in the body. Each time they train, they break down the muscle tissues. If swimmers eat properly and recover sufficiently, those muscle tissues rebuild larger, stronger, and more functional by the time they practice again. Muscles become stronger and get better at working together, the energy-supplying mechanisms function better, the heart and lungs get stronger and pump more blood to the muscles, and the body becomes better at tolerating pain. There are three key ingredients required: proper amount and intensity of exercise, adequate nutrients, and adequate rest.

Progressive Overload

Training stresses the body; during a period of recovery, the body adapts to this increased stress and creates a new normal. The body is now better in some way; it is stronger, or faster, or has better endurance depending on the kind of training performed. But once the body has adapted to a particular amount and intensity of a type of exercise, only an increase in amount, intensity, or both will stimulate the body to adapt again. If continued stress is not placed on the body at this new higher level in a reasonable length of time (a day or two), the body loses its new capacity and reverts to its previous level of normalcy.

Different kinds of training require different amounts of recovery time. The more stressful the training mode, the longer the time required for regeneration. Repeat a certain kind of training too soon and the body will not yet be recovered; it will not be ready to improve with the second bout. Repeat the training too late and the body will have lost some of the first training effect by the time of the second bout. Generally, the time course of adaptation for aerobic or endurance work (the kind of work that forms the foundation of age-group training) is short, so swimmers can repeat aerobic training every day and keep getting better from it without breaking down and failing to adapt to the stresses. The time course for high-intensity sprint training is much longer, and swimmers need two or three days of lower-stress work to recover.

The balance between stress and recovery is delicate and requires careful manipulation of three variables—training volume (how much), intensity (how hard), and density (how much rest between training sessions)—all with an eye to the physiological goals of the training for the swimmer and for the group. The swimmer needs enough stress to force an adaptation but not so much that he gets sick or injured. Then he needs enough rest to adapt but not so much that he reverts to previous levels.

Regarding sickness and injury, it has been my experience that the swimmers who are most often sick or hurt are those who are least consistent with their training schedule and effort. This may seem counterintuitive. One would expect that those swimmers who come to practice every day and work the hardest would get hurt more often since they place more stress on their bodies. But hard-working, consistent-training bodies adapt to the stresses of training. The bodies of inconsistent trainers never get strong enough to handle training stress and are more likely to break down under the load.

> The bodies of inconsistent trainers never get strong enough to handle training stress and are more likely to break down under the load.

Specificity

Different kinds of training develop different physical capacities; the body improves in specific ways when kids exercise. In other words, swimming will improve kids' swimming more than running will. Swimming butterfly will improve their butterfly more than swimming backstroke will, and training race-pace fly will improve their fly race times more than training slowly will. If life were simple and specificity were absolute, training athletes would be easy: Swim race pace in each swimmer's specialty whenever possible at every practice. But any coach knows that such training would quickly result in injured or overworked swimmers. Many considerations muddy the waters of specificity.

First, you are dealing with kids, not mature adults. Young swimmers are physiological generalists who respond aerobically to almost any physiological stress or stimulus. High-intensity anaerobic training will not evoke the same training response in age-groupers as it will in senior athletes. Also, age-group training aims at building long-term physiological capacities, not at being fast by Friday. Swimmers need to establish a technical and fitness base now to build high performance upon later. Further, kids today are not as fit as they used to be, so cross-training with dryland exercises helps to build general athleticism and cardiorespiratory fitness.

Second, you are trying to build swimming all-rounders. Although it may be true that training fly makes flyers, making flyers is not the aim. You want young swimmers to be strong in all strokes. They can specialize when they are seniors getting ready for college. Even if a swimmer has a favorite stroke right now, training all strokes provides natural recovery, helps prevent overtraining in any one stroke, and provides a new best stroke should the swimmer hit a plateau.

Third, race-speed swimming is stressful and takes a relatively long time to recover from. No one can handle the physiological (or psychological) stresses of swimming the same stroke at race pace all the time. That is a recipe for failing adaptation and performance plateaus. Again, you are not training young swimmers for success at the meet next weekend but rather training them to have the engine, efficiency, and mind-set to be extraordinary several years down the road.

> You are not training young swimmers for success at the meet next weekend but rather training them to have the engine, efficiency, and mind-set to be extraordinary several years down the road.

Individuality

Not everyone gets the same result from the same training program. Kids are different, and what works for one swimmer doesn't necessarily work for all. Heredity and environment both matter. There are many factors that come into play:

- **Age and stage of biological development.** Certain kinds of training are more beneficial at certain times of life. Also, the older kids get, the wider the disparity between their responses to certain kinds of sets. A group of 12-year-old girls will likely respond similarly to a particular training set, whereas a group of 14-year-olds will respond very differently to the same set.

- **Training age.** How the body responds to and tolerates training depends on how long the swimmer has been training and what kind of training he has been doing.

- **Psychological makeup.** Some swimmers whose bodies are perfectly suited to distance swimming are not temperamentally suited to the training volume, consistency, and rigor that distance success requires.

- **Motivation levels.** Some swimmers who work hard and consistently take advantage of opportunities to improve; others slog through practice and bore themselves silly.

- **Consistency and correctness of training.** Some swimmers come to practice every day and perform the training sets as prescribed; others show up occasionally and do as they please.

- **Geometry of the body.** Some swimmers have longer limbs than others, some have longer torsos than others, some have wider shoulders than others, and some have leaner bodies than others. While swimmers are growing, all these variables are changing. These differences are important in determining how swimmers move through the water, how much strength it takes them to do so, and how they respond to training.

- **Muscle composition.** Swimmers have different proportions of fast-twitch and slow-twitch muscle fibers, and these differences determine whether swimmers are physiologically built for distance swimming, sprinting, or middle distance. Further, the size, length, and number of muscle fibers determine whether a swimmer is naturally strong.

Reversibility

The idea here is simple: Use it or lose it. Training benefits (adaptations) are lost if training stops or if the training load does not increase to force new adaptations. Taking weeks or months off from training is not wise because swimmers lose the speed and endurance benefits they worked hard for, and their bodies revert to fitness levels from previous weeks or months. This is called *detraining*. The wise approach is to work hard for a season and then use that improved fitness and performance as the foundation for further improvements the next season. Otherwise, the only result of working hard is getting tired.

Consistency of training is crucial, especially for younger swimmers: They add a pebble with each practice until they have a mountain. Cardiorespiratory endurance, the bulk of the work that young swimmers do, is especially sensitive to detraining. Two weeks off from training can require two to three weeks of hard training just to get back to the fitness levels achieved before the swimmer's vacation. Many programs give their age-group swimmers as much as a month away from the pool between seasons. The reasoning behind this practice can be sound—the kids need a physical and mental respite from the grind—but breaks should never be so long that swimmers lose fitness and feel for the water. As General George S. Patton noted, "Never yield ground. It is cheaper to hold what you have than to retake what you have lost." Short breaks are preferred, at most a week at the end of the winter and spring season and maybe a week and a half after the summer season. Even when they are away from the pool, swimmers need to stay active and fit, riding their bikes, playing in the backyard, and so on. Practice should be so enjoyable that swimmers can't wait to be back at the pool with their coaches and their swimming friends.

Since the world is not ordered by swimming coaches, sometimes it happens that swimmers will go on family vacations in the middle of the season, and even the soundest arguments cannot change the situation. This can seriously disrupt the training routine and preparations for the upcoming championship meet. If swimmers absolutely must be away, coaches should strongly recommend that they find a legitimate team to train with wherever they are staying. Training in a hotel pool—no doubt, a pool 10 yards (9 m) long and shaped like a lima bean that has 90-degree water, a myriad of distractions, and no pace clock, lane lines, or backstroke flags—is not adequate for swimmers who care about being fast.

Confluence

Your aim is to develop a training program that will give kids what they need when they need it so that training and biological growth dovetail. A swimmer's body will let you know when it is biologically ready to improve with certain types of training. It is the difference between walking through an open door and crashing through a closed one—improvements come easier when a swimmer is in a critical period for a particular physiological or neuromuscular capacity. Improvements in a certain kind of training will proceed at a certain rate for a time and then skyrocket. The attentive coach will notice the accelerating rate and give the swimmer or the group more of that kind of work so that the capacity in question increases optimally.

Having watched this cycle with generations of swimmers several years in a row has resulted in a basic program for training groups that is formulated to take advantage of these periods. Thus, our 10-and-under swimmers do different work from the 11- to 12-year-olds, who do different work from the 13- to 14-year-olds. All the while, coaches must recognize that no two kids are identical and must try to account for these individual differences.

Recommended Age-Group Training Program

I owe many of my ideas on training to my time coaching with the North Baltimore Aquatic Club and to the help of coaches Murray Stephens and Bob Bowman, who opened my eyes to what swimmers are capable of, what fast is, and the finer points of training young swimmers. Much of what follows can be traced to the North Baltimore way, with adjustments based on my experience and study. This program has proven effective, but of course it is neither the only way to organize and prioritize a program nor set in stone. Coaches should learn continually, and their programs should evolve continually as a result.

An age-group swimming program is similar to a marathon, requiring long-term thinking, planning, and decision making. The focus is on training for the future, slowly building physiological capacities over months and years that serve as the foundation for future high-level athletic performance. Thus, every swimmer is an individual medley swimmer now so that she has options later. With each training group, we have one program for all, with little choice. On a butterfly day, everybody does fly; on a backstroke day, everybody does back. We give all our swimmers the same base training and skills. They can diverge from the path later, when their bodies have decided what kind of swimmers they will be.

Attitude and Expectations

As has already been discussed, we take mental training seriously. How a swimmer thinks determines his performance, so we consciously steer swimmers into certain helpful currents of thought. It's all about getting better. In our training environment, we make the *agon*, the struggle or the competition, fun. Racing is commonplace, motivating, challenging, and unthreatening. Swimmers are setting goals all the time, continually striving to reach higher. This is *kaizen*, or continual improvement, and this is how we define success. Daily practice performance is emphasized even more than performance at monthly meets. We expect *arete*, or excellence—we do things right all the time, and swimmers are held to high standards. We applaud and expect commitment, two of whose markers are attendance and work ethic.

Technique

Next to attitude, technique is the biggest help or hindrance to a swimmer's progress. Using the stroke catechism as the basis of our technique work, we swim full stroke with a technique focus, working on one aspect of the stroke at a time, cycling through the various stroke fundamentals like the colors of the rainbow. In particular for the age-groupers, distance per stroke (DPS), as measured by the number of strokes taken per length (S/L), is given priority over tempo or stroke rate (SR). We try to groove in long and efficient strokes, and many technique sets are swum with goal stroke counts every length. In our main sets, we emphasize good technique most toward the end, when swimmers are tired and nearing race paces (i.e., when they are feeling race pain and maintaining technique is crucial to maintaining speed).

During the age-group years, swimmers go through puberty and the adolescent growth spurt. These can cause serious problems with technique. Swimmers must adjust their strokes to their continually changing bodies, and some swimmers may lose their strokes and their feel for what they are doing in the water. Long, lanky girls who have grown quickly often are not strong enough to control their long limbs, leading to many technical challenges. To some extent, daily technique work can help smooth the growing process.

Individual Medley Base

Age-group swimmers should be all-rounders and should not specialize their training in any one stroke or distance. We focus most of our daily work on one stroke, though we will often begin with a short technique or speed set of the stroke that will be the next day's focus. The main set is usually a substantial aerobic set in which the intensity builds throughout. We often follow the main set with a kicking set before finishing with a few dive sprints or relays before we warm down. Because we switch main training strokes each day and thereby change the motor patterns that are stressed, the swimmers have natural recovery days, so they stay fresh and fast. Within a workout, too, we cycle the stresses, recovering from one kind of stress by stressing something else. Swimmers focus better since they are not asked to keep their minds on one thing for a long time.

> Age-group swimmers should be all-rounders and should not specialize their training in any one stroke or distance.

This approach provides implicit recovery through the structure of the training week and session. Further, by hitting each stroke every week, we keep the swimmers moving forward across a broad front. Progress in any one stroke may not be as rapid, but plateaus are less likely. No one event or stroke gets too much pressure put on it psychologically ("My whole season is ruined if I don't swim well in my 100 fly!"). An example of a typical training week with major and minor emphases is shown in table 9.1.

For sample training weeks for 9- to 10-year-old swimmers, 11- to 12-year-olds, and 13- to 14-year-olds, see figures 9.1, 9.2, and 9.3 starting on page 134.

TABLE 9.1

Sample Training Week With Major and Minor Emphases

	Major emphasis	Minor emphasis
Monday	Freestyle	Butterfly (technique)
Tuesday	Butterfly	Super walls (see page 123)
Wednesday	Individual medley and kicking (best stroke)	Backstroke (technique)
Thursday	Backstroke	Breaststroke (power)
Friday	Super walls and racing dives (combined work with seniors for the first 40 minutes) and breaststroke	
Saturday	Freestyle and kicking (weak stroke)	

FIGURE 9.1

Sample Training Week for Strong 9- to 10-Year-Old Swimmers in Early to Midseason[1]

MONDAY: Fly Focus

Warm-Up

400 IM, 400 fly drill, 400 IM

Minor Backstroke Set

1,200 backstroke build[2], alternating 50 kick, 50 drill, 50 full stroke

Major Fly Set

5 rounds of 4 × 50 fly drill on 1:00, varying stroke focus by round

12 × 50 fly kick on 1:00

First 3 50s on back with hands at sides, second 3 on side, third 3 with kickboard, and last 3 on back with hands up

40 × 25 alternating moderate freestyle and fast fly:

First 20 with fins on :30, using rainbow focus (page 72)

Second 20 without fins on :35, using rainbow focus

Warm-Down

300 swimmers' choice

TUESDAY: Backstroke Focus

Warm-Up

400 IM, 400 backstroke with ankle buoy, 400 IM

Minor Breaststroke Set

400 breaststroke kick on :15 rest

300 one-pull–two-kick breaststroke drill on :15 rest

200 breaststroke for maximum distance per stroke (DPS) on :15 rest

4 × 25 breaststroke sprint on :40

Major Backstroke Set

16 × 50 on 1:00, alternating one-arm backstroke drill and backstroke kick

2 rounds of the following:

200 backstroke on 3:20 (group A), 3:30 (group B)

150 backstroke on 2:30 (A), 2:40 (B)

100 backstroke on 1:40 (A), 1:45 (B)

50 backstroke on :50 (A), :55 (B)

500 backstroke with fins, build pace and do 6 underwater dolphins off each wall

Warm-Down

300 swimmers' choice

WEDNESDAY: Breaststroke Focus

Warm-Up

400 IM, 400 breaststroke drill, 400 IM

Minor Freestyle Set

8 × 100 freestyle balance[3] work on 1:40

12 × 50 freestyle on :50, using rainbow focus

Major Breaststroke Set

18 × 50 alternating breaststroke kick on 1:05, breaststroke drill on 1:00, breaststroke full stroke on 1:00

75 breaststroke, completing 25 of kick, drill, and full stroke on :15 rest

150 breaststroke, completing 50 of kick, drill, and full stroke on :15 rest

225 breaststroke, completing 75 of kick, drill, and full stroke on :15 rest

300 breaststroke, completing 100 of kick, drill, and full stroke on :15 rest

24 × 25 breaststroke on :30, alternating moderate freestyle and fast breaststroke

Warm-Down

300 swimmers' choice

THURSDAY: Freestyle Focus

Warm-Up

400 IM, 400 freestyle long and smooth, 400 IM

Minor IM Set

20 × 50 IM order, 1 stroke focus per repeat, descend by rounds of 4
    First 8 × 50 on :55
    Next 12 × 50 on 1:00

Major Freestyle Set

10 × 100 freestyle kick
    First 5 100s on 2:05 (A), 2:10 (B)
    Next 3 on 2:00 (A), 2:05 (B)
    Last 2 on 1:55 (A), 2:00 (B)

20 × 25 on :30, alternating 2 freestyle kick and 2 full-stroke freestyle with 6-beat kick focus

12 × 100 freestyle, descend 1 to 4, 5 to 8, 9 to 12
    Group A: 4 on 1:40, 4 on 1:35, 4 on 1:30
    Group B: 4 on 1:45, 4 on 1:40, 4 on 1:35

Warm-Down

300 swimmers' choice

(continued)

FIGURE 9.1   *(continued)*

FRIDAY: IM Focus

Warm-Up
400 IM

Relay Starts
Relay starts with seniors for about 45 minutes

IM Main Set: IM Amphibious Operation
Swim free IMs[4] followed by this dryland exercise set:
  Dryland: plank (hold 30 s), 3 push-ups, 16 single-leg pike-ups (8 per side), 8 scapular push-ups
100 free IM, dryland set
200 free IM, dryland set
300 free IM, dryland set
400 free IM, dryland set
500 free IM, dryland set
600 free IM, dryland set
700 free IM, dryland set

SATURDAY: Freestyle Focus

Warm-Up
400 IM, 400 freestyle kick, 400 IM

Minor Fly Set
5 rounds of the following:
  100 fly kick on back on 2:00
  2×50 fly drill on 1:00
  2×25 fly swim sprint on :30

Major Freestyle Set
3 rounds of 3×200 freestyle on 3:10, alternating focus on balance, DPS, and 6-beat kick for the 200s in each round
800 freestyle prone flutter kick with fins
3 rounds of 3×100 freestyle on 1:35, alternating balance, DPS, and 6-beat kick for the 100s in each round

Warm-Down
500 swimmers' choice

---

[1]All workouts are short-course meters (25 m pool). Adjust intervals for swimmer ability and short-course yards.

[2]Build pace within a repeat.

[3]Balance indicates swimming freestyle repeats in which swimmers breathe once every three strokes for 1/4 of the distance, on every left-arm stroke for the next 1/4, on every right-arm stroke for the next 1/4, and once every five strokes for the last 1/4. The focus is on keeping the stroke balanced left to right and breathing to the nonbreathing side, with every stroke equally efficient.

[4]Free/IM is an individual medley used with freestyle in the place of butterfly (i.e., free, back, breast, free).

FIGURE 9.2

Sample Training Week for Strong 11- to 12-Year-Old Swimmers in Early to Midseason[1]

MONDAY: Backstroke and Breaststroke Transition Focus

Warm-Up

400 IM, 400 backstroke and breaststroke alternating by 25s, 400 IM

Main Back–Breast Switching Focus

6 × 100 (50 backstroke, 50 breaststroke) on 1:40

6 × 50 freestyle moderate pace at base[2] strokes per length (S/L) on :50

6 × 150 (75 backstroke, 75 and breaststroke) on 2:25

6 × 50 freestyle moderate pace at base S/L on :50

6 × 200 (100 backstroke 100 breaststroke) on 3:20

6 × 50 freestyle moderate pace at base S/L on :50

   Note: Boys can do dryland exercises instead of moderate 50s between BK/BR sets.

Backstroke Technique Focus

1,200 backstroke with fins, build[3] pace, alternating 50 kick, 50 one-arm drill, and 50 swim

TUESDAY: Fly Focus

Warm-Up

400 IM, 400 fly kick and drill, 400 IM

Main Fly Set

12 × 50 fly drill on :55, alternating stroke focus

5 rounds of the following:

   100 Sarah Dotzel (alternating 25 free and 25 fly) very fast on 1:30

   50 backstroke on 1:00 with perfect technique

8 × 50 fly kick on back descend on :55

5 rounds of the following:

   200 Sarah Dotzel (alternating 25 free and 25 fly) with fins descend to crazy fast on 2:50

   100 backstroke with fins and perfect technique on 1:40

8 × 50 fly kick on back fast on 1:00

Fly Finishing-Speed Focus

24 × 25 fly with fins, alternating moderate freestyle and sprint fly

   First 12 on :30 and second 12 on 1:35

Warm-Down

300 swimmers' choice

WEDNESDAY: Freestyle and Backstroke Technique Focus

Warm-Up

400 IM, 400 backstroke, 400 IM

(continued)

FIGURE 9.2 *(continued)*

Freestyle Focus: Technique

2 rounds of the following:

    8 × 50 freestyle with paddles on :50; focus on high-elbow catch and pull

    6 × 50 freestyle on :50 at base S/L; focus on (distance per stroke) DPS

    4 × 25 freestyle sprint on :30 at base + 1 S/L; focus on DPS

    4 × 100 balance[4] on 1:30 (change breathing pattern each 25); focus on balance left to right and breathing to nonbreathing side

    4 × 100 freestyle on :10 rest, alternating with ankle buoy (use finger drag recovery) and regular (use finger drag recovery and 6-beat kick); focus on directness, straight forward, and straight back

Backstroke Focus: Technique

4 rounds of 8 × 50 on :05 rest, alternating one-arm drill and regular backstroke

    Round 1 with paddles; focus on clean entry, strong catch, and long pull

    Round 2 regular; focus on clean entry, strong catch, and long pull

    Round 3 with ankle buoy; focus on body line and no wiggle or sway to legs

    Round 4 regular; focus on body line and no wiggle or sway to legs

THURSDAY: IM and Backstroke Focus

Warm-Up

400 IM, 400 kick primary stroke without boards, 400 IM

IM and Backstroke Main Set

8 × 200 descend (alternating backstroke and free/IM[5] on 200s) on 3:10 (group A), 3:20 (group B)

8 × 50 freestyle or backstroke long and smooth with fins on :50, underwater dolphin kick to 10 m off every wall

8 × 200 descend, alternating backstroke and free/IM:

    4 on 3:00 (A), 3:15 (B)

    4 on 2:55 (A), 3:15 (B)

8 × 50 freestyle or backstroke long and smooth with fins on :50, underwater dolphin kick to 10 m off every wall

4 rounds of the following:

    2 × 50 kick choice moderate pace on 1:10 (A), 1:15 (B)

    1 × 100 IM sprint on 1:30 (A), 1:35 (B)

Warm-Down

6 × 50 easy pace on :50

FRIDAY: Breaststroke and Fly Technique Focus

Warm-Up

400 long and smooth

Relay Starts

Relay starts with seniors for about 45 minutes

Breaststroke Focus: Technique

20 × 25 flutter-kick breaststroke pull with fins on :30, using rainbow focus (page 72)

10 × 50 one-pull–two-kick breaststroke drill on :55 (A), 1:00 (B), focusing on kick technique, finishing kick, and streamlining

5 × 100 breaststroke on 1:40 (A), 1:45 (B) Focus on DPS

20 × 25 breaststroke on :30, alternating DPS focus and sprint

Fly Focus: Technique

12 × 50 fly drill on :55, using rainbow focus

20 × 25 fly with fins on :25, alternating moderate freestyle and fast fly with rainbow focus

20 × 25 on :30, alternating moderate freestyle and fast fly with rainbow focus

Warm-Down

6 × 50 easy pace on :50

SATURDAY: Freestyle Focus

Warm-Up

400 IM, 400 freestyle kick, 400 IM, 400 freestyle with ankle buoy

Freestyle DPS Focus

3 × 200 freestyle kick descend on 4:00 (A), 4:15 (B)

1,200 freestyle straight, balance work by 25s

900 freestyle straight, alternating by 25s with base − 1 S/L, base S/L, and base + 1 S/L

18 × 50 freestyle on :50
    For every 3 repeats, alternate 1 moderate at base S/L, 1 build at base S/L, 1 sprint at base S/L + 1.
    For each set of 3, choose 1 stroke focus.

Freestyle Kick Focus

8 × 100 freestyle kick descend:
    Group A: 2 repeats on 1:55, 2 on 1:50, 2 on 1:45, 2 on 1:40
    Group B: 2 repeats on 2:05, 2 on 2:00, 2 on 1:55, 2 on 1:50

8 × 50 freestyle kick sprint on 1:00 (A), 1:05 (B)

12 × 25 freestyle kick super sprint on :35 (A), :40 (B)

Freestyle Aerobic Set

400 freestyle on 5:40 (A), 6:00 (B)

300 freestyle on 4:15 (A), 4:30 (B)

200 freestyle on 2:50 (A), 3:00 (B)

100 freestyle on 1:25 (A), 1:30 (B)

100 easy-pace backstroke on 1:50 (A), 2:00 (B)

5 × 100 freestyle fast on 1:30 (A), 1:40 (B)

Warm-Down

8 × 50 easy pace choice on :55

---

[1]All workouts are short-course meters (25 m pool). Adjust intervals for swimmer ability and short-course yards.

[2]Base S/L means base stroke count per length. It should be determined for each swimmer during the first few weeks of the season. Base − 1 S/L means base stroke count per length minus one, so the strokes are very long. Base + 1 S/L means base stroke count per length plus one, so the strokes are slightly shorter but always accompanied by more speed.

[3]Build pace within a repeat.

[4]Free IM is an individual medley used with freestyle in the place of butterfly (i.e., free, back, breast, free).

[5]Balance indicates swimming freestyle repeats in which swimmers breathe once every three strokes for 1/4 of the distance, on every left-arm stroke for the next 1/4, on every right-arm stroke for the next 1/4, and once every five strokes for the last 1/4. The focus is on keeping the stroke balanced left to right and breathing to nonbreathing side, with every stroke equally efficient.

FIGURE 9.3

Sample Training Week for Strong 13- to 14-Year-Olds in Early to Midseason[1]

MONDAY: Back and Breast Transition Focus

Warm-Up

400 IM, 400 back and breast by 25s, 2 × 200 IM, 400 back and breast by 50s, 4 × 100 IM

Walls

12 × 50 freestyle with fins and underwater dolphin kick to 10 m, alternating on :50, :45, :40, and :35
6 × 100 backstroke with fins and underwater dolphin kick to 10 m, alternating on 1:25, 1:20, and 1:15

Backstroke and Breaststroke Main Set

3 × 200 backstroke descend on 2:50 (group A), 3:00 (group B)
6 × 100 breaststroke descend on 1:40 (A), 1:45 (B)
6 × 200 (100 backstroke, 100 breaststroke) descend intervals and swimming speed to race pace:
    Group A: 2 repeats on 3:05, 2 on 3:00, 2 on 2:55
    Group B: 2 repeats on 3:10, 2 on 3:05, 2 on 3:00
    Group C: 2 repeats on 3:15, 2 on 3:10, 2 on 3:05
300 free at base[2] strokes per length (S/L), long and smooth
12 × 100 IM fast on 1:30 (A), 1:40 (B)

Warm-Down

6 × 50 freestyle easy pace at base S/L on :50

Dryland Training

30 minutes of core work

TUESDAY: Fly Focus

Warm-Up

400 IM, 400 fly kick on back, 2 × 200 IM, 400 fly drills, 4 × 100 IM

Fly Prep Set

2 rounds of the following:
    200 fly kick on back on 3:20
    150 fly single–double B-form drill on 2:30
    100 fly kick on back on 1:40
    50 fly single–double B-form drill on :50

Fly Main Set

2,000 pyramid fly medley:
    Swimmers use one-arm B drill, single–double B-form drill, fly kick on back, and fly sprint.
    They swim 25 of each drill, 50 of each drill, 75 of each drill, and 100 of each drill to go up the pyramid.
    Then they repeat 100 of each drill and move back down the pyramid to end with 25 of each.
    Swimmers should swim strong, and pyramid should be timed and times recorded.
12 × 50 fins fly kick on back, alternating 1 moderate on :50 and 1 very fast on :40
12 × 25 fly kick on back sprint on :30

20 × 50 on :50, alternating moderate freestyle and sprint fly
  First 8 50s on :45, the next 8 on :50, and the final 4 on :55
36 × 25 alternating moderate freestyle and sprint fly
  First 18 25s on :25 and the next 18 25s on :30

Warm-Down

6 × 50 freestyle on :50

Dryland training: 30 minutes of arm and leg strengthening

WEDNESDAY: Freestyle and Backstroke Technique

Warm-Up

400 IM, 400 freestyle with ankle buoy, 2 × 200 IM, 400 backstroke with ankle buoy, 4 × 100 IM

Freestyle Focus: Technique

2 rounds of the following:
  4 × 100 freestyle paddles on 1:25, focusing on high-elbow catch and pull
  6 × 50 freestyle on :45 at base S/L, focusing on distance per stroke (DPS)
  4 × 25 freestyle sprint on :30 at base + 1 S/L, focusing on DPS
  4 × 100 freestyle balance[3] on 1:25, changing breathing pattern each 25, focusing on balance left to right and breathing to nonbreathing side
  4 × 100 freestyle alternating with ankle buoy (with finger drag recovery) and regular (use finger drag recovery and 6-beat kick), focusing on directness, straight forward, straight back
15 × 25 freestyle on :30
  For every 3 repeats, alternate 1 moderate, 1 build[4], and 1 sprint.
  For each set of 3, choose 1 stroke focus.

Backstroke Focus: Technique

6 rounds of 8 × 50 backstroke on :05 rest, alternating one-arm drill and regular backstroke each 50
  Round 1 use paddles; focus on clean entry, strong catch, and long pull
  Round 2 regular; focus on clean entry, strong catch, and long pull
  Round 3 use ankle buoy; focus on body line and no wiggle or sway to legs
  Round 4 regular; focus on body line and no wiggle or sway to legs
  Round 5 use parachutes; focus on clean entry, strong catch, and long pull
  Round 6 regular; focus on clean entry, strong catch, and long pull
15 × 25 backstroke on :30
  For every 3 repeats, alternate 1 moderate, 1 build, and 1 sprint.
  For each set of 3, choose 1 stroke focus.

Warm-Down

6 × 50 on :50, alternating freestyle and backstroke

Dryland training: 30 min of core work and stretching

THURSDAY: Breaststroke Focus

Warm-Up

400 IM, 400 breaststroke kick, 2 × 200 IM, 400 breaststroke drill, 4 × 100 IM

Backstroke focus: wall and speed

5 × 200 backstroke gradual descend, work walls, on 2:50/3:00
16 × 50 backstroke on :50, alternating moderate and fast

(continued)

FIGURE 9.3   *(continued)*

Breaststroke Main Set

8 rounds of the following:

    50 breaststroke for maximum DPS on :50 (A), :55 (B)

    50 one-pull–three-kick breaststroke drills on :55 (A), 1:00 (B)

    50 breaststroke for maximum DPS on :50 (A), :55 (B)

    50 dolphin-kick breaststroke pull on :50 (A), :55 (B)

4 × 200 breaststroke descend to very fast on 3:20 (A), 3:30 (B)

8 × 50 fins backstroke on :50 (long and smooth) with underwater dolphin kick to 10 m

8 × 100 on 1:35, alternating moderate freestyle and very fast breaststroke

Warm-Down

6 × 50 on :50, alternating breaststroke and backstroke

Dryland training: 30 minutes of arm strengthening and breaststroke leg flexibility

FRIDAY: IM Focus

Warm-Up

400 IM, 8 × 50 IM order on :50, 2 × 200 IM, 16 × 25 IM order on :25, 4 × 100 IM

Short Freestyle Ladder With Stroke Technique Focus

100 freestyle at base S/L on 1:20 (A), 1:25 (B)

200 freestyle balance on 2:40 (A), 2:50 (B)

300 freestyle at base S/L on 4:00 (A), 4:15 (B)

400 freestyle balance on 5:20 (A), 5:40 (B)

IM Main Set: Amphibious Operation

Swim IMs and free/IMs[5] followed by the specified dryland exercise set:

    Dryland A: plank (hold 30 s) and 8 burpees

    Dryland B: 5 push-ups, 16 single-leg pike-ups (8 per side), 10 scapular push-ups, 16 legs-up twisting
        crunches

100 free IM, dryland A

800 IM, dryland B

300 free IM, dryland A

600 IM, dryland B

500 free IM, dryland A

400 IM, dryland B

700 free IM, dryland A

200 IM, dryland B

900 free IM, dryland A

Finishing-Speed Focus

16 × 25 IM order sprint

    First 8 25s on :30, next 4 on :35, and last 4 on :40

Warm-Down

6 × 50 easy pace on :50

Relay Starts

Relay starts with juniors for about 45 minutes

SATURDAY: Freestyle Focus

Warm-Up
400 IM, 400 freestyle with ankle buoy, 2 × 200 IM, 400 freestyle kick, 4 × 100 IM

Freestyle DPS Focus
4 × 100 at base S/L on 1:25

800 freestyle speed play, alternating 25 moderate at base S/L and 25 fast at base + 1 S/L

32 × 25 freestyle sprint at base + 1 S/L on :30

16 × 25 freestyle on :35, alternating easy pace at base − 1 S/L, super sprint at base + 2 S/L

Main Freestyle Set
Janet Evans 150s set:

    1 × 150 freestyle moderate pace on 2:10

    3 × 150 freestyle fast pace on 1:55

    2 × 150 freestyle moderate pace on 2:05

    2 × 150 freestyle fast pace on 1:50

    3 × 150 freestyle moderate pace on 2:00

    1 × 150 freestyle fast pace on 1:45

Freestyle Kicking Set
2 rounds of the following:

    8 × 50 freestyle prone flutter kick on 1:00 (without kickboards and with hands at sides)

    8 × 25 freestyle kick sprint on :35

2 rounds of the following with fins:

    4 × 50 freestyle prone flutter kick on :50 (without kickboards and with hands at sides)

    8 × 25 freestyle sprint on :30

Warm-Down
8 × 100 freestyle at base S/L on 1:30, long and smooth

---

[1]All workouts are short-course meters (25 m pool). Adjust intervals for swimmer ability and short-course yards.

[2]Base S/L means base stroke count per length. It should be determined for each swimmer during the first few weeks of the season. Base − 1 S/L means base stroke count per length minus one, so the strokes are very long. Base + 1 S/L means base stroke count per length plus one, so the strokes are slightly shorter but always accompanied by more speed.

[3]Balance indicates swimming freestyle repeats in which swimmers breathe once every five strokes for 1/4 of the distance, on every left-arm stroke for the next 1/4, on every right-arm stroke for the next 1/4, and once every three strokes for the last 1/4. The focus is on keeping the stroke balanced left to right and breathing to nonbreathing side, with every stroke equally efficient.

[4]Build pace within a repeat.

[5]Free/IM is an individual medley swam with freestyle in the place of butterfly (i.e., free, back, breast, free).

As noted in chapter 3, USA Swimming's Individual Medley Xtreme program, or IMX, can be used to encourage swimmers to work hard in all four strokes. The events in the IMX differ from one age group to another but generally are middle-distance freestyle races; the longer back, breast, and fly events; and one or two individual medley events. Times are scored using a power points system—the faster the swim, the higher the score. In order to be entered in the system, swimmers must swim all the IMX events, so they cannot avoid their weak strokes. Since the events are middle distance rather than sprints, aerobic training of the sort recommended in this book leads to higher scores and rankings. The purpose of the IMX program is to ensure that age-group swimmers develop their skills across a range of strokes and distances that are integral to long-term success.

We talked with the swimmers all the time about IMX, improving their scores, and working hard to improve their weak events. But we still needed to give meaning to the numbers. What is a good score? How do we evaluate and compare? After many mind-numbing hours relating times to scores for each sex and age, I compiled a scoring system with seven performance levels ranging from diamond at the top down to tin at the bottom. The diamond level is exacting and requires faster-than-AAAA times across the board, whereas the tin level is relatively lenient and allows most swimmers who complete the IMX events to be introduced.

Competitive kids love lists, they love seeing where they rank, and they love trying to reach the top. IMX encourages these proclivities. After each meet, coaches can post IMX scores and their details (total score and score for each event) by age group. Encourage swimmers to improve their scores by decreasing the range from their worst to their best event score. A good sign that you are developing versatile swimmers is for the group's normal range to be fewer than 100 points. Right next to these rankings we post our team's performance-level qualifiers and our IMX team records for each age and sex. At the end of each season, we post a permanent IMX honor roll consisting of national rankings and team performance levels. Kids want to make the wall, and we strongly encourage them to do it.

Endurance Base

Kids are aerobic sponges. Because sprinting capacity is generally linked with maturation, skinny young swimmers at early stages of their physical development are not yet built for sprinting. However, their aerobic capacities seem infinitely elastic; their bodies are predisposed to huge increases if exposed to endurance training. Put simply, kids are physiologically built for distance events. The strength and the sprinting ability will come later. For now, endurance training will help them more than sprinting, and it will build a firm foundation for their speed. If you don't give swimmers distance training when they are young and their bodies are most receptive, it is difficult to make up the aerobic deficit later. They will be trying to build a house on sand.

> If you don't give swimmers distance training when they are young and their bodies are most receptive, it is difficult to make up the aerobic deficit later.

Endurance training gives swimmers options. There is no way to tell, based on race results or temporary favorite strokes, what a young swimmer's eventual specialty will be. But an early and steady diet of sprinting limits a swimmer to sprint events later on, even if her body isn't finally suited to sprinting. Early endurance training gives a swimmer the flexibility to choose any event. It is a coaching axiom that you can race down from what you train but not up—if you train for sprints, you will not be able to swim a good distance race, but if you train for distance, you can drop down and sprint fairly well, especially when speed is maintained with regular sets of short sprints.

Endurance training also harmonizes with motor learning principles. Technical precision and efficiency in stroke mechanics is easier to attain at the slower speeds and stresses of aerobic training. Once you have grooved long, strong strokes into a swimmer's brain and body, then you are ready to build the tempo and work on speed. But if you routinely subject a young athlete to high-stress sprint work, he will develop short, choppy, ugly, inefficient strokes. He will be fast for a 25 but not for much longer, and those dead-end strokes will be set in stone, resistant to change no matter how many hours of stroke work he does.

Though swimmers may straggle out of an endurance practice feeling half dead, their bodies recover quickly from the aerobic training. By the next day, they are new and improved. With aerobic training, kids don't get destroyed and broken down as they do from high-stress sprint training. Further, when sprinting is combined with early specialization, as it often is, you have a recipe for overuse injuries. Endurance training, especially when combined with individual medley training, is easier on the body in that the stresses are smaller, and the variety of strokes ensures that no single stroke pattern gets overworked.

For all these reasons and more, short-rest aerobic work should be the meat and potatoes of age-group training programs, usually with repeat distances of 200 to 400 yards or meters (I love 300s). Over the course of a season, decrease the intervals as the swimmers improve aerobically. One important distinction between a program for age-groupers and one for senior swimmers is that young kids respond aerobically to all kinds of physiological stressors, so precise energy-system work is relatively pointless. If you give a group of senior swimmers a steady diet of mile repeats, their sprint times will not budge, and they may get worse. If you give young swimmers repeat miles, they will get better across the board in distance events and sprints. Specificity does not apply to the extent that it does with mature athletes.

Often age-group coaches shy away from giving swimmers long sets, fearing that the swimmers need to be entertained constantly and will get bored. It is true that age-groupers need to be reminded frequently what they are to be thinking about or working on, but coaches should not be afraid of giving kids long sets they can sink their teeth into. Most swimmers like the longer sets, even the long, straight swims of 2,500 and longer. They love racing each other on the long swims, and they feel appropriately tough, proud, and confident when they have done well. With a well-developed set of hand signals formulated to your needs and emphases, you can convey stroke information to swimmers while they swim without their having to stop. They make stroke changes on the fly, so you don't have to watch lap after lap of ugly swimming. Also, longer swims allow swimmers to stretch their strokes out, which they cannot do when the intensity is high. We do one very long swim each week, cycling between freestyle, backstroke, and individual medley (or free/ IM, where freestyle is substituted for fly in an individual medley).

One especially effective format with age-groupers is a long aerobic set with double descending rounds, meaning that the intervals and the swimmers get faster from round to round. For example, they might swim four rounds of 3 × 300 freestyle, with round 1 on 4:00, round 2 on 3:55, round 3 on 3:50, and round 4 on 3:45. The swimmers get faster from start to finish, and each round has its own stroke emphasis. A short break between rounds allows the swimmers to regroup mentally, review what they just did, and decide on new goals for the upcoming round—then off they go.

It is most effective to focus on the times or paces the kids are swimming at, not on their heart rates or on the energy systems being stressed. Also, though we do repeat particular sets from time to time, we do not do test sets per se. "All else being equal" never is, so comparing one test set with another is often comparing apples and oranges. Priorities often get mistaken to the point that improving on the test set, rather than improving in meets, becomes the coach's focus of training in the period between tests. The tail ends up wagging the dog. You want your swimmers improving every day on all types of sets, swimming faster, splitting better, and looking more beautiful. Every set they do is a test set.

Training the Racing Stroke

If swimmers are going to race pretty and race tough, it is crucial to marry technique, endurance, and speed. The faster (and prettier) they can swim aerobically, the better. One frequently ignored but crucial aspect of training is its neuromuscular effect. Training does more than make a swimmer a cardiorespiratory specimen; the work she does affects her technique while it increases the size and functioning of her engine. The kind and structure of the sets you assign should help ensure that the work affects technique positively.

Especially important for helping swimmers improve both their physiology and technique are descending series, in which swimmers control their paces and gradually get faster as a set progresses. Swimmers range from moderate to race speeds, focusing on technique points all the while, particularly the points that give them trouble. They focus especially on maintaining stroke integrity at the crucial times for an athlete—when fatigued and at race speeds.

Too many swimmers look good and swim efficiently only at slow speeds—they compartmentalize and use different techniques for different occasions. Swimmers should aim for one good, beautiful, and efficient stroke that they use across a broad spectrum of speeds. Swimmers can train technically across this range of speeds to meet this aim. This aim is more easily reached when training short course (yards or meters); tempos can be higher and paces faster because of the natural recovery that turns provide. This is especially true with breaststroke and butterfly, which are inherently demanding.

> Swimmers should aim for one good, beautiful, and efficient stroke that they use across a broad spectrum of speeds.

Some of the many positive effects of descending series include the following:

▪ **Physiological effects.** Swimmers train the specificity and feel of race pace without being overwhelmed by high-intensity sprint sets, so they can swim fast every day.

▪ **Neuromuscular effects.** Swimmers train to maintain technical efficiency and good stroke rhythm under stress; they can feel stroke nuances even at high speeds and under physiological distress. They have the neuromuscular flexibility to adapt to the changing needs of the moment in races, picking up the pace to attack or answer an attack without losing rhythm or stroke integrity.

▪ **Conditioning the racing stroke.** Swimmers feel race pace several times each practice session, and they get more opportunities to swim at race pace aerobically. This last point is key: Aerobic swimming can be maintained.

▪ **Psychological effects.** Swimmers can swim especially fast as their bodies gradually pick up speed through a descending series—often even surpassing their best meet times—and this boosts confidence. Also, swimming very fast when very tired hurts exactly the same as it will hurt in the last quarter of a race. When the piano falls on the swimmer's back in a race, he knows he can handle it and still push the pace.

▪ **Sense of pace.** Swimmers get accustomed to fine-tuning their pacing because they rarely get stuck swimming at one speed for long periods of time. They can make small adjustments in speed by adjusting stroke tempos and ranges of motion.

▪ **Stroke discipline.** Swimmers go through a gradual spectrum of speeds, not night-and-day contrasts between a training stroke and a racing stroke. They do not see their racing stroke as completely different from the one they use to train with but rather a slight variation on a comfortable and habitual theme. Swimmers learn versatility through changing speeds.

Walls

For the longest time I held the opinion that I had taught my swimmers how to turn correctly; if they chose to do 200 sloppy and slow turns each practice, that was too bad for them. But that attitude doesn't work. One swimmer in a hundred (if a coach is lucky) will be driven and conscientious enough to improve her walls in that situation. One out of a hundred isn't a good enough percentage. You still might not take large blocks of time to focus on turns, but incorporating turn work into training sets a few times a week is beneficial.

Use super wall sets (refer to page 123) of repeat 25s, 50s, and 75s, usually totaling about 1,000 meters. Expect swimmers to kick six to eight underwater dolphins (or past a mark at 8 or 10 meters off the wall), deep and fast and streamlined, off every wall. Even on normal wall sets, the requirement should be four dolphins (or 6 meters) before a strong breakout. Realistically, normal walls can be sustained over a long time, but super walls cannot. Only ask your swimmers to do all the time what they can sustain all the time. Demanding what swimmers simply cannot do is a good way to be ignored.

> Only ask your swimmers to do all the time what they can sustain all the time.

Speed

Because age-groupers do not have the hormones that mature adults do, they do not have the anaerobic capacities of adults. Therefore, the effect of strength or speed training on young swimmers is primarily an improvement in neuromuscular coordination, not brute strength—they can use what they have with less neural interference. This coordination is important if swimmers are to race fast, so although we favor endurance training over sprint training, on most days our swimmers race some short sprints, focusing on maintaining long, fast, pretty strokes. We stress technique with the rainbow-focus format discussed in chapter 5 (see page 72). Also, most of our sprinting is done side by side, with match racing and keeping score, to cultivate competitiveness.

Kicking

We treat kicking sets like swimming sets, with challenging intervals and high expectations. Kicking is not social hour. In order to overload one motor pattern, we kick the same stroke the whole set. Sometimes this is the same stroke we just swam in the main aerobic set, but at other times the kids choose their primary stroke or their weak stroke. Quite often we kick without boards, with the arms down at the side to save the shoulders. Even the longest, hardest swimming set is not nearly as detrimental to shoulder health as holding the arms on a board in a position of continuous impingement for an entire set of kicking.

Often coaches assume that slow kickers just aren't trying. In some cases, this may be true, but many poor kickers are working just as hard as the fast kickers, they just aren't using good kicking technique. Therefore, talk about and practice kicking correctly. This is just as true of flutter and dolphin kicks as of the breaststroke kick. Also, at least some of our indirect kicking sets are done swimming full stroke while emphasizing a strong kick and proper timing of the kick to the body roll and pull.

Because proper technique and speed are impossible for flutter and dolphin kicks without good range of motion in the ankles, we do ankle flexibility exercises almost every day. A strong breaststroke kick requires flexibility in the hips, knees, and ankles that most kids do not have naturally, so several times a week our swimmers do a special set of breaststroke leg stretches that are described in the Dryland Training section.

We probably kick less frequently than most programs, but when we kick, we kick long and hard. If we assume that it takes 500 to 600 yards or meters to loosen the legs and begin kicking fast, then a set lasting only slightly longer than that stresses the legs for only a few minutes and is essentially wasted time. A long, challenging kick set of 1,600 to 2,000 meters more effectively overloads the legs, especially when it concludes with several short sprints of match racing.

Dryland Training

It is a truism among coaches that kids these days are not as fit, coordinated, or athletic as they were 10 or 15 years ago. If our kids are not good enough athletes to be good swimmers, we must somehow make up the athletic deficit with dryland training to supplement what they do in the water. For age-groupers, the aim for dryland training is general: to build coordination, agility, explosiveness, body awareness, and strength; to develop optimal ranges of motion in the key joints, especially in the legs for breaststroke; to strengthen the body core as a foundation for good technique and strong pulling and kicking; and to balance the musculature to help prevent future injuries, especially in the shoulder complex. With more advanced 13- to 14-year-olds, we add specific swimming strengthening work, both in and out of the water. Typically, our exercises are basic and are not targeted to specific swimming actions. We use minimal equipment, and most of our exercises are body-weight activities. You do not need to be fancy or spend a lot of money to get strong.

We frequently incorporate games, especially during the warm-weather months when we can play outside. Games such as Ultimate Frisbee, a favorite of our team, build speed, endurance, agility, coordination, and competitiveness. Games make the kids better athletes, get them outdoors, and are fun. (And the coach can play, too.) Also, in keeping with my admiration of and respect for the U.S. Navy Seals, some of our dryland training is done in the form of amphibious operations, meaning that water and dryland training merge. There are many variations, but as an example we might do five to eight rounds alternating a 400 IM or 400 freestyle swim with a short dryland routine, such as 25 sit-ups, 10 push-ups, 6 burpees, and 3 pull-ups—and we race while doing so. The coach loves the effort the swimmers put out, the kids love the variety, and the whole group gets stronger. Everybody wins.

As in the water, on dry land we emphasize that exercises be done correctly, with proper rhythm, tempo, and body position. No ugliness or sloppiness is tolerated. The goal is not to crush the kids or to build super strength but to be perfect. Ideally, dryland exercises are done after the water training session, because we do not want dryland training to take away from pool performance and because young swimmers should be fresh when they perform technique work in the water. Sometimes this will not be possible due to lack of deck space, pool-use pressures, or problems with coaching coverage.

We do very little stretching of the shoulders. The more time I spent in our local medical library reading about shoulder structure, function, and injuries, the more concerned I became about many of the traditional shoulder stretches. Physical-therapist and orthopedic-surgeon friends seconded my concerns, so we stopped—and we became essentially free of shoulder troubles.

We spend 15 to 30 minutes every day doing dryland training, usually alternating one day focusing on flexibility and arm and leg strength with one day focusing on body core and stability. We include many exercises in our dryland program. Following is a short summary of 10 key dryland exercises for age-groupers and four breaststroke leg stretches. For more information about dryland training for swimming, as well as an expanded set of recommended exercises, see *Complete Conditioning for Swimming* by David Salo and Scott Riewald (Human Kinetics, 2008).

FIVE EXERCISES FOR ARMS AND LEGS

A variety of exercises can strengthen the arms and legs. Five important exercises are described here. Rope climbing and pull-ups require equipment—a rope hung from the ceiling and a pull-up bar—but the equipment is relatively inexpensive and the exercises are invaluable. The other three exercises require no equipment and can be done anywhere. All of these exercises can be performed by swimmers young and old.

Rope Climbing

Swimmers climb up and down the rope. A protective mat underneath the rope is necessary if the rope is not over the pool. Three levels of proficiency can be used. Level 1 *(a)* kids use their arms and legs to move up and down the rope. Level 2 kids use their arms to move up the rope and use their legs only to hold their position. The strongest kids, level 3 *(b)*, use only their arms with no help from their legs. Athletes at all levels should come down the rope slowly, hand over hand, without letting go of the rope and dropping to the mat.

Rope climbing: level 1.

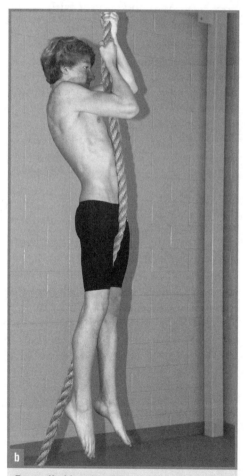

Rope climbing: level 3.

Pull-Up

The athlete should hang from a pull-up bar with the arms extended. Palms may face toward or away from the athlete. The different positions work slightly different muscle groups. The athlete pulls herself up so her chin passes the bar and then lowers herself to the start, keeping the body straight and taut.

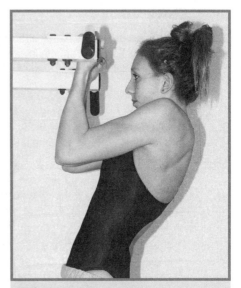

Pull-up.

Burpee

From a standing start, the swimmer drops down with his weight on his hands and feet *(a)*, then shoots the feet back together, putting the body in push-up position. The swimmer performs a push-up and then jumps to bring the feet forward underneath him and positioned next to the hands. Finally, the swimmer jumps as high as he can with arms stretched overhead in a streamlined position *(b)*. Keeping good body lines throughout the exercise is difficult but important.

Burpee: drop down position.

Burpee: streamlined vertical jump.

Push-Up

The athlete places the hands about shoulder-width apart with the body straight and taut and the toes on the floor. The athlete lowers herself until the chest touches a kickboard placed under the torso and then pushes up until the arms are straight. Several variations are also useful:

▶ For oblique push-ups, the hand placement changes so that one hand is about 6 inches (15 cm) in front of the usual placement and the other about 6 inches (15 cm) in back of the usual placement. The hands are diagonal to each other *(a)*.

▶ For scapular push-ups, the hand position is the same as the regular push-up. For the movement, instead of the elbows bending, the arms stay nearly straight. The swimmer lowers the body by retracting the shoulder blades until they touch *(b)*, and then she raises the body by protracting the shoulder blades until they are as far apart as possible. This variation strengthens the muscles around and under the shoulder blades, improving shoulder stability.

▶ For rotational push-ups, the hand position is the same as the regular push-up. When the swimmer pushes up, she puts her weight on one hand and turns the body to face out, extending the other arm, stretching it above the body *(c)*. A straight vertical line runs from hand to hand. The swimmer returns to the starting position by falling back into push-up position and then flies away to the other side.

Oblique push-up: starting position.

Scapular push-up: retracting the shoulder blades.

Rotational push-up: extending arm above the body.

Squat

The swimmer stands with feet shoulder-width apart and arms out in front. He squats and bends the knees to at least a 90-degree angle while keeping the back straight and posture perfect, heels on the ground, and knees straight (i.e., not letting the knee wobble). The swimmer then extends the legs until the knees are straight. The tempo is steady and the rhythm smooth. For a jump-squat variation, the swimmer squats, jumps as high as he can, and then lowers himself smoothly into the squatting position again with no pause.

Squat.

FIVE EXERCISES FOR THE CORE MUSCLES

A dryland routine for abdominal and core stability and strength should contain many exercises. A few of the proven fundamentals are described here. All are simple and require no equipment.

Forearm Plank

For the plank (also known as a bridge or triangle), the swimmer lies facedown, supporting the weight of the upper body on the forearms. The swimmer lifts her body, creating a straight, taut line from head to toes *(a)*. For more of a challenge, the swimmer lifts one foot or one forearm, which adds instability. For a side forearm plank *(b)*, the swimmer starts by lying on the side, supporting the upper-body weight on one forearm, and then lifts the body so the shoulders and hips are in line.

Forearm plank.

Side forearm plank.

Alternating Single-Leg Pike-Up

Starting from a streamlined position lying on the back, the swimmer bends at the waist, lifting one leg and the torso and arms to vertical positions so the hands touch the feet. The other leg remains flat on the ground. She returns to the starting position and repeats the motion with the other leg. Straight body lines and smooth, quick rhythms are key.

Alternating single-leg pike-up.

Lunge

Lunges improve posture and balance as well as strengthening the legs. The swimmer stands with hands on the hips. Keeping the torso taut and vertical, the swimmer steps forward with one leg, bending the knees until the knee of the front leg is directly over the foot and the knee of the back leg nearly touches the ground. Staying balanced and keeping the torso vertical, the swimmer drives off the lead foot and steps forward to lunge with the other leg. One lap of lunges around the pool deck is sufficient.

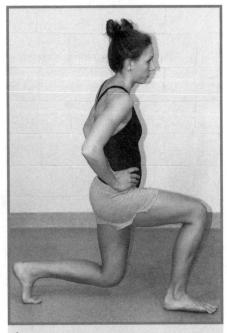

Lunge.

Legs-Up Twisting Crunch

The swimmer lies on her back with the hips flexed to 90 degrees and the knees flexed to 90 degrees. The thighs are perpendicular and the lower legs are parallel with the floor. The hands are behind the head. The swimmer curls up with the upper body and twists so that the outside of one arm touches the opposite knee. The swimmer returns to the starting position and repeats the motion to the other side.

Legs-up twisting crunch.

Flutter Kick

The swimmer lies as flat as possible on her back with the hands at the sides. Keeping the knees straight and moving at the hips, the swimmer flutters the legs steadily and quickly. The feet may separate, but no more than a foot (30 cm).

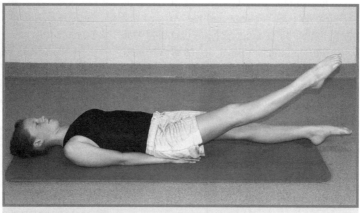

Flutter kick.

BREASTSTROKE LEG STRETCHES

Many traditional leg stretches should be practiced to increase flexibility in the hamstrings, quadriceps, ankles, hip flexors, iliotibial band, and other muscles. The following series of stretches prepares the legs for breaststroke kicking. Hold stretches for 20 to 30 seconds. Swimmers should feel the stretch but not pain. Complete the series twice.

Flare

The swimmer kneels on a towel or a kickboard and flares the feet outward so that the toes are pointing sideways. The lower legs should be pointing directly backward. The closer to the ground the heels are, the more water the swimmer will be able to hold with the breaststroke kick.

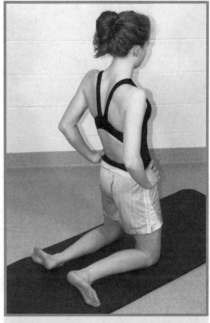

Flare.

Half Breaststroke

The swimmer lies with the back flat on the ground. He keeps one leg straight and bends the knee of the other leg to 90 degrees and places the foot on the ground and out to the side. Then, the hip and knee of the bent leg move as close to the ground as possible.

Half breaststroke.

Butterfly.

Butterfly

The swimmer sits on the ground with the soles of the feet together and the knees spread apart. The swimmer pulls the feet toward the groin and presses the knees toward the floor.

Full breaststroke.

Full Breaststroke

The swimmer lies with the back flat on the ground and pulls both heels toward the hips, planting them just outside the hips. The feet and toes should point to the side, and the knees should remain close together and as close to the ground as possible. This is difficult for many nonbreaststrokers, who may have to sit up at first in order to get the legs in position.

Program Benefits

There are a number of positive consequences to a champion-thinking, beautiful-technique, distance-medley training program over and above the pleasing knowledge that swimmers are on a well-trodden road to excellence. What helps them most in the long run also benefits them every day.

■ **Focus and interest.** Swimmers can never be bored when training distance since there is always so much to think about: pacing, technique, time goals, turns, breathing patterns, stroke counts, race strategies, racing with teammates, and so on. More variety is possible with distance training than with sprint training. Properly executed distance training uses the brain intensely, and getting the brain fully engaged is the key to keeping swimming interesting.

■ **Improvement.** When athletes quit swimming, the foremost reason is that they didn't see any improvement. With distance swimming, improvements are easier to make and to spot. As noted, kids are physiologically suited to distance swimming and with reasonable effort can improve from day to day. A swimmer may not notice a three-tenth improvement in a 50-yard repeat, but he cannot miss a five-second drop in a 500. Swimmers can see that they are getting faster, and this will keep them swimming longer.

■ **Success.** Like it or not, distance events and standards are soft nowadays. Qualifying for and doing well at local, state, regional, and national championships is easier in the distances than in the sprints—success awaits anyone willing to do the work. When swimmers are successful, they tend to like swimming more, and they get excited about working hard and being fast.

■ **Variety overcomes plateaus.** Every athlete hits a plateau now and then, and these plateaus are hard psychologically. If a swimmer specializes in one stroke or event, a plateau means her career is stalled. But when swimmers are training in all four strokes, something will be working right at any given time, no matter how stuck one stroke might be.

■ **Versatility.** By training distance, young swimmers can race well in any event from a sprint to the mile. With individual medley training, the advantages are even greater: Swimmers are solid in every stroke and every distance. Versatile swimmers are also more valuable to the team because they score more team points and help fill in the team's gaps.

■ **Work ethic.** Distance training demands consistent hard work. Consistency, persistence, and toughness are great qualities to instill in a person, and they infuse other areas of a swimmer's life. Whereas sprinting often rewards size and strength, which are mostly determined by heredity, distance swimming rewards not the supremely talented but the tough. Toughness is within anyone's grasp, even if genetics didn't make you extremely tall.

■ **Long-term thinking and training.** It takes years to make a distance swimmer; no get-rich-quick schemes will play out. Distance swimmers tend to be patient and methodical. They are willing to delay gratification, they understand they need to stick to the plan, and they proceed step by step.

■ **Self-knowledge.** Distance swimming is as much an intellectual and moral undertaking as it is a physical one. Swimmers are constantly bumping up against self-imposed limits and driving past them. They face down their demons every day.

CHAPTER 10

Planning for the Short and Long Term

Chapter 9 examined training principles as they apply to young swimmers, and using those principles, built a training program with its various parts and their priorities. This chapter takes that training program and discusses planning—executing the training program over the course of a year, a week, and a training session. The training year is broken down into phases, each with the kinds of training that are most appropriate. With the training year as a guide, you move from the general to the specific: what you are going to do in training this week and this practice.

Planning Challenges

Planning is simple in theory: Take an honest look at exactly where you are and how you got here, then decide where you want to go and how you will get there. But planning is complicated in the details because no season goes according to plan from start to finish, and there are so many moving parts in our machine.

You need to be flexible. A plan is a road map, not a straitjacket, and there are many routes to any destination. If there is road construction or a bridge wiped out by a flood, you have to find a way around them. When things in the pool aren't going as expected, find something to do successfully. When things are going well, build on that success until the returns diminish. Meets show you what is working and what is not; this is true for both individual swimmers and for a program. When a meet alerts you to shortcomings, use that data to adjust your course so that you are headed in the direction of your goal again.

Just as important as good aim is the speed at which you are moving toward your goal. Keeping swimmers healthy is crucial to making good time. An injured or sick swimmer is a swimmer who isn't happy and isn't getting better, and he is more susceptible to sickness or injury the next time. Every year, we have a three- to four-week period where a lot of the kids in our area get sick. The schools get hammered, and the swim team gets hammered in its turn. This is frustrating, but because it is inevitable, and we must work around the problem. When the epidemic begins, we lower the stresses of practices, knowing that almost all the swimmers are either about to get sick or are sick now but not showing it yet. Going full speed ahead in this situation is a good way to bury your team. It's better to lose a few days by backing off the throttle than to lose a few weeks by being stubborn and wedded to a plan.

Injuries also stop the train. They can be a big problem both physically and psychologically: An injured swimmer cannot train well, yet she wants to. A single injury could stem from a multitude of causes. However, a pattern of injuries means you have shot over their heads. Then again, 9- to 12-year-old boys are inventive at finding ways to get hurt. Someone is hobbling into practice just about every day ("Fell down the stairs at school, Coach," or "My sister pushed me into a cactus, Coach"), no matter how careful you are in planning your training.

In a related matter, every year around January life gets cold and dark in our part of the world. Our junior swimmers come to and leave practice in the dark every day, and this affects everyone psychologically. If we add daily training drudgery to this environment, we create first training and then racing plateaus. If a similar problem exists in your location, try to add a little spice to the routine, perhaps by doing more relays to finish practice, more match sprints to get kids racing and excited, or more amphibious operations for variety. This is a little adjustment, but it keeps kids happier and more motivated to swim and work hard.

Planning a Year and a Season

During the short breaks between swimming seasons, coaches may be far from the pool, but their heads are still swimming, going over meet and practice results from the previous season, analyzing what worked and what didn't, talking with coaching colleagues about potential tweaks to the program, reading books and articles in search of guidance and inspiration, and generally planning for the next season.

Analyzing the previous season and trying to tie together cause and effect is difficult, maybe even impossible. No coach operates in a hermetically sealed laboratory executing a controlled experiment using the scientific method. Real life is messy and complicated, and we do many things in an almost infinite number of combinations. How do we determine the one particular thing that led to a particular result? Just because we did more kicking this season doesn't necessarily mean that more kicking was the reason we did better or worse than before.

The more practice and meet data you have, the better, but this information is only valuable if it is accurate, measures the right things, is representative, and is comprehensive from all parts of the season. To further complicate the situation, the more the coach is spending time writing

> The more practice and meet data you have, the better, but this information is only valuable if it is accurate, measures the right things, is representative, and is comprehensive from all parts of the season.

down numbers, the less he is teaching and coaching. There is as much art as science here, and a coach's assumptions about what is important largely determine the answers he comes to.

Assuming we have an understanding of where we are, how we got here, and where we want to go, we take a look at the calendar. Looking at the training year, an obvious first question is, how do we break it up? How many seasons and how many championship or target meets do we plan for? Given the local competitive offerings and my preference, I plan for two seasons in each year. We have a long short-course season with four or five parts (see the following sections) that lasts from late August until the championships in late March, and then we have a shorter long course season with the same parts but truncated, lasting from early April to early August as shown in table 10.1.

It is unfortunate that the more important season of the two, the summer long-course season, is by far the shorter of the two. Despite this, and despite not having access to a long-course pool, our program is formulated for long-course success. The meets we discuss most, pump up the kids about most, and focus our training on most are at the end of the summer.

Planning a training year for age-groupers is different from planning for senior athletes. Age-group training and the parts of the season are more general and less specific—think shotgun, not rifle. We are not training to maximize performance at the end of the season, though of course we do want to swim fast at the championships. Rather, we are training for long-term physiological and neuromuscular benefits. We do not focus the training phases on stressing particular energy systems; instead, using the current cliché, we are training to train. This is true even for those age-group swimmers, usually girls, who have reached a national level of performance.

TABLE 10.1

Sample Year of Age-Group Training

Training phase	Time of year
Short-course season	
Variety and building phase	Late August through all of September
Quantity (aerobic buildup) phase	From October to mid-January
Quality phase	From mid-January to early March
Sharpening phase	Mid- to late March
Active rest phase	Early April
Long-course season	
Variety and building phase	Mid-April
Quantity phase	Late April to mid-June
Quality phase	Mid-June to mid-July
Sharpening phase	Mid-July to early August
Active rest phase	Early to mid-August

In planning our season, we begin with the championship or target meet and work backward, filling in the important bump meets (meets in which athletes take psychological and physical steps forward) and then the minor meets. (See chapter 14 for more on meet selection.) The general idea of the season is simple: We prepare ourselves mentally and physically to handle the upcoming stresses, then we increase the mileage while lowering the send-offs, then we loosen the send-offs while increasing the intensity, improving all the while and swimming our best at the end of the season. All year long we do the same things, but we emphasize different things at different times, and we emphasize different things at different levels and ages.

The five basic parts of our season, as shown in table 10.1 on page 163, focus on creating anatomical adaptation (variety and building phase), building volume and aerobic capacity (quantity phase), building intensity and speed (quality phase), honing race paces and details for the target meet (sharpening phase), and recovering from the season (active recovery phase). The length of each phase depends on the season and on the age and performance level of the swimmer or training group.

Variety and Building Phase

The swimming year begins in late August. The first month or more of the short-course season is characterized by variety. Here the general rule of one stroke a day does not apply; practices are stocked with shorter sets that have widely differing foci and stresses. The training load may be lighter than during the later phases of the season, but we still have a lot to do every day. We gradually get the swimmers' bodies ready for the more stressful swimming to come. This anatomical adaptation should be taken seriously to keep swimmers healthy, particularly their shoulders and knees.

Psychologically, this phase is for setting (or resetting) the tone and the expectations for the group. In every training group, new swimmers need to be socialized into the group's habits and expectations. Teach them what to do, how to do it, and why. We spend time each day discussing how to be a champion, talking about the importance of dreams, goals, daily attitudes, doing things right all the time, commitment, practice attendance, and hard work.

Physically, this phase focuses on anatomical adaptation: strengthening the muscles and joints for the stresses to come. We do a higher proportion of pulling and kicking than we will later. We especially focus on breaststroke kicking, pulling freestyle and backstroke with an ankle buoy for resistance and body line, and short, fast breaststroke pulling for power and technique.

Many programs swim mostly freestyle in the early season because they can get more mileage doing freestyle. We do not, and mileage is not a primary consideration. It is the time spent doing an exercise at a particular intensity that matters to the body, not how many yards or meters have been done. In other words, 30 minutes of backstroke swimming is physiologically equivalent to 30 minutes of freestyle swimming if done at the same intensity, even if the freestyler swam 150 more meters. If you aim to make physiological improvements, time matters, not volume. It is helpful in the long run to spread out the training among the four strokes so that swimmers build good technique, stroke rhythm, and strength in each stroke.

Technically, this phase emphasizes stroke fundamentals. The early season is a good time to watch elite stroke film. Review and practice the stroke catechism focal points, making sure that every swimmer understands what you're looking for—what each of the cues actually means. You can also introduce any stroke drills that you plan to use throughout the season.

In dryland training, we introduce all of our exercises (see chapter 9), making sure that the kids can do them perfectly without their technique falling apart. Once the exercises are learned, we do almost all of them every day—not much of each, so that the stresses stay small, but having the swimmers do the exercises correctly without cutting corners and gradually building strength in key positions and movements.

Our first meet occurs after five or six weeks of training as we are ending this phase. Age-groupers are ready to go fast, but we avoid their best events. We want the swimmers making strides in their supporting events or off-events because this improvement makes them more interested in working hard in these events.

When we begin the long-course season, the need for the physical and mental lessons of this introductory phase is not as great. Because we take such a short break after the short-course championship meet, the swimmers' bodies are already adapted, so we need no long and protracted anatomical adaptation. We may take a week or two to review the basics of our training, revisit stroke fundamentals, and set expectations for the upcoming season, but then we build up quickly.

Quantity Phase

The second phase of the season focuses on aerobic buildup. For 11- to 14-year-old swimmers in particular, this phase needs to be long because aerobic adaptations are the primary physiological goals of the training program as a whole. This buildup lasts a little over three months, from early October through mid-January. Here we do more work with less rest. The idea is to do a lot of a little: Following the progressive overload principle, we are forcing the body to adapt to a stress. You have to do enough of an activity to force an improvement or adaptation. In the past, I often made the mistake of trying to do too many things, wanting to keep things interesting for the kids and cover all the bases. Our practices consisted of a little of everything, and we were always jumping from one thing to another, bamboozled with variety but not getting much of anything done. We never focused enough time and effort on any one thing to improve in it, and the results were not good.

> You have to do enough of an activity to force an improvement or adaptation.

Because this phase is protracted, we can gradually increase the training loads without overdoing it. Distances slowly go up, intervals slowly come down, and paces continually get faster. Most of our main sets are short-rest descending series. We are, as usual, working all four strokes, and we begin stressing one stroke per practice. Though we may not spend as much time doing technique sets as we did earlier, we still emphasize making continual technical improvements and ensuring that swimmers' strokes adjust positively to the training sets. Assuming that attitudes are good (i.e., the early mental training worked), we scale back the explicitly psychological aspects of the program. During this phase, we set aside time twice a week for a philosophy talk. I take a pertinent subject, such as recent practice or meet performances, upcoming meets, or team goals, and discuss it with the kids. For dryland training, we apply the same principle of less is more: We alternate stresses, but one day we will focus on championship thinking, the next day on strengthening arms and legs, and then on core work.

During this phase we have the first and maybe second of our major benchmark bump meets. We may reduce the intensity slightly for a couple of days beforehand, but generally we work through these meets and still swim fast. If the meet starts on Friday, we will train fairly fast on Monday, very fast on Tuesday, and longer but easier on Wednesday and Thursday rolling into the meet. The swimmers get a small bump from the Tuesday practice and a bigger one from the training we have done for the month or months previously. I tell them they can swim fast with little rest, so they do.

Toward the end of this phase is our annual Christmas training camp. When the swimmers are out of school for the holidays, we keep our evening practices the same but add morning practices every day. These practices are open and recommended to everyone. The aim is not to crush the swimmers with a traditional mega-mileage hell week. I am not interested in watching mile after mile of slow swimming, and I am not interested in the injuries that often result from sudden massive increases in training volume. We increase the workload somewhat, but we use the camp as much to educate as to get a physiological bump. We give seminars for both swimmers and their parents on nutrition and swimming, stroke mechanics, swimming in college, effective study habits and time management, and so on. We also do a lot of underwater filming, and we run video sessions for each stroke, comparing our swimmers with the world's best.

Quality Phase

The third phase of the season takes the aerobic gains made in the quantity phase and raises the ante. Generally, we loosen the intervals a little. With only slightly more rest, the kids swim considerably faster. For the older age-groupers, the 13- to 14-year-olds, this phase may last two months in the short-course season and one month in the long-course season; for the younger swimmers, this phase is shorter and the previous aerobic buildup phase proportionally longer. In this phase we add some alternating easy–fast sets, and with fly and breast we may do more sets alternating moderate pace freestyle and very fast stroke. Dryland work is more intense, with more demanding exercises and more resistance. If the weather cooperates, we may be able to do some of the dryland training outdoors, which helps overcome the cabin fever that some of the kids fall prey to by winter's end. Competitively, in this phase we have the last of our major bump meets, but overall there is a lot of training and not much racing in this phase.

Sharpening Phase

We sharpen only for our target or championship meet at the end of the season. I don't have a lot of faith in resting young swimmers. At their championship meet, they swim as many events as they are allowed to, and we assume they will make finals in every event. They are going to be swimming an awful lot at the meet if we add the race totals to all the warming up and down. They have to be aerobically fit to withstand the rigors of the championship, so we cannot rest much even if we wanted to.

Although I do not recommend a traditional taper for either age-groupers or seniors, I do at least respectfully bow in the direction of the taper gods. For the last three weeks heading into the target meet, we keep the volume up but do a higher proportion of starts, turns, super walls, race pace, and broken swims. Emphasize the importance of hitting goal race paces and talk more about the meet. You might think of the sharpening phase as a more intense continuation of the quality phase. During the last four or five days, do less fast swimming, more long and smooth swimming with perfect technique, and some fast wall work. Then let the greyhounds loose.

Active Rest Phase

This phase is the vacation from swimming training between seasons, about one week long in the spring and one and a half weeks long after the summer season. Instruct swimmers to stay active by playing with their friends in the backyard, riding their bikes, hiking with their parents, swimming in the ocean, and so on. The point is to recharge the mental and physical batteries. The vacation should be long enough for the swimmers to miss coming to practice but not so long that they become comfortable with a daily schedule that does not include training. You want them antsy to get back in the water.

Planning the Week and the Day

Begin planning the practices for the week by looking at where you are in the big picture: What part of the season are you in, and what are the basic priorities for this phase? Then review the previous week of practices: What went well? What did not and why not? What did you neglect? What did you overdo? Then take a simple one-page planning sheet that shows the week at a glance and start filling in the blanks with the major and minor emphases for each day. Don't think that you need to stuff everything into one practice; it is better to do a few things well than several things poorly. You are involved in a marathon, not a sprint. If something doesn't get done today, you can do it tomorrow or next week.

Once you know what the week looks like, you can start being more specific, even if you are still not including particular sets. For instance, on Monday you may want to focus the freestyle technique work on high-elbow catches and the aerobic set on 300s with a set total distance of 2,400 meters. Table 10.2 on page 168 provides an example of a typical midseason training week with major emphases.

It is important to know what you want to do and why you want to do it. What are the swimmers getting from each set? How do those benefits interact with the other things that you are doing the same day, that you did yesterday, or that you will do tomorrow?

TABLE 10.2

Sample Training Week

Day	Stroke	Technique focus	Aerobic work	Additional work
Monday	Freestyle	High-elbow catches	300s (2,400 m)	
Tuesday	Butterfly	Short repeats with short rests (rainbow focus)	50s alternating with freestyle (1,600 m)	Super walls: 25s and 50s
Wednesday	Individual medley		200 free IMs (2,400 m)	Kicking (best stroke): 100s then 25s (1,600 m)
Thursday	Backstroke	Quick, clean entries	Ladder 100 to 400 (3,000 m)	
Friday*	Breaststroke	Pull and kick acceleration	1,200 mix drills: 50s fast (2,000 m)	Super walls and racing dives
Saturday	Freestyle		Pyramid 100 to 700 to 100 (4,900 m) Focus should be longer and harder for an aerobic bump	Kicking (weak stroke): 200s then 25s (2,000 m)

*Practice combined with seniors for 40 min.

There are several schools of thought about the best time to plan daily practices. Some coaches prefer to write a week's worth of practices at a time, devoting Sunday afternoon each week to detailed planning. Other coaches don't plan at all and wing it. I have to plan things out beforehand, but not too long beforehand. I need to see one practice before I can plan the next one. So each morning, with a cup of coffee in hand and Beethoven playing in the background, I review my weekly plan, review the practices from the previous day or two, and write the detailed practice for that afternoon. Even so, much can change from the time of writing to the time of doing. It is almost never the case that the practice I write is identical to the practice we actually do.

Control the Stresses

Planning practices means planning stresses. Controlling the stresses on swimmers is one of the most important tasks of a coach. This is a delicate balance: You need enough stresses for them to get better but not so much that they get injured. You have to pay close attention to the kids, how they look in the water, what they say (especially under their breath or to each other), their body language, and so on. Don't be afraid to adjust a practice if it turns out to be too easy, but also recognize when a group or an individual has had enough and pushing farther is either useless or harmful. Once again, the adage, "Optimal, not maximal," applies.

> Don't be afraid to adjust a practice if it turns out to be too easy, but also recognize when a group or an individual has had enough and pushing farther is either useless or harmful.

Spread the Stresses

You can spread the stresses by switching strokes each day, giving swimmers a built-in recovery of particular motor patterns. Further, you can alternate a day of breaststroke or butterfly (symmetrical strokes that are naturally power and strength oriented) with a day of freestyle or backstroke (asymmetrical strokes that are more naturally aerobic). You can also spread the stresses within a practice. For each practice, the sets should be ordered such that each can be done correctly. For instance, you can follow a shoulder-oriented main set with a kicking set where the arms are down by the sides to let the shoulders rest. If it looks like you're close to redlining on one thing, you can switch the stress to another stroke or part of the body, thus keeping the swimmers' heart rates elevated but letting them recover in the process.

Set order is especially important with longer practices. It is easy to bury the swimmers during the first half hour of a Saturday practice and then watch them struggle for the last two hours doing nothing well or fast. The coach gets irritated, thinking that the kids just aren't working hard enough, while the kids get frustrated as they keep failing to meet the coach's expectations. This situation is more often the fault of the coach and a poorly written practice than a result of the kids' failure to try. If the coach plans the practice well, each kind of set can be done well and the swimmers can be successful from start to finish.

As a general rule, plan for the technique work to come first, the distance-per-stroke work second, the speed and strength work after that, the intense aerobic work next, and the moderate aerobic work last. You do not have to have a cookie-cutter routine that you follow every day; still, certain kinds of work are better performed when placed earlier or later in a practice session.

Focus on Aerobic and Skill Work

As should be obvious from the discussion thus far, aerobic and skill work predominate in an age-group practice. Even if you have not planned for a technique set, emphasize technique points in every set you do, no matter how long or how fast. The main set each day will usually be aerobic. Plan for some speed work—short sprints—almost every day. Think of every set you do as a test set and compare the results with similar past sets. Once you have completed the buildup phase, the daily volumes should be relatively stable, around 7 to 8 kilometers for the stronger 13- to 14-year-olds, 5 to 6 kilometers for the 11- to 12-year-olds, and 4 to 5 kilometers for the 10-and-under swimmers.

Emphasize Training Improvement

Getting faster in practice is the basis of getting faster in meets. Take improvement any way you can find it—swimming the same pace on a tighter interval, swimming faster on the same interval, swimming the same pace for longer distance, swimming with fewer strokes per length, swimming the same speed easier, and so on. Long aerobic sets consisting of descending rounds (refer to chapter 9) are especially effective with age-groupers.

> Take improvement any way you can find it.

Between rounds the swimmers rest for a moment while the coach reminds them about the emphases of the work to come, and the swimmers review what they just did and set goals for what they are about to do. The swimmers practice precision pacing, they get faster from start to finish, each round builds on the previous one, and each round (or even repeat) has its own stroke emphasis, giving the swimmers something to focus their minds on.

Running Effective Practices

Trying to decipher a coach's logbook is like looking at a skeleton and trying to figure out what the living person looked like. A bare-bones log does not explain how things are done, what the tone of a practice is like, or how well the swimmers did. Even if two coaches start with identical practices on paper, they will likely end up with two different practices in the pool.

There is *what* you do, and then there is *how* you do it. Writing a theoretically perfect practice is one thing; running an effective practice is another. The flow, rhythm, tempo, or pace of a practice matters. It is similar to conducting a great symphony. The conductor takes the notes on the page—the sets in a log—and transforms them into something beautiful. The following strategies can help you get the most from each practice.

- **Be glad to see them.** Show your swimmers that the best part of the day is the time you spend with them. If practice is drudgery for you, it will be drudgery for them.

- **Focus on the swimmers.** What you learn about the kids during practice is in part a function of your assumptions and intelligence, but most of all, it is determined by your level of focus. Look for trends and patterns in the group and in individuals, and try to figure out how and why they are being created. Show interest in and talk to each swimmer every day. One minute of helping a swimmer during warm-up goes a long way toward keeping her motivated and making her feel valued. This is especially true for swimmers on the lower end of a group who may not get as much attention as those at the top.

- **Read your swimmers.** Pay attention to their body language, what they say, how they say it, and how they look in the water. When things simply aren't working, know when to bail and try something new. When things are going well, don't slow them down or get in the way. Be a catalyst for their discovering how fast they are. Complement the flow of the practice.

- **Have an exalted view of their potential.** Expect excellence in details, pacing, effort, technique, and attitude. Have the kids swim fast every day. Have them set their expectations by their good days, not their bad days. They have no idea of how good they can be or what is out there for them to achieve. Create situations in which they discover they can swim fast even if they don't feel good and conditions aren't perfect. This discovery will save them at big, tiring, stressful meets.

- **Create and protect group morale.** Only certain attitudes are acceptable at the pool. Good attitudes are contagious, but so are bad ones, and malcontents can never be allowed to infect the group. It is important to nip jealousy in the bud and to quarantine complainers. Talented kids will not get there anyway if the group culture tolerates or even enforces mediocrity.

- **Challenge them all the time.** Do not sacrifice the progress and dreams of your best swimmers by setting the level of the group at the level of the mean. Have intervals to challenge each tier of the group so that every swimmer can get better. Sometimes that requires having a different interval or even a different set for every lane.

- **But don't squeeze the lemon dry.** Fast swimming excites coaches, and faster swimming excites them even more. A willingness to push to high achievement is one of the distinguishing marks of a good coach. But there comes a point, especially when working with young swimmers, when it is time to stop. You have seen enough work and enough speed for the day. You do not have to plumb the depths of a swimmer's abilities right this second; there is always tomorrow, next week, and next month. Pushing too far often results in sickness or injuries, and the extra bit you were so pleased with today gets subtracted over the next week. Also, it is better to finish when the athlete is pleased with his improvement, even if you suspect that more is still hidden. Use what you saw today as the starting point tomorrow.

- **Have them set goals all the time.** Goals are not just for the end of the season. Have swimmers set goals constantly for each set, repeat, split, and so on. Constantly remind the swimmers of the relation between practice and meet performance. Notice their little successes, make sure they notice them, and build their confidence on the foundation of those little successes. Manufacture those successes if necessary.

- **Create good competitors.** Whenever possible, have at least two lanes for each of the top intervals so that kids can race. Have them race all the time, and switch swimmers from lane to lane to create good matchups. Have them keep score to spice things up.

- **Create leaders.** The key factor here is Brooks' Law of Lane Order, which states, "The eagerness of a swimmer to lead is directly proportional to how far and how high a swimmer will get." Consistently moving to the front of a lane signals a hard-working, competitive swimmer who is willing to be held accountable for her performance. Conversely, consistently moving to the back of a lane signals passiveness, a desire to hide, a distaste for hard work, and an unwillingness to be held accountable. Kids who lead make quick progress; kids who hide do not. Do not allow talented kids to hide. Manipulate lane order when necessary, making them lead lanes and not be content to be a follower.

- **Use time wisely.** Every second of every practice is precious. Make every set and every repeat count. Know the purpose of every set you do. There is no time for garbage yards or filler sets; recovery should mean a new challenge, not a lack of challenge. Create a sense of urgency—if swimmers do not understand that this set matters, they will be unlikely to do it well. As concretely as possible with each swimmer, connect what they are doing now with future racing.

- **Keep them moving.** Don't let the fastest kids stand around waiting for the slowest kids to finish. When one group finishes, give them the next set and send them off. Young kids shouldn't have much rest between sets; you want to keep their heart rates up. Young kids also have short attention spans, so keep impromptu lectures, admonitions, and set instructions short and sweet—preferably under one minute. Nothing destroys the flow of a practice more than having kids stand around waiting or pretending to listen.

- **Train technique all the time.** Work for gradual, continual stroke improvements. Train for perfect technique at a range of speeds from slow to race pace. Never assume that a swimmer's stroke is perfect, that it will stay that way, or that you can relax. Bad habits and inefficiencies creep in when you are looking the other way.

- **Train all four strokes.** Build versatile swimmers with options for the future, and give them natural recovery from training stresses.

- **Get and keep their attention.** They won't get much better if they're thinking about what's for dinner. Give them something to focus on, and continually change that focal point so their minds can't wander far.

- **Be vigilant.** Kids do not naturally do everything perfectly. If you are not on top of them all the time, they will wander from the path of righteousness. Nag, nag, nag—in a nice way (Humor gets the point across without a swimmer feeling like he is being attacked.).

- **Make them accountable.** Constantly reinforce that actions have consequences. No miracles are allowed, so if swimmers want to race fast, they had better train fast. Keep things honest by making sure that swimmers' goals are in line with their training performances. Reinforce every day that hard and conscientious work leads to improvement and success.

- **Measure the things that need measuring.** To ensure they are paying attention, ask the swimmers questions about how they are swimming. Ask their times, splits, and stroke counts frequently. Because sometimes kids miscount, spot-check their numbers. A good policy is to trust but verify.

- **Watch your tone.** Often kids will pay more attention to how you say something than what you say. The goal is to get the behavior you want, not to let off steam if you are upset. So don't just react emotionally; instead, think like a chess player, several moves ahead. No matter how frustrated you may be, let them know that you are on their side. Your goal is for them to get better, even if the lesser angels of their natures are getting in the way and driving you crazy.

- **Work to find the right approach for each swimmer.** The goal is for every single swimmer to leave better than she came. What works for one will not necessarily work for all. Different kids need to be treated differently and talked to in different ways. Know your kids.

- **Finish on a high note.** No matter what has happened the rest of the practice, find a way to make sure swimmers do the last set well. When they leave happy, they are eager to come back.

CHAPTER 11

Working With Parents

A crucial part of a swim coach's job is developing good swim parents. This is just as difficult as developing good swimmers. The longer I coach, the more I value the role that parents play in a swimmer's development. They do much more than pay the dues and drive their kids to practice. Parents' attitudes toward swimming, the program, the coach, and their child's participation are keys to the child's attitude and performance.

Often the young swimmer takes parental cues negatively. If parents show by word, deed, facial expression, and so on that they do not value swimming, that they do not appreciate having to drive to practice or sit in the stands during meets, or that morning practices or team meets are optional, then chances are good that the child will lack commitment, have little success, and eventually lose interest in swimming. On the positive side, when parents support their child's interest in swimming by showing that they value both swimming and the lessons learned while swimming, then their children are implicitly taught to enjoy the sport and are more likely to stick with it.

Ensuring a Good Fit

Because of this strong parental influence, it is crucial that the values and behaviors taught at home mirror those taught at the pool. If the current at home is flowing in the opposite direction from the current at the pool, there will be big problems. Thus, coaches must ensure a good fit between family and program before a swimmer joins the team. Speak with prospective parents and swimmers about the principles, values, expectations, and philosophy of the program. Give them a lot of team literature. Ask them to read it carefully, and let them know that unless they buy into the program wholeheartedly, they probably will not be happy with the experience.

Give parents enough information so they know what they are getting into. You want only those families who are going to fit in and improve the program, not families who don't believe in what you are trying to do. Continual problems are likely to occur with parents and swimmers who do not subscribe fully to the goals of the program. These families are likely to be unhappy from the start and may try to spread that unhappiness. Their fit with the team is about more than just swimming fast; it is about two cultures, the team's and the family's, and whether or not they coincide.

This method isn't perfect—there are always surprises, both good and bad, but the retention rate is much better than if you simply leave it to chance and take the money of whoever walks in the door. Of course, screening prospects may seem to conflict with a desire to build team numbers and improve the financial bottom line, but in the long run, it pays off. When a family that never fit in walks away mad, it is not good for business or public relations.

Educating Parents

Once families are on the team, it is the coach's job to educate them. How receptive the parents are to your instruction depends to some extent on your credibility. This, in turn, depends to a large extent on the performance of the swimmers and the team. When the swimmers do well, the parents think you know what you are doing and are more likely to trust you. New coaches are looked at warily; they have not yet proved themselves.

Even when the team is improving rapidly, there are still hazards to avoid. As a general rule, no parent is unhappy when her child is swimming well, and no parent is happy when her child is not swimming well. An entire group but one can be setting the world on fire, and the parents of the one laggard will still be disgruntled. It is never the case that everyone will be pleased, but the best way to decrease the number of parent problems is to run a good program and to persuade more and more of your swimmers to do what you ask.

There are a myriad of ways to get your message to parents. Most teams have newsletters, Web sites and blast e-mails, team handbooks, and philosophy or position papers. Most coaches run individual and team meetings and have informal conversations before and after practice. All of these are valuable methods of communication.

Next comes the question of what parents need to learn. The coach's main educational task is to socialize the parents into the culture of the team and its expectations, values, and priorities. Team cultures are as different as national cultures. Paris feels completely different from New York or London; there are a thousand little shocks to your ordinary way of doing things. Even though most teams do many of the same things, they do them differently, and these idiosyncrasies need to be learned before families will feel at home.

New parents often want to know everything all at once, and they expect the team handbook to have all the answers. But patience is both a virtue and a necessity. Guidebooks can help the traveler understand a new culture, but most of all he has to live in that culture and pay close attention to what is being done and said before he can appreciate its nuances and can think and act like a native. This process does not happen overnight, because some things have to be experienced to be understood. The same applies to joining a new team. No handbook can answer every question and take into account every contingency that a novice swim parent might think of. A valuable complement to a team handbook is a human handbook. Place veteran, trustworthy, and sympathetic parents in the foyer where parents wait for their kids. These parents can answer questions and relate the complexities of meet entries, team T-shirts, or meet hotels.

You must teach parents how to be good swimming parents. They can either learn this slowly and painfully through trial and error, with their unfortunate swimmers on the end of the yo-yo, or you can try to bring them up to speed artificially. Our club has an extensive memo that I wrote a long time ago and have tinkered with ever since. Its purpose is to teach parents how to further their child's happiness and performance in the pool. Most swimming parents were not national-level athletes in any sport when they were young, so they have no idea what to expect as their child grows up as an athlete and progresses from novice to national. They need to understand the steadily growing commitment required as their child ages.

Alert them of the milestones to come—what will happen and why, both in their swimmer's career and in their role as swimming parents—so that each new experience has the air of the familiar. When parents know what to expect, they are better able to take their child's victories in stride and are less likely to overreact to each setback. They will see both the ups and downs as necessary parts of a long process. You need to teach them to see the big picture and to take a long-term perspective. This is analogous to the stock market; when stocks are trending upward, only a foolish investor panics at the tiny daily adjustments in price.

> When parents know what to expect, they are better able to take their child's victories in stride and are less likely to overreact to each setback.

Convince parents of how important they are in their kids' performances. By their behavior, they are teaching their children how to behave. By their handling of success and failure, they are teaching their kids how to handle success and failure. By living and teaching hard work, discipline, consistency, and commitment at home, they are teaching their kids to be hardworking, disciplined, consistent, and committed swimmers. By supporting the swimming program and coach, they are teaching the child to respect and obey her coaches so that the lessons they are trying to teach get learned.

Day-to-Day Communication

Even when parents have been socialized into the program, there is a need for day-to-day communication. People want to know what is going on. Nature may abhor a vacuum, but rumor loves a news vacuum. So keep the parents informed about what has happened, what is happening, and what is about to happen. Critique the last meet and give your view of how the season has progressed. Inform them about upcoming meets and their importance in the context of the season. Alert them to any areas of general concern. If there is a message being circulated, make sure that message is yours.

It is important to let parents know how and when to communicate with you if they have questions or concerns. For instance, my parents know not to come on deck during practice to talk with me unless there is a life-and-death emergency. I am available after practice if they would like to talk about the ordinary issues of swimming life. Every team has its own protocols, its proper times and places for communicating, and parents need to know what they are. Further, it is often helpful to let parents know the best ways to communicate with you. In the past, I have given a little workshop letting parents know which approaches work best so that communication proceeds efficiently and civilly.

Ask parents to let you know if there are things going on at home or school that are likely to affect swimming practice. The pool does not exist in a vacuum. What happens in one place often happens in another, and what happens in one place often affects what happens in another. If there are familial problems that are upsetting the child, you will likely see these in his training or his interactions with coaches or other swimmers. Even if parents do not feel comfortable going into detail about their home life, a short version of what is going on can reveal the roots of atypical behavior and give you insight into the problem and how to manage it.

Working With Swimmers

Whom should the coach talk to when a problem arises, the parent or the swimmer? Coaches differ here. Whenever possible, it is best to deal directly with the swimmer. If a behavior or attitude problem is a little one, discuss it with the swimmer to solve it right away. Young kids are often testing the limits, and mischievous behavior that is not malicious does not warrant a summit meeting with the parents. You do not want to make something big out of something little. A minor course adjustment is all that is required.

Conversely, if a swimmer has a problem or question, it is better to hear it from the swimmer than from the parent. For instance, if a swimmer doesn't like her events in the upcoming meet, you might tell her to give you a good argument and you will change the program. Is it difficult for a 12-year-old to stand up for herself to an authority figure like a coach? Yes. Is it ennobling for the swimmer? Yes. A large part of our program aims at teaching kids to be self-reliant, to take responsibility for their swimming. This is why we expect the swimmers to figure out for themselves when to warm up for their races, to pack their own swim bags, to take care of their own equipment and pick up after themselves, to get their own times on repeats, and so on. Discussing important issues directly with athletes rather than through a middleman is a part of this constellation of behaviors.

Sometimes there will be an issue that is obviously under the control of the parent, such as repeated tardiness, missing team meets, or untimely vacations. Sometimes repeated attempts to work out a problem with the swimmer fail and superior forces must be brought in. In these instances, discussing the matter with the parent is warranted.

Alert parents to small but growing problems. Don't wait for a problem to snowball and for parents to approach you. If you approach parents about their child's behavior, you can better direct the agenda and control the tone of the conversation, making the problem easier to resolve. Of course, how you do this matters. Attacking parents and putting them on the defensive is sure to result in a bigger problem than the one you started out with. Instead, an approach implying that you are both on the same side and have the welfare of the child at heart works much better. For instance, to open up helpful communication, you might say something like, "I am seeing this behavior at practice. It concerns me and I'm sure it concerns you, too, and I want to make sure we stop this immediately. Do you have any suggestions?" Often the swimmer is telling the parent a different story from the one you are living at the pool, so setting the record straight is appreciated.

> Don't wait for a problem to snowball and for parents to approach you.

Dealing With Conflict

No matter how good a coach and communicator you are, there will be problems. A family's approach to child rearing may be different from yours. The particular way they prioritize family, athletics, and academics may not be to your liking. When you hear, "Are you trying to tell me how to raise my kid?," you know you have trodden on toes and have lost the argument. It is to be expected that swimming will play a more important role in your life than it does in the life of a typical swimming family. You will think that swimming should be more important to them than it apparently is, because you know how valuable the sport can be to a child's life, and because you see talent that is going undeveloped. Families, like swimmers, make their choices, and coaches have to live with those choices and do the best they can.

The biggest parental change I have seen since beginning coaching is the increased number of parents who think their child can do no wrong. Some kids frequently make excuses for not doing what they should be doing, and they blame others when things do not go well. These kids usually have parents who make excuses for the child not doing what he should be doing, and who blame others when things do not go well. Attitudes—good or bad—often run in families. Swimming coaches have little control over these attitudes, even if you do your best to warn about their consequences down the line.

Conflict of some sort may be inevitable, but this is not necessarily a bad thing. When done politely, conflict clarifies positions, gets people off the fence, and forces decisions that can lead to real progress. It is your job as a coach to tell parents what they *need* to hear, not what they *want* to hear. Adhering to the philosophy and policies of the program despite pressure to give in—in short, having a backbone—is an important trait of a leader and of a good coach. Your job is to educate, not palliate. You are there to be the coach, not their best friend.

PART IV

Developing the Competitive Edge

CHAPTER 12

Racing Attitudes and Tactics

For most swimmers, racing is the reason for swimming. Meets are the emotional highlights of the season. From a coach's perspective, you ask the swimmers to do in practice what you want to see them do when they race.

This is the first of three chapters on racing, and it discusses three topics leading to competitive success: the attitude of a champion and the rules for racing, tactics for races, and common racing patterns and how swimmers can improve their competitive habits. Chapter 13 discusses meet management, or how to help swimmers make good choices at a meet so that they race their best consistently. Chapter 14 concerns selecting meets and events at meets.

Rules for Racing: Attitude Matters

Daily training builds the engine, but a swimmer's competitive personality determines how much of that engine's power she will have access to when she races. Everyone has seen swimmers who train well but melt under the pressure of meets, and everyone has seen swimmers who do not train well but who love to race; they continually swim over their heads at meets. How kids think about racing and how they think when they are racing really matters.

Two points, or essentials, for fast, consistent racing are confidence and competitiveness. As coach John Wooden wrote, "Confidence comes from being prepared." Swimmers who work hard and smart in daily training, who are used to setting goals and working to reach them, and who are getting better every day will generally be confident in their abilities. As far as competitiveness goes, both coaches and swimmers should try to create a love of it and competing in practice. Swimmers should race all the time, and they must learn to take pleasure in the contest. If they only race once or twice a month and only a few races each meet, they do not get much practice at it, and it is much more likely that

> Swimmers should race all the time, and they must learn to take pleasure in the contest.

they will develop mental hang-ups about the pressures of racing. But if they race a hundred times a day in training, if they see every single repeat as a race against their teammates, the clock, and themselves, then they become veteran racers who are better able to put racing into perspective—winning is fun but not guaranteed, and losing isn't disastrous but rather a challenge to do better the next time. When practices are constructed to encourage racing, swimmers get used to racing, challenging themselves and others, winning, losing, and having fun doing it.

The following nine rules of racing lead to high performance, and champions live by them. Coaches can help swimmers build the right attitudes and actions every day in practice. Teach the rules, expect them to be followed, and train the team mentally and physically so that these expectations can be met.

Rule 1: Win the Close Races

If a swimmer is even or nearly even with someone with 15 meters to go, she should do whatever it takes to get her hand on the wall first, no matter what. That touch-out will likely get her the cut for a championship, into finals, or on the podium. Swimmers are racing not only the seven others in their heat but also everyone from the heats before and after theirs. They must do things right to maximize their chances of touching out these invisible competitors.

Winning touch-outs in meets comes easily when swimmers have practiced winning touch-outs a hundred times a day in workouts. Coaches can easily teach swimmers how to finish properly; the challenge is getting them to practice this every time they finish a repeat and to approach every finish as if their life depended on getting their hand on the wall first.

Rule 2: Swim Fast in the Morning

It is painful for swimmers to attend a big meet and have to watch finals from the stands, knowing that if only they had raced respectably in the heats, they were ready to do something special at night. If swimmers are prepared to swim fast, they must do what they need to do in the morning to give themselves the chance. At any major meet, only a few swimmers achieve best times in the morning, and those swimmers rocket up the standings.

Kids are pragmatists; they will do what works. Local heroes can swim slow in the prelims of a local or regional invitational and still make it back for finals, so they often put out minimal effort and do only what is required. They do not consider morning swims to be worthy of a good effort. Accordingly, they often establish physical and mental habits that serve them well enough locally but backfire when they progress to the next step. At a championship, an established superstar may be able to get away with a less-than-stellar morning effort, but swimmers working their way up the national ladder have to swim best times in the morning to get an opportunity for a second swim at night.

Throughout the season, coaches must reinforce the idea that morning swims are important and expectations high. Just because a swimmer made finals today doesn't mean the effort was acceptable. Yet at every meet, you hear coaches commenting, "That was good for a morning swim," and "Nicely done—fast enough to make it back." But swimmers need to think ahead and raise their sights. They need to aim at the time it will take to get a second swim at their championship meet, not at the time it will take to make finals in this event at this meet. They should not settle for the minimum and swim to local standards and expectations. Instead, they should use local invitational meets as rehearsals for major championships. They should practice seeing the big picture, so they can be one of those swimmers at nationals who come out of nowhere and surprise everyone by moving up 50 spots from their seeding.

Rule 3: Always Swim Faster at Night

Swimming fast in the morning is necessary but not sufficient. Swimmers must show that they earned their places in the final by stepping up again. In any evening final, usually six of the eight swimmers will swim faster than they did in the morning and two will swim slower. If swimmers want to be competitive, they must be one of the six. The decision to succeed is made before they even get on the blocks to race. It is made by their bodies every day in practice and then by their minds well before the race starts. They should not be satisfied just to be in the final or to be getting a medal but should aim to swim even faster and place even higher.

Rule 4: Cherish Relays and Swim Even Faster

Relays are races, they are important, and they count double points. Being named a member of a relay is an honor and a privilege, and it should be regarded as such. When a swimmer is on a relay, he is competing with his teammates and competing for his team. He should give his best, and that means always swimming faster on a relay than he did in his individual event.

Swimming on a relay is a privilege, and swimmers must bring their full competitive efforts to the race.

Coaches must do their part to show by their words and their actions that they value relays. Talk up the importance of the races to come, including potential team records, national top 10 finishes, and qualifications for major championships.

Rule 5: Improve as the Meet Progresses

By the last day or two of a long meet, everyone has swum multiple events, handled the pressure of racing repeatedly, and sat around for hours. Everyone is tired, but the champions somehow manage to ignore how they feel and swim fast anyway.

> Swimmers must find a way to swim fast, no matter the circumstances.

How do they do this? They *decide* to. Fatigue is no excuse for slow swimming. Swimmers must find a way to swim fast, no matter the circumstances—first day or last, first event or last, best event or worst. In the words of hall-of-fame coach Paul Bergen, "It doesn't matter how you feel. Do the job." This is almost entirely a matter of will, intention, and preparation. As the meet progresses, a swimmer needs to tell herself, "I always get better and swim faster as a meet goes on. When my competitors are dwindling down to nothingness, I am growing stronger and stronger. I swim fast all the time and fastest when others are thinking up excuses to back off or give up. I am mentally tough. I *decide* to swim fast."

Coaches can help by ensuring that swimmers have many opportunities in daily practices to swim fast when they are tired. When coaches expect swimmers to finish every repeat, every set, and every practice strong, and when swimmers assimilate these expectations, they will be strong down the stretch of a long meet.

Rule 6: Get Tougher for Tougher Conditions

I have spent many meet days on deck in cold and rainy weather. I have heard choruses of coaches, swimmers, and parents chanting, "You can't expect too much with weather like this." Ridiculous! If you throw a bunch of competitive kids together in a tank of water and tell them to race, they can swim fast, whether it's blistering hot, mild and sunny, or cold and rainy.

Swimmers can perform at their peak in terrible weather so long as they think right, make good decisions, and take the weather into account in how they manage the meet. Swimmers can always define the present circumstances as less than ideal, so they will always be able to come up with excuses not to perform their best. But they can just as easily decide that the present circumstances (whatever they are) are right (or at least irrelevant), and go to the blocks and swim fast. No matter how awful the conditions, a number of kids always swim well and make huge drops.

That swimmers can swim fast no matter what is a crucial lesson for them to learn. What are they going to do if the most important meet of their lives is swum under less-than-ideal conditions? The worse the conditions, the more champions step up, prove their championship qualities, and separate themselves from the crowd. They focus on the task at hand, don't worry about what they cannot control, and don't waste their effort thinking up excuses for not swimming fast. Whenever I wake up on a meet morning and see rain out my window, I cheerily think to myself, "A perfect day—the tough kids are going to shine!"

Rule 7: Expect to Swim Fast

The decision to excel is made before swimmers get on the blocks, and in large part, their expectations will determine the quality of their performance. If they have practiced swimming fast even when tired, and if they truly expect to get on the block and swim fast no matter what, then chances are good that they will do just that. If, on the other hand, swimmers expect to get up and swim slow because this is midseason and it doesn't matter, and it's not their best event anyway; they're tired, they didn't sleep well, they don't really care how they do, then they are going to swim poorly. It is distressing to watch so many athletes sabotage their performances with low expectations that have little correlation with their abilities.

Coaches have a huge impact on how swimmers mentally approach meets and races. A well-placed team meeting a few days before a meet can work miracles. Tell the swimmers what you are expecting of them and what they should be expecting of themselves, where this meet fits in the context of the season, how it represents a wonderful opportunity to set themselves up for the meets and championships to come, and so on. To a large extent, swimmers adopt the coach's expectations, so let them know where you stand.

The big question for swimmers who don't expect much is how are they going to get better if they only expect to swim fast once a season. Swimming slow throughout the year and then relying on a miracle is an effective way of slowing progress to a crawl and ensuring that swimmers stay home from the major meets, or if they do manage to qualify, that they are mired at the bottom of the standings. The way to get good in this sport is to expect a lot. Swimmers have to walk to the blocks having already said to themselves, "I have trained my guts out and I'm going to do whatever it takes to swim fast, *no matter what*." A focused laser beam will cut through anything in its way.

Rule 8: Race Hard and Finish the Job

Many swimmers set high goals, train hard to reach those goals, and then fall just short at a meet by losing a touch-out, placing ninth when only eight swim in finals, or barely missing the qualifying standard for a major meet. They were in position to succeed but faded and let victory slip from their grasp. This should not happen. If a swimmer is well positioned with 10 or 15 meters to go, then he should finish the job. That is what racing is all about. If you are climbing Everest, you don't stop a few feet from the summit. You get your hand on the top and plant your flag!

One of the challenges in life is that you never know if you need to give every ounce of effort until after the fact, when it's too late to change what you've done. Nothing is worse than the feeling of regret, knowing that you could have broken through *if only* you had tried a bit harder, or that you could have won *if only* you had competed a bit smarter. Swimmers must bring their best with them to the blocks every time. They must plumb their depths, and if the strength is there, use it. They should leave it in the pool and save themselves the effort of feeling regret, disappointment, or anger. They should finish the race with a smile.

Coaches can inculcate this standard by constantly preaching the importance of finishing strong and by expecting every finish in practice to be fast and technically

> Coaches must stress the importance of reaching and surpassing goals, not just coming close.

perfect. Also, coaches must stress the importance of reaching and surpassing goals, not just coming close. Habitually coming close and being satisfied with the effort sets swimmers up for disappointment at a meet. They definitely will not be satisfied when they miss the Olympic trials cut by .01 second and have to watch the meet on television.

Rule 9: Learn From Experience

Meets—and big meets in particular—provide good opportunities for swimmers to take stock. How is their training going? How is their racing going? What are they doing particularly well, and how can they foster these strengths? What are they doing that is holding them back, and how can they fix these problems? Further, what did they see other people do that seemed to work well? What did others do that obviously hurt them?

Swimmers with dreams of greatness must be willing to confront their weaknesses and improve them. This is a lesson that coaches must teach, but it does not always take. I have coached swimmers who made the same obvious racing mistakes for several years running, despite my continual efforts to get them to change and despite their competitors having brought these mistakes to their attention forcefully. Changes are hard to make for both swimmers and coaches, but they are necessary nonetheless.

Aside from being opportunities to race, meets can be wonderful educational opportunities. When we go to an important meet, our team always has a range of swimmers along, some at the top, some in the middle of the pack, and some who barely qualified for the meet. Big meets can be even more important for the swimmers on the bottom than for those fighting for titles. They can watch what it takes to be fast. I will often use the top swimmers as examples: "Look at how he dolphins off his walls." "See how her feet accelerate as she kicks out the back of her fly stroke." Fast swimmers are fast for a reason. Having inexperienced swimmers watch a living, breathing example of excellence is more effective than lecturing them for 10 minutes after a race.

Swimmers who do not qualify for finals should attend evening sessions anyway. They may not currently be fast enough to make the final, but they should try to figure out what makes the finalists faster than they are and then go home and work to make up the difference by the next meet.

Racing Tactics

How one swims a race matters, and there are many ways to race poorly and spoil good training. Physiologically, an even-paced race takes best advantage of a swimmer's energy resources. This is true for elite senior swimmers who are driven, mentally tough, and used to hurting and who will use all the energy they have. For them, swimming too fast at the beginning means going overly anaerobic early on, which destroys finishing speed.

For most age-groupers, even-paced racing may not necessarily be best. There is more to racing than physiology. An age-grouper's mental state during a race determines how much she will push herself—her willingness to use all her available physiological resources. Often if a young swimmer sees that she is so far behind to be effectively out of the race, she will stop trying and not take another hard stroke. It doesn't matter how much energy a swimmer has in her body if she has no interest in using it. Alternatively, if she thinks that she has a chance to succeed, then she will give all she has and surprise you with her toughness. The swimmer's thinking here is simple: "I will only hurt myself if I have a good reason to."

I prefer guts to intelligent pacing. Too many young swimmers understand pacing to mean racing passively, which results in falling too far behind early. A swimmer is more likely to maintain effort in a race if she is competitive from the beginning. It is also easier to start with kids who will race their guts out and rein them in a bit, than it is to start with kids who are wimpy racers and make them courageous and willing to hurt.

Note that having guts does not mean going on a reckless and foolish quest for speed from the moment the gun fires. I've seen enough kids try to no-breathe the first 50 of a 500 to know that frying and dying does not work. Instead, you want *intelligent aggression*. Adapting physiologist Jack Daniels' suggestions for running races, you want them to swim the first quarter of the race with their brains, the middle half with their training, and the last quarter with their guts. They focus on a couple of concrete cues to stay controlled and easy but fast out the front, and then they let loose as the race progresses.

General Tactical Points

The following tips apply to just about any race. They form a template on which the particular race plan and tactics can be placed.

- **Be aggressive.** Swimmers must give themselves a chance to do something special.

- **Make a move in the third quarter.** Almost everyone lets up during the third quarter of a race; if a swimmer speeds up when everyone else slows down, he can take over a race.

- **Use the walls.** Speed in, speed out. Walls are a place for picking up speed, not for taking a break.

> Walls are a place for picking up speed, not for taking a break.

- **Manage breathing patterns.** Swimmers should breathe more at the beginning so they can breathe less at the end. Fly and freestyle races should start with a breathing pattern swimmers can maintain until close to the finish, when they put their heads down. Breathing a lot when tired and poor stroke technique and body position contribute to reduced speed.

- **Fight fatigue with focus.** Almost everyone looks good the first 25 meters of a race, but fewer do the last 25. Fatigue compounds stroke problems and aggravates poor body position, so swimmers should focus on keeping the stroke long, smooth, and powerful at the end of the race. They should be strong when others are weak.

Tactics for Specific Races

This section discusses tactics for particular races. Obviously there will be adjustments from one coach to another, one swimmer to another, and one stroke to another, but these guidelines are sound. These tactics should be rehearsed in daily practice so that swimmers arrive at a meet knowing their race plans and feeling comfortable about what they want to do.

50s

Most young swimmers cannot control their technique at top speed; sprints often become competitions to see who can splash the most. Coaches and swimmers should train instead for controlled fury.

- Take the race out fast but under control. Swimmers should build into their race tempo over the first several strokes. They tend to spin their wheels if they try to hit full tempo from the first stroke.
- Use long, fast, and relaxed strokes, with a strong kick for control and power.
- Nail the walls. In short course, don't even think of breathing anywhere near the turn.
- Win the close races. There is an art to getting a hand on the wall first, and this art should be practiced every day, not just at meets.
- On freestyle and butterfly, learn to race the 50 with as few breaths as possible.

100s

Most young swimmers tend to chop their strokes and try their hardest from the first stroke. But the 100 distance, even in short course, lasts too long for swimmers to maintain top speed the whole way. Racing a good 100 requires an intelligent building of speed.

- Go out fast, emphasizing long strokes. Remember to breathe the first 25.
- Swimmers should power the second 25 but keep their strokes long and not spin their wheels. A pull isn't effective if the arm slips quickly through the water but the body stays put.
- Hit the legs hard coming off the 50 wall. This shifts the swimmer into a higher gear.
- Gut out the last 25. Swimmers should increase their stroke tempos, maximize their kicks, and (in free and fly) put their heads down the last 10 to 15 meters.
- Win the close races.

200s

Racing a good 200 requires a killer mentality combined with intelligence. Too many swimmers treat the 200s as mega-distance races, going out too slowly, swimming too slowly in the middle, and coming home too slowly. These events need to be approached as long sprints. We will treat the 200 butterfly and individual medley separately.

- Swimmers should go out fast but long and relaxed. On freestyle, they must remember to breathe (Try a breathe-every-three pattern, because it can be maintained from start to finish and it helps balance the stroke.).

- Lay off the legs for the first 100. This does not mean that the legs should float; it means swimmers should not focus on them and should not overkick. Swimmers should save them for the last 100. They provide an extra gear.

- Attack the 100 turn and the third 50. Almost everyone backs off on the third 50 of a 200 race. If swimmers reverse this strategy by surging the third 50, they gain an immediate advantage that adrenaline will help them keep to the finish.

- Maintain distance per stroke at the end. Focus on holding good stroke mechanics when fatigued.

200 Fly

The 200 butterfly is a 200 race like any other, so the previous suggestions apply. But swimmers and coaches alike know there is something special about it. Swimming a good 200 fly requires aerobic speed that can be maintained, which requires training of the sort recommended in chapters 7 and 9.

- Use relaxed speed for the first 100—comfortable, relaxed, long, and easy. Swimmers want to hit the midway point feeling good and ready to go full tilt to the finish. If they are already tired at the 100, it's going to be a long race.

- Hit the legs hard coming off the 100 wall for both body position and power.

- Come home with the big three: race tempos, strong legs out the back of the stroke, and a one-up, one-down breathing pattern. (These were discussed in chapter 7.) With these in the swimmer's favor, he maintains his speed while others struggle.

- Swim with a racing stroke, not a survival stroke. This is mostly in the mind. If swimmers consider the 200 fly a distance race, they will flounder through it with a survival stroke. If they approach it as a two-minute race, they will race it.

200 IM

Like its fly counterpart, the 200 IM deserves special treatment. Each swimmer has stronger strokes and weaker strokes, and the tactics of exploiting strengths and hiding weaknesses are key to competing well.

- Swimmers should be in a position to use their weapons. The stroke just before a swimmer's strongest stroke is probably her key stroke since it sets up her weapon. If she is well beaten when she gets to her strongest stroke, she wastes her weapon just catching up instead of using it to pull away and dominate her opponents.

- Build the butterfly leg. The second 25 is key; swimmers need speed and momentum for the transition to backstroke.

- Punch the backstroke hard. Even good backstrokers often ease off during this leg and fail to exploit their advantage. Of course, swimmers want to go fast when everybody else is going slow, so they should increase the tempo by emphasizing the shoulder roll, but they should lay off the legs a little.

- The breaststroke leg is crucial for sorting out the medals. A breaststroker should attack, and a swimmer who is not a breaststroker should get on top of the water, increase the tempo, and try to control the bleeding.

- Get on the legs hard and sprint the freestyle from the first strokes. Many swimmers go easy the first 25, then realize they have a lot of energy left and explode the final few meters—too little, too late. They should put their heads down the last 10 to 15 meters.

400 IM

The idea of weapons and key strokes is doubly important in the 400 IM, especially the long-course version, since swimmers can lose so much ground on their weak strokes that they get into a hole so deep they can never climb out. As with the 200 IM, we offer suggestions for each stroke to maximize the overall performance.

- Relax the first 50 of butterfly, and build momentum in the second 50. Most swimmers foolishly swim too fast during the first 50 of fly and then fade and struggle into the changeover to backstroke, hurting both strokes with their tactics. They should come into the backstroke transition wall at full speed.

- Punch the backstroke. Lay off the legs and emphasize the shoulder roll and fast tempo. Most swimmers don't perform well on the back leg because they are tired after fly, saving up for breaststroke, or both.

- Make the most of the breaststroke. The time difference between fast and slow breaststrokers is huge. Thus, more ground can be won or lost on this leg than on any other in the long IM race. Faster breaststrokers should exploit their advantage and attack with guns blazing. Slower breaststrokers, in particular those with poor kicks, must rely on a quick tempo—if they cannot kick like Kitajima, they should not glide like Kitajima. Also, to be competitive, poor breaststrokers must surround this leg with strong backstroke and freestyle legs so that they have a lead when breaststroke begins and can catch up once it ends (Hard, focused work in practice helps ensure that the breaststroke will be less of a problem next time.).

- Begin the freestyle leg with a sense of urgency. If swimmers are ahead, they should try to exploit their advantage immediately while their competitors are still doing breaststroke. If they are behind, they should aim to catch someone right away and not wait until the last 50. By starting strong, a swimmer can often blow by competitors who are waiting cautiously for their final sprint. In the last 50, of course, swimmers should race their guts out and kick like crazy to the wall. Especially tough kids put their heads down the last 15 meters. Everybody hurts by this time, and the more swimmers push themselves and faster they swim, the sooner the pain stops.

Racing Patterns

One concrete way to have swimmers understand themselves as racers is for them to complete a racing pattern checklist such as the one in figure 12.1 (page 192). Each of the patterns listed is either a positive competitive trait that swimmers should practice or a negative competitive trait that they should avoid. Many of the patterns appear as antithetical pairs: A swimmer either gets a best time in the morning preliminaries or she doesn't; a swimmer makes finals or he doesn't. Also, there are more negative patterns than positive. As noted, there are many ways to spoil good training by making poor racing choices.

Swimmers should go over the list carefully while thinking about their racing history over the previous year or so, which should give them enough data for a true assessment. The object is for swimmers to take stock of their racing habits, both their strengths and their weaknesses. Next to each pattern, they check *yes* or *no*. After swimmers have completed the checklist, they review their answers, concentrating on patterns they noted with a *yes*: These are their racing habits. For every habit, they decide whether it is a positive, helpful habit that leads to competitive success or a negative, harmful habit that holds them back competitively. Then they write down their five most important competitive strengths and their five most important competitive weaknesses (see figures 12.2 and 12.3 on pages 193 and 194) and determine how to solidify the strengths and change the weaknesses.

With the coach's help, they think through the positive steps they can take to improve their racing habits. Swimmers do not have to wait until the next meet to work on these positive racing patterns. Kids usually race as they train. A swimmer who shows one trait consistently in meets is almost assuredly showing similar traits in daily practices. For instance, a swimmer who takes his races out too fast and then fades will almost always fade coming home in training repeats and training sets. A swimmer who consistently steps up when challenged by a teammate or a coach in practice will usually thrive under the pressure of a big meet or championship final.

Because of this strong correlation between meets and practice, swimmers should work to improve their racing habits in daily workouts. Every time they are in a key situation that corresponds to a habit they need to ingrain, they should practice responding correctly until that positive response becomes a habit. These habits are as much psychological as physical, so they take time and repetition, but once solidified, they are relatively easy to transfer to race conditions.

The racing patterns checklist should be revisited frequently. Swimmers can see their racing improvement by completing the checklist after each meet, or at least after each important meet, and noting how they are evolving as racers. In this way, every meet becomes an opportunity for them both to race and to learn about themselves as racers. They think through what they do well and what they do poorly, and they consciously, dispassionately, systematically, and progressively improve themselves. This is the way of a champion.

The coach, too, can use the racing patterns checklist, either directly or indirectly, when reviewing meet results. Discovering what your swimmers are like under a variety of competitive situations—big meet versus small meet, local meet versus travel meet, best events versus worst events, prelims versus finals, first day versus last day, early season versus end of season—is a primary means of discovering what is going on in their heads and thus how best to help them improve.

FIGURE 12.1

Racing Pattern Checklist

YES	NO	
☐	☐	Wins every touch-out situation, often in creative ways.
☐	☐	Loses every touch-out situation, often in creative ways.
☐	☐	Gets better and stronger as a long meet progresses.
☐	☐	Gets worse and weaker as a long meet progresses.
☐	☐	Swims fast in prelims and faster in finals.
☐	☐	When makes finals, swims slower than in prelims.
☐	☐	Gets energized by a competitor's fast time in a previous heat.
☐	☐	Gets psyched out by a competitor's fast time in a previous heat.
☐	☐	Swims bored in small meets but gets energized at big meets.
☐	☐	Swims well in small meets but gets psyched out under pressure in big meets.
☐	☐	Swims well in best events but doesn't seem to care in off events.
☐	☐	Swims well in off events but poorly in best events.
☐	☐	Swims consistently well across the board in best and in off events.
☐	☐	Swims fast against fast competitors but slow against poor competitors.
☐	☐	Races strong no matter the level of the competition.
☐	☐	Slows down the third quarter of the race, saving for the finish.
☐	☐	Speeds up the third quarter of the race, then adds another gear at the finish.
☐	☐	Takes races out too slowly, then finishes furiously, usually just doing enough to lose.
☐	☐	Takes races out too aggressively, slowing progressively and never holding a pace.
☐	☐	Paces races intelligently and finishes well.
☐	☐	Outswims competitors but loses races because of poor walls.
☐	☐	Gains advantage because of fast walls.
☐	☐	Folds under the pressure of a competitor pressing them or attacking.
☐	☐	Responds energetically to the pressure of a competitor pressing them or attacking.
☐	☐	Gives best effort only if there is a strong possibility of winning; otherwise, backs off.
☐	☐	Gives best effort every race, whether behind, ahead, or even.
☐	☐	Makes the same mistakes every race at every meet.
☐	☐	Fixes previous mistakes; gets better at racing.
☐	☐	Responds to a poor race by moping and swimming even worse the rest of the meet.
☐	☐	Responds to a poor race by forgetting it and refocusing for upcoming races.
☐	☐	Frequently just falls short of a standard (winning, qualifying, or making finals).
☐	☐	Frequently just squeaks in.
☐	☐	Seemingly swims with no patterns whatsoever—a pattern of randomness.

From M. Brooks, 2011, *Developing Swimmers* (Champaign, IL: Human Kinetics).

FIGURE 12.2

Five Competitive Strengths

MAJOR STRENGTH 1

_____

Positive daily steps to foster this strength:

1. _____

2. _____

MAJOR STRENGTH 2

_____

Positive daily steps to foster this strength:

1. _____

2. _____

MAJOR STRENGTH 3

_____

Positive daily steps to foster this strength:

1. _____

2. _____

MAJOR STRENGTH 4

_____

Positive daily steps to foster this strength:

1. _____

2. _____

MAJOR STRENGTH 5

_____

Positive daily steps to foster this strength:

1. _____

2. _____

From M. Brooks, 2011, _Developing Swimmers_ (Champaign, IL: Human Kinetics).

FIGURE 12.3

Five Competitive Weaknesses

MAJOR WEAKNESS 1

_____

Positive daily steps to overcome this weakness:
1. _____
2. _____

MAJOR WEAKNESS 2

_____

Positive daily steps to overcome this weakness:
1. _____
2. _____

MAJOR WEAKNESS 3

_____

Positive daily steps to overcome this weakness:
1. _____
2. _____

MAJOR WEAKNESS 4

_____

Positive daily steps to overcome this weakness:
1. _____
2. _____

MAJOR WEAKNESS 5

_____

Positive daily steps to overcome this weakness:
1. _____
2. _____

From M. Brooks, 2011, *Developing Swimmers* (Champaign, IL: Human Kinetics).

CHAPTER 13

Managing Meets for Racing Excellence

High performance is all about preparing to succeed. The best teams are the best prepared teams, and the best athletes are the best prepared athletes. Preparation means not leaving things to chance but taking control of performance: taking care of the big picture and the small details, the thousand and one factors that make for a series of great races at a big meet against fast competition. Thorough preparation allows swimmers to get the most out of themselves, to compete to their potential. They never have to wonder afterward how fast they could have been.

The most obvious area of preparation for high performance is building the physiological capacities to swim fast—speed, endurance, and neuromuscular facility. This is long-term preparation, and swimmers do this in training every day. No matter how motivated swimmers are at the meet and no matter how badly they want it, unless they have trained well, it's not going to matter much. When they get on the blocks, it's too late to start to care.

Preparation for success is similar to making a cake. From the beginning of the season, swimmers have been making their cake. With every practice they have attended and every practice effort they have given, they have been adding the ingredients in various proportions. If the training recipe has been just right, they have the right amounts and proportions of flour, shortening, eggs, and sugar. If training has been lacking, they have too much of one ingredient and not enough of something else. When they get to the meet, it is time to put that cake in the oven, and it's too late to change the ingredients. At the meet, it is too late to build more or different physical capacities. Training does that, and training is over.

Coaches and swimmers may discover certain shortcomings, and they can tackle those shortcomings in practice the day after the meet. But for now, there is nothing to be done about them, and swimmers have to race with what they've got. That said, there are simple ways to get the most out of what swimmers have right now, no matter the ingredients—the proper baking will optimize the taste of what they have put in. How swimmers behave at the meet goes a long way toward determining whether they are going to use all they have when they race.

Consistency Through Planned Meet Management

It is difficult to swim well from start to finish of a big meet. Championship meets and major invitationals last three to six days. Age-groupers will often swim three individual races in the morning, then the same again in the evenings with added relays, day after day. Each race is expected to be a maximum effort and a personal best performance. Morning sessions can start early in the morning, sessions can seem to last forever, and evening finals can stretch until fairly late at night, after which the family or the team needs to eat dinner. This makes for long, tiring, stressful days. Often, the environment does not cooperate. Indoor meets can be plagued with poor ventilation and acoustics, making the coughing of the swimmers louder than the shouting of the spectators. For outdoor meets, in certain areas spring meets entail racing in four days of cold rain, and summer meets mean enduring heat and humidity that bake the brain and sap energy. All the while, maximum performance is expected every time.

These conditions can be challenging in the best of situations, but swimmers can make matters worse with poor choices. Some kids have no idea what events they are swimming; others have never warmed up for their races and never plan to and you can't make them. A sizable minority of the youngest swimmers hover over the coach's shoulder, asking 50 times when they swim next. Then there are the boys who walk directly from their candy bar and video game to the blocks, or the girls who are so busy listening to their MP3 players and dancing to the music that they don't notice they're supposed to be on the blocks next! There are the high-level swimmers who forget to drink for four days and are so dehydrated by the last day that they can barely finish their races. There are kids who make all the right choices before their favorite events but who don't care how they swim in their off-specialty events. Also, there are swimmers who are tired and decide that they cannot swim fast. Swimming meets are never boring amid this human comedy.

> You need to create good habits in swimmers that result in consistently good performances.

When huge natural challenges are combined with the artificial challenges created by swimmers' poor choices, the result is roller-coaster inconsistency—some swims are wonderful, some mediocre, some awful, and none predictable. For all the time that both coaches and swimmers spend around the pool, this is not good enough. You need to create good habits in swimmers that result in consistently good performances. These skills can be taught and practiced, and they must be.

You can do this by formulating and practicing effective racing routines—in other words, by practicing meet management. Most simply, meet management is planning ahead, creating a mental and physical routine for consistent peak performance that is practiced at every meet, before and after every swim, and before and after each session of a meet. Swimmers learn to make every decision during a meet based on what is going to help them race their best, maximizing the recovery after one race so as to prepare for the next. It means making good choices about how to act at a meet. A few of the many areas to consider include planning for the conditions, paying proper attention to the meet and to where the swimmer's races fit into its flow, preparing for and recovering from each race with appropriate warming up and warming down, and fueling the body with adequate food and liquids. There are a lot of choices to make, all of which affect a swimmer's performance. Learning how to make these choices is an important step toward elite performance.

Early and midseason meets should be used as meet management practice so that by the time of the championships, swimmers are comfortable with their routines, with taking care of themselves, and with making good choices. Each meet becomes an exercise in taking care of their goals and learning to take care of all the little details without anxiety—they do so naturally, automatically, and habitually so that their minds are free to focus on racing. Through practice, swimmers get better at doing meets, and their performances improve in the process. As this happens, coaches are better able to see the results of their programs because patterns of performance emerge.

Process of Meet Management

This section breaks meet management into its parts and offers instructions for how to do a meet properly. Swimmers learn how to act in the days leading up to the meet, what to do when they get to the pool, how they should best prepare for each race and recover afterward, and how to maintain their energy and focus as a demanding meet progresses. All of these skills can be taught by coaches; they can be practiced by swimmers, and when they are made habitual, they result in fast racing that makes everyone happy.

Before the Meet

The structures that follow concern the calm before the storm. This includes when the swimmers are at home or at the hotel the night before and the morning of the meet and when they reach the pool but before the racing begins.

1. **Get adequate rest.** Most swimmers understand the importance of getting to sleep early the night before a meet. But it is more important for swimmers to get a good night's sleep the two nights before a meet. This will make a difference in their energy levels at the meet.

2. **Eat a carbohydrate-rich dinner the night before the meet.** Swimmers need to fill the energy tank before a demanding weekend.

3. **Eat a carbohydrate-rich breakfast the morning of a meet, and avoid greasy or heavy foods (this includes crowd favorites bacon and sausage).** Swimmers can't race their best without fuel in the tank, and they need the right kind of fuel. It's worth getting out of bed 20 minutes earlier to eat something nutritious.

4. **Wear the team uniform to the meet: suit, cap, T-shirt, sweats, jacket, and so on.** Swimmers need to show everyone they are proud to be members of the team.

5. **Dress for the weather.** Swimmers should be prepared for both the morning and evening lows and the afternoon highs.

6. **Be on time.** Teams are usually on a fairly strict timetable with team meetings or common warm-ups, and swimmers who are late may miss out on something important or be out of phase with their teammates. We report to the team area 75 minutes before the meet starting time, but each coach has her own protocols. Swimmers need to plan ahead to take care of the little details that could prevent them from getting to the meet on time.

7. **Check in with the coach, and if necessary, check in with the clerk for deck-seeded events (usually distance races).** Swimmers must let you know they are present and accounted for. If the officials call for scratches and you think certain kids are still absent, you are in a bind: to scratch or not to scratch? When swimmers show up on time and let you know they have arrived, uncertainty is eliminated.

8. **Stretch out and warm up with the team.** When a team stretches together, gets in together, and warms up together, it looks professional. The team members look like they know what they're doing, and that can deliver a devastating psychological blow to teams that are less organized. For age-group swimmers, it is probably best to have a standard meet warm-up for the training group. When everyone knows the warm-up, they can get in and do it, policing themselves without the coach having to tell them each step and without a lot of standing around. On our team, the standard warm-up is about 2,000 yards or meters with speeds and intensities gradually building throughout and working all four strokes. Practice the meet warm-up for the last couple of workouts leading up to each meet. Then, at the meet, the kids know the warm-up, and you won't have to micromanage them.

Bookend Breaks

Many swimmers and their parents decide they need a break the day before a meet and the day afterward. The decision regarding race preparations belongs with the coach, so it must be made clear that swimmers should not self-taper by skipping practice unless they are explicitly told to do so. The meet and its effects are taken into consideration when coaches plan the workouts for those days.

Before Each Race

Some swimmers race best if they are social before a swim, others if they sit by themselves with a towel over their head, others if they listen to music and dance. Prerace rituals are individual, and it often takes some experimenting until a swimmer finds what works best. No matter how they get there, swimmers need to don a "laser-beam focus, whatever it takes, race your guts out" mentality by the time they step on the blocks.

Swimmers should talk to the coach before every race. You need to know that they are focused on their race plan and ready to race with intent. I used to talk at swimmers for quite a while before they raced, going over every little detail. I probably hurt more than I helped, making them more anxious than they already were. Now I stick to a few race cues based on both the racing tactics discussed in chapter 12, the swimmer's past history, and current strengths and weaknesses. Swimmers should have rehearsed their races in practice, so nothing you say will be new. Remind rather than inform. Further, look at body language: What does the swimmer's face or posture tell you about his state of mind? If necessary, try to get the train back on the tracks. If all seems well, you might only add, "Go race your guts out, champion," to the few tactical cues and send the swimmer to the blocks.

Swimmers also need to warm up well. In practice, swimmers aren't asked to swim fast before they've swum 2,000 or 3,000 yards building up to speed. It takes the body a while to get into a racing rhythm, yet many age-groupers seem to think they can march directly from eating candy and drinking soda to the blocks and race their best. For swimmers to race optimally, the body needs to get warmed up, the heart needs to get pumping, the blood needs to be flowing through the muscles, the strokes need to be grooved, and the aerobic system needs to be switched on and functioning well. Swimmers must warm up and get into racing mode before every race.

> Swimmers must warm up and get into racing mode before every race.

An important consideration is when to warm up. A race warm-up done too early is worthless. It is always mystifying—and frustrating—to see swimmers start to warm up an hour before a race, swim a couple hundred meters, then stand around for 55 minutes before they compete. In order for the warm-up to fulfill its purpose—to prepare swimmers to race to their maximum in the upcoming race—timing is critical. On our team, swimmers jump into the warm-up pool about 23 minutes before they race. They swim progressively faster for 12 to 15 minutes. By the end of the warm-up they are swimming fast and feeling grooved. They dry off quickly, put on their jackets, and get to the blocks with four or five minutes to spare. A good rule of thumb is, the shorter the time between the end of the warm-up and the beginning of the race, the better. If they finish the warm-up an hour before the race, they may as well have been playing video games for all the good it will do them. (See page 202 for tips about what to do if a warm-up pool isn't available.)

It is the swimmers' responsibility to know when to get in. They must learn to study the heat sheet and work backward from their event and heat. Swimmers new to our team frequently ask me, "When do I warm up?" My cryptic answer is, "Warm up when it is appropriate to do so." When they look at me quizzically, I continue, "If you do not know when that is, Caleb or Julia will help you figure it out." (Caleb and Julia are two of our national-level seniors.) In this way, the older kids have the responsibility for helping the younger kids figure out how to be self-reliant racers, and I can concentrate on coaching.

Once swimmers are in the warm-up pool, they have to know what to do there. Most age-groupers do little or nothing. They don't swim enough, and they don't swim hard enough. Again, a race warm-up that doesn't prepare swimmers to race to their maximum is worthless. A working rule of thumb for distance is as follows:

- For 10-and-under swimmers, 500 to 600 yards or meters
- For 11- to 12-year-olds, 600 to 700 yards or meters
- For 13- to 14-year-olds, 700 to 800 yards or meters

Exactly what to do is to some extent up to the swimmers and coaches, who should experiment with formats to find what works best. And to some extent it depends on the specific race to come. But the same rule applies as to the general presession warm-up: Stretch out the strokes, gradually increase the intensity, get the heart rate elevated and the aerobic system turned on, and feel the racing stroke and rhythm with some short sprints.

Swimmers need to be responsible for warming up at the right time and in the right way.

During Races

Chapter 12 discussed racing attitudes, rules, and habits (good and bad) and how coaches can help swimmers adopt these behaviors and attitudes through daily training. In a nutshell, you want swimmers giving everything they have in every race they swim. They should never dog it, whether they are 50 meters behind or 50 meters ahead. They should never save up for the next race or their favorite race. They should respect their competitors, the sport, and themselves by giving their best effort and racing their guts out.

After Races

After swimmers finish a race, they can bask (quickly) in the glory of having done well, thanks to good race preparation. Then they should get out of the pool and walk quickly to the coach. They should not stop to talk to teammates or parents, count laps for seven heats of 500s, get a hot dog, or do anything else. They talk quickly with you, keeping the conversation short and hitting the highlights. If there is a logjam of swimmers waiting to talk with you and they could be waiting a while, it may be preferable for them to swim down first and talk to you afterward.

After that brief talk, swimmers should jump into the warm-down pool and swim. On our team, swimmers have a goal of splashing down in the warm-down pool within two minutes of finishing their race. To meet this goal, they have to hustle. The sooner they start warming down, the better and more effective the recovery. Presuming they have raced hard, they need to not only loosen tired, tight muscles but also relax the mind after a stressful time. Swimmers should consider warming down to be the first step in preparing for their next race.

> Swimmers should consider warming down to be the first step in preparing for their next race.

Not warming down properly is the most common meet mistake made by competitive swimmers at all ages and levels. Warming down means swimming, not sitting in the water talking to friends, playing sharks and minnows, or grabbing onto the gutter and watching the meet. It means swimming straight at a respectable pace, stopping only for sips of water or sport drink. Several Olympians must warm down for more than a half hour to get their bodies properly recovered from racing. Such a long warm-down may be unnecessary and impractical for age-groupers with several races each session, but older swimmers generally warm down longer than younger swimmers, and even the youngest should warm down for at least 10 minutes after a race.

The first half of the warm-down should be in the stroke just raced, the last half in the stroke to be raced next. The prerace warm-up distance guidelines apply for postrace warm-downs:

- For 10-and-under swimmers, 500 to 600 yards or meters
- For 11- to 12-year-olds, 600 to 700 yards or meters
- For 13- to 14-year-olds, 700 to 800 yards or meters

Regarding the intensity of the warm-down, after a couple hundred meters of long, smooth swimming, swimmers should increase to a respectable pace. This helps the muscles recover faster and more effectively than does slogging through a few slow, ugly laps. After the last race of the day, swimmers should add a few hundred meters to these numbers. After a particularly hard effort in a distance race, swimmers should swim down as long as it takes to feel good; the more they do in warm-down, the better their next race will be.

Between Races

Quite often swimmers have time between races—time that is usually filled with playing video games or card games, messing around in the locker room, or wandering around the pool deck in packs. It is good for swimmers to relax and conserve their energy for their races, but there are better and worse ways to use this precious recovery time.

1. **Rest for the next event.** Swimmers should stay off their feet as much as possible.
2. **Cheer for teammates.** Even if kids aren't swimming the distance events (which are often last in the event list), you should encourage them to stay and watch their distance swimming teammates. A 1650 free race goes by more quickly when one's teammates are lining the side of the pool and cheering.
3. **Keep warm.** Swimmers should be fully clothed from head to toe. Warm, relaxed muscles are fast muscles.
4. **Pay attention, and learn to use the heat sheet.** In order to know when they will race, swimmers must know their own event with heat and lane, the order of events, which race is currently in the water, and how many heats are in the events just before theirs. They also need to plan out their preparation for their next race. That is a lot to keep track of. Not paying attention often leads to swimmers not being ready to race—everyone has seen the swimmer running to the blocks with goggles in hand—or even missing races. The worst offenses are missing an event for which there is a positive check-in (i.e., distance events) or missing an evening final. Penalties usually involve the swimmer being automatically scratched from his next race or kicked out of the meet entirely.
5. **Eat and drink appropriately.** This will depend on when the swimmers' next events are. If there is not much time between events, swimmers should just have some sport drink. With more time, they can also eat something light, nutritious, and easily digested, such as a bagel or piece of fruit. Coaches should ban and confiscate candy, chips, donuts, soda, and other junk foods.

Special Considerations

Multiday preliminaries and finals meets challenge even the best meet managers. The stresses of these meets are cumulative. If swimmers make poor decisions early in the meet, the consequences of these choices accumulate and they will be running on fumes by the end of the meet. Between sessions of a preliminary and finals meet, swimmers need to rest, stay off their feet, relax their bodies and minds, and rest some more. Between days of a preliminary and finals meet, they need to eat good meals and go to bed early. Teaching swimmers to use these downtimes for appropriate recovery will increase the chances that they maintain their strength throughout a meet while their competitors fade. The swimmers' focus over the several days of the meet should be racing fast and using the time between races to prepare to race fast the next time.

Ideally, every meet will have a separate warm-up and warm-down pool available throughout the meet so that swimmers can practice perfect meet management from start to finish. Unfortunately, this is often not the case, and kids have to make do with what they have. In the absence of a separate pool, sometimes meet directors place frequent, short breaks throughout a session, during which the pool is available for warming up. If this is the case, swimmers must make sure they know when the breaks are, be ready for them, and use every available second to warm up, no matter when their last race was or when the next one will be. Also, if swimmers cannot swim before or after their races, they must do the next best thing—get the heart beating and the blood flowing faster by doing calisthenics or jogging in place. Swimmers could also stand in a hot shower and stretch out or massage their muscles. Even if it isn't perfect, it's better than nothing.

Meet management becomes even more important when conditions are not ideal and stress loads are great. When the weather is blazing hot, swimmers who are taking care of their hydration will stay more consistent and energetic than those who are voluntarily parched. When the weather is cold and miserable, swimmers who have brought warm, dry, water-repellent clothes and who stay warm and dry behind the blocks until the last second will have the advantage of swimmers who are wet, cold, and shivering as they prepare to race. In situations of high stress, when swimmers are already nervous and on edge, it doesn't help them to have to worry about when to warm up or what to drink or eat. If they have established a routine that they have followed and practiced, then the decisions about how to act come naturally with no thought or anxiety.

> If they have established a routine that they have followed and practiced, then the decisions about how to act come naturally with no thought or anxiety.

Team Travel Meets

Meets are meets are meets. Swimmers get on the blocks and swim fast, whether at their home pool, the rivals' pool across town, a special pool like Indianapolis or Austin, or the Athens or Beijing Olympic pools. However, team travel meets are a slightly different breed. They entail traveling across the country, staying in hotels, rooming with teammates, obeying the coaches, eating out for every meal, riding in cramped team buses or vans, and racing people they've never seen before from teams they've never heard of. All in all, swimmers cannot control their environment to the extent that they can back home, and because their parents aren't there making all the decisions and smoothing over every problem, they have to take much more responsibility for making good choices than they ordinarily do. All these factors make travel meets a little different and much more important. Travel meets teach swimmers to deal with numerous challenges.

- For time changes, swimmers must plan ahead, adjusting their living, eating, sleeping, and even workout schedules.

- When traveling on team buses, the usual format is to hurry up and wait. Everything takes more time, so swimmers must expect the delays and learn patience. There is a balance between planning for every contingency and being very flexible.

- Meals with the team (especially with a large group) take seemingly forever, and often the imagination is taxed to find nutritious choices.

- Kids don't get their own rooms or beds. Their teammates' habits may irritate them, but they have to learn to live together, respect each others' intentions to swim fast, and when necessary, stick up for their goals.

- Swimmers will not be placed with their best friends, so they must get to know previously unknown or little-known teammates. They travel as one team, not five training groups.

- Kids are often left with a lot of free time, and they have to learn constructive ways of filling that time that will aid their overall mission of swimming faster. They should rest between sessions, and they should stay at the meet to cheer for their teammates. They learn how to be a part of a team.

- Some kids simply are not going to be serious about swimming, and serious swimmers must learn to prevent anyone else from hurting their performance. It is ultimately their responsibility to stick up for themselves and protect their goals.

- Since they are not racing the same old competitors, the pecking order is abolished for a weekend, providing new possibilities for breakthroughs.

- There are more opportunities than usual to be distracted, so swimmers get more opportunities to practice focusing and making good decisions.

- Because they are on their own, swimmers learn how to be independent, make good choices, and figure out how to solve problems. Independence builds strength.

- Meets important enough to travel to tend to be big and fast. What better atmosphere for swimming fast than getting a whole bunch of fast kids from a large geographical area to race together?

- Travel meets aren't normal, predictable, or perfect. They rip swimmers out of the usual routine and comfort zone. This is a good thing.

- Swimmers have more freedom and hence more responsibility as they make many more choices than they usually do. They have to practice making good choices (with the coaches' help, of course). "What's going to make me swim faster?" should be the question that guides their decision making.

- With just the coaches and swimmers (and perhaps a few chaperones), travel meets provide wonderful opportunities for coaches to get to know the swimmers better, to see how they react in different situations (and even everyday situations that the coaches rarely see), and to teach the way of a champion for an extended period of time.

Travel meets represent concentrated meet management. They accelerate a swimmer's competitive development through their challenges and their lessons. They are massively educational—the most valuable meets that swimmers can attend.

CHAPTER 14

Selecting Meets and Events

This chapter concludes the discussion of factors affecting swimmers' performances at meets. Chapters 12 and 13 discussed the importance of attitudes (what is going on in the swimmers' heads), tactics (how they swim races to maximize what they've got inside them), and meet management (how they act at a meet to prepare for and recover from races), each of which can help a swimmer race better when done correctly and slow a swimmer down when done incorrectly. In this chapter the focus is on which meets swimmers compete in and which events they swim at those meets. A well-constructed meet schedule and planned event lists can aid immeasurably in keeping swimmers improving steadily and continually.

Principles of Meet Selection

Controlling the meet schedule means controlling your swimmers' progression. How a coach chooses meets is important. The following principles can give consistency to meet choices and lead to consistent swimmer improvement.

Make Meets Important

The racing schedule needs to be planned if the coach wants to be able to expect—and not just hope for—good performances throughout the season. Every meet should serve a purpose. There are different ways of being important. Some meets are *administratively important*. In the YMCA leagues and most local dual-meet leagues, in order to be eligible for the championships, swimmers must compete in a certain number of in-season meets. Most championships at any level have qualifying standards, and early-season meets and smaller invitationals are administratively important for making qualifying standards for these bigger meets. Other meets, such as bump and target meets, are *competitively important*. Try to schedule administratively important meets early in the season, when the team is gradually building momentum.

Meet choices need to reflect the goals of the program and training group. They need to be scheduled at the right times, and the competition needs to be at the right level for the swimmers. Never be at the mercy of the local racing calendar. Choose meets because they fit your plans, not because they are convenient, even if that requires traveling more than might be desired. When kids swim fast because the coach has made wise choices, the extra miles on the car and the hotel stays are forgiven.

When swimmers race too frequently, they court staleness. Meets need to be special, with high expectations. They are not special when you are attending them every weekend. It is optimal to race about once a month. The swimmers should improve at every meet, and they need time to improve. For developing swimmers, training is the most important factor leading to gradual, continual improvement, which is the key to keeping kids interested and motivated. In daily practice, swimmers learn to swim better, faster, stronger, prettier, tougher, and smarter, and they gain confidence in their abilities by making small improvements. In meets, they get to show off these improvements publicly, but without good, hard, consistent training, there are no improvements to show off. Race improvements follow from practice improvements.

Keep a Clean Calendar Before Big Meets

Heading into a championship, it is crucial to maintain consistent training rhythm. Having frequent meets in the weeks before a peak meet is the most effective way to destroy training rhythm and ensure poor performances at the big meet. If possible, it is best to have no meets for at least three weeks before the target meet. Of course, sometimes two championship meets will piggyback and there is nothing to be done about it (e.g., in the United States, state meets and zones, high school regional and state meets, sectionals and nationals, nationals and junior nationals). When this happens, sometimes you need to compete in both, with one given priority. But sometimes the overriding importance of the final meet necessitates skipping the lead-up meet entirely.

Realize That Success Matters

You set swimmers up to succeed by your meet choices. In theory, they can improve no matter what meet they attend and no matter whom they race against. However, the psychology of a child or an adolescent complicates this picture a bit. No two meets *mean* the same thing to a single swimmer. A given meet will represent different psychological climates for swimmers of different levels depending on how they expect to do at the meet. Do they have a chance to win? A chance to final? A chance for a second swim? Are they mired at the bottom of the standings? Each of these situations brings unique pressures for the swimmers. This matters! Under what circumstances will each swimmer have the best chance of swimming well? Despite what coaches say about doing one's best, results matter to the kids both before the race (the psychological climate of a swim) and afterward (when evaluating a swim). There must be a chance to succeed if the swimmer is to pull out all the stops and give a maximum performance. It's hard for a child to think like a winner if she finishes 73rd.

> You set swimmers up to succeed by your meet choices.

Results matter to kids so make meet choices that give them a chance to swim well.

Value Performance Over Convenience

Teams can stunt the progress of their swimmers by treating swimmers of different levels and with different needs as if they were the same. For instance, it is easiest and most convenient to find meets that the whole team can attend. Everyone races the same weekend, so it is easy to coordinate coaching coverage, and families with kids of varying ages and abilities do not have to be in two places at once. This can work in either direction: Teams can choose low-level, take-all-comers meets that often do not challenge the top end, or they can choose higher-level meets where the bulk of the kids barely qualify and then get crushed. Meet decisions have consequences for the program as a whole and for the progress of the individuals in it. Every swimmer needs to be challenged. Generally, top-end swimmers should attend high-level competitions and low-end swimmers should attend the all-comers or no-time-standards meets.

Along the same lines, many swimmers automatically attend a meet if they make the qualifying times, but this practice raises important questions. Do you send a swimmer to a meet that she just recently or barely qualified for, perhaps has only one event to swim, and where she will likely finish near the bottom with no hope of a second swim? Or do you have her attend a lower-level meet where she can swim several events and improve across a broad front, where she can be competitive and can expect to do well, and where a good morning swim gets her a second swim at night? The swimmer and her parents will usually argue loudly for the former route, but the latter probably results in much faster meet performances, where the swimmer progresses to being a contender in the upper-level meet much faster. She doesn't attend meets for the experience (i.e., for the experience of swimming slow) but to swim fast. Swimmers shouldn't attend meets simply because they qualified but because they are prepared to succeed and to take a step forward in performance.

Competing at a meet that is currently over a swimmer's head can be useful for the motivational aspects of the competition. If swimmers have aspirations of national- or international-level performance, attending a Grand Prix meet and getting to rub shoulders with and race against the sport's superstars can be tremendously motivating. Swimmers get a taste of the atmosphere of high performance, they learn by watching how elite performers do their job, and they head home determined to reach that level as quickly as possible. This can be extraordinarily educational and provide a boost to the next level. But perhaps this is a midseason experience, not a season-ending championship one.

Think Beyond the Cuts

Few experiences are more frustrating than going to a big (and long and expensive) meet with a swimmer whose primary goal was simply to qualify for the meet. The usual result is spending five days away from home so she can swim one event, race poorly, finish 97th, and be perfectly content because she made nationals—not very satisfying. On the other hand, few experiences are as wonderful as going to big meets with kids who have prepared themselves mentally and physically to attend the meet and who are ready to rocket up the standings. It is important for coaches to have structures in place to motivate swimmers to think beyond the cuts. Good goal setting helps. When we discuss season goals, we talk about steps to championship swims. Step 1, which is necessary but not sufficient, is to make the qualifying standard, first in one event and then in several. Step 2 is to improve in practice and prepare to swim fast at the meet. We talk about this all the time. Making cuts early in the season (or, better, the previous season) allows time for swimmers to reset their goals and refocus their expectations and intentions.

Further means of getting kids thinking beyond simply qualifying for a meet are to compile and distribute goal sheets that include both meet qualifying standards and a list of probable times to final. For each of the major meets, review the previous year's results and estimate the times it will take to final this year, assuming that this year will be a little faster. This lets swimmers know how fast they need to swim to be participants and how fast they need to swim to be contenders. Again, often we have a requirement that swimmers must qualify for several events to attend a championship meet so that they are not sitting around for five days to swim one event. Racing several events spreads the pressure, rendering stress levels more manageable, and it helps swimmers get into the rhythm of the meet. Our individual medley and all-around training makes this requirement easier to meet. Finally, for some travel meets, we require that swimmers meet a certain number of standards equivalent to what it took to final the previous year.

Season Meet Planning and Periodic Bumps

It is common to see kids swim slow throughout the season, then turn around and expect miraculous improvements at taper time. Often, their whole swimming lives depend on the results of one race at one big meet, which sometimes leads to tremendous breakthroughs but more often leads to tremendous meltdowns. Even when this process works, swimmers only race fast once a season, so they only make progress once a season. Most of the time they are treading water or moving backward from where they were six or eight months previous.

A sounder approach is to plan for continual and cumulative progress. As an age-group coach, you should expect best times pretty much all the time, and you should expect consistent effort and performance across the range of events, with no wild swings from in-season slow to taper-meet fast. Age-groupers can swim fast all season long, not just once at the end, and they should take several small to medium steps forward. This should happen with little to no rest before meets, even important invitationals.

Swimmers can meet these expectations because of focused training and strategic meet choices. First, fast racing begins with fast training. Meet performances are largely a function of swimmers' expectations; when they are swimming fast and improving in practice, they expect to swim fast and improve in meets. They are ready physiologically and psychologically. Ensuring that practice performances lead to improved meet results is a main task of the coach. Continually tie swimmers' practice performances to meet performances and vice versa. When they train well, tell them what that might mean when they race next: "If you can hold 59s on this set, you should be under 5:00 in the 500 at the next meet!" When they race well, use those race times to establish practice expectations. For instance, "Since you are now a 1:01 flyer in a meet, I want you to start training like a swimmer who plans to break a minute!"

> Ensuring that practice performances lead to improved meet results is a main task of the coach.

Second, try to plan the meet schedule well, with the right meets at the right levels at the right times, so the athletes can take small to medium steps forward all season long. These psychological and physical steps forward are called *bumps*. Bump meets are fairly important invitationals, and they are practically built for swimming fast: good teams from a wide area, kids they haven't raced before (so there is no established pecking order letting them know how they are supposed to finish), a fairly high level of competition, and a preliminary and finals format. The swimmers get practice getting comfortable with the expectations and stresses of swimming fast in two sessions a day. Using their previous training and adding to it the raised expectations that come with a meet like this, swimmers get a bump in performance—best times and nice steps forward, both of which help them to rearrange their goals and expectations for training and racing in the future.

Each bump is important because it keeps the swimmers moving forward, which keeps them motivated. They see themselves getting faster regularly and almost automatically. They start to expect more of themselves in training, which leads to increased capacities and even faster swimming. Without these regular bumps, swimmers tend to plateau in practice, get bored, and end up racing flat at the championships.

An example of a planned short-course season for North America, which can be easily adapted to other calendars, would follow this pattern:

1. **Building phase.** This phase includes minor local invitational or dual meets in late September or early October. For my YMCA team, this period presents an opportunity to get requirements out of the way and to make qualifying standards for upcoming major invitationals or championship meets. The faster swimmers who already have cuts should avoid their best events.

   For newer swimmers or kids getting their feet in the door, these early-season minor meets are critical. If they don't race early, they don't qualify for the later, faster meets. Coaches must emphasize to the swimmers and parents the importance of regular attendance at team meets for swimmers to progress. You are not asking for their every weekend, but you want them racing when the team has a meet. Bump meets don't work for a swimmer if he cannot attend them. And no one wants to be left home from a championship meet that he was fast enough to swim in, if only he had attended the qualifying meets.

2. **Quicker building phase.** This phase includes minor local invitational or dual meets in November. There is more pressure to swim fast here than in September and October, but the plan is still to avoid the major events for the faster swimmers and to emphasize making standards for swimmers at a lower level.

3. **Bump meet 1.** This meet should be an important benchmark (multistate) invitational in early December. Expectations are high. Swimmers will race their best events and should take reasonable steps forward across the board.

4. **Bump meet 2.** This meet should be an important benchmark (multistate) invitational in mid-January, preferably long course. Because the team swam fast in December, is swimming fast in practice, and has just gotten out of a winter holiday training camp, the swimmers are ready to swim long-course best times. This gives them a psychological jump start on the summer season, setting expectations for the April and May long-course meets. If there is no long-course meet to be found, then a short-course mid-January bump meet should focus on swimmers' supporting events (see the housecleaning phase).

5. **Bump meet 3.** This meet should be an important benchmark (multistate) invitational in mid-February. The emphasis should be on major events. If the previous bump was a long-course meet, it has been two months since the swimmers raced short course, and they are ready for serious improvements.

6. **Housecleaning phase.** This phase includes a minor invitational in late February or early March. Use this meet to shore up supporting events, and avoid best events if cuts for championship meets have already been achieved. You want the swimmers to be fast, but not too fast, three to four weeks out from the championship. If they are too good here, especially in their major events, this may mean that you have seen all the improvement you are going to see and that they will race flat at the target meet. This meet should be relatively low stress, with timed finals, and no more than two days long—easy to recover from and get back into training rhythm.

7. **Target meet.** This is the championship meet in mid-March to early April, depending on the level of the swimmer. Sometimes there are two meets almost in tandem, such as a state championship and then a regional championship or a regional championship and then a national championship. Swimmers focus on their best events. This is obviously the meet where expectations are highest, bumps are largest, and performances are strongest.

The goal of season meet planning is for the swimmers to improve and swim fast all season long, not just once at the end. Coaches can engineer this improvement by planning training, planning meets, and establishing proper expectations so that progress happens naturally and continually.

Principles of Event Selection

Controlling events means controlling the progression of a swimmer. As with the choice of meets, the choice of events affects how much and how consistently swimmers improve throughout a season. When choices are haphazard or at the mercy of swimmers' whims, the results are just as haphazard.

Coaches Choose the Events

Unlike the young swimmer or the parents, the coach has broad perspective. In my program, I know where the team is going, and I see each meet in the context of the entire season or year. I know when we are going to get an opportunity to swim certain key events and thus when we must swim those events to open up greater opportunities down the road. I will not be entering the swimmers in the same events over and over or just in their best events. I will not just enter them in whatever events they did best at last meet (which are their favorite events this month). I will not allow them to avoid strokes they don't like. I will make sure they swim everything and not allow them to specialize. Most importantly, I will make sure they swim their best events at the right times, not every time. It is safe to assume that swimmers would not follow these guidelines if left to themselves.

Improve Along a Broad Front

By training swimmers appropriately and then entering them in as many events as they are allowed to swim, you increase the likelihood that they will improve across a broad front. Age-groupers should get used to racing a lot at meets—a lot of events, strokes, and distances. For most kids, downtime at meets is just wasted time or time to get in trouble messing around in the locker rooms. Further, steer swimmers toward the longer events, which are more important in the athletes' long-term development than are the sprints. Generally, the shorter the race, the worse the stroke technique. This is especially true for younger swimmers, who rarely have the motor control

> Age-groupers should get used to racing a lot at meets—a lot of events, strokes, and distances.

necessary to hold a good stroke at full effort. It is also the case that longer events offer greater opportunities for success and improvement, at least for those swimmers who are willing to work hard in practice.

Plan With the Whole Season in Mind

Choosing events intelligently requires planning and foresight. Figure out which meets you will attend, what the qualifying standards will be, what the level of competition will be at each meet, and what events will be offered. (In our area, neither the distance events nor the longer-form stroke events for age-groupers are offered frequently, so we must be on the lookout for meets with broad event offerings). Have the entire season in front of you and plan it out, in particular for the stronger kids. You will probably be thrown some curveballs by the meet directors and by your swimmers. The latter will sometimes swim faster than you had expected and sometimes slower, so you must be adaptable.

Make a Swimmer's Best Events Special

With the whole season in front of you, decide when you will have a swimmer swim his major events. The rule is, not often. Make each time special, with high expectations. Don't overswim an event and allow a swimmer to bore himself into a coach-created plateau. On teams that race often, you can frequently see a good swimmer racing his best events every single meet. By midseason the swimmer has usually flatlined. On the other hand, if your team races about once a month, the kids may swim their best events only three or four times during the short-course season and fewer during the long-course season. With distance swimming, this few-but-ripe rule counts double: You are neither going to see a swimmer race too many high quality miles each season nor should you expect him to.

Rotate Away From Success

After a breakthrough or a big time drop in an event, a swimmer will almost never race that event at the next meet (unless absolutely necessary, such as at a championship), because the odds of another improvement are almost nonexistent. This decision will often be controversial since the swimmer and her parents will extrapolate from that recent quantum leap and expect another huge gain at the next meet. When this leap doesn't happen at the next meet—and it won't—the result is a huge deflation instead of motivation and excitement. Stand your ground and wait a while. Give the swimmer time to train and get better. Similarly, coaches should avoid events where the swimmer is not ready for an improvement (based on her practice performances). Take preventive measures and, when at all possible, do not allow plateaus to happen. Find events where the swimmer is ready for a bump.

Make a Second List of Supporting Events

One way to keep swimmers moving forward across a broad front is to have a second set of supporting events in addition to a swimmer's main set of events. Supporting events set up and correct swimmers' weaknesses in their main events.

In tandem with rotating away from success, use the time between races of main events to prepare the way for another time drop by focusing on supporting events. For instance, if a swimmer's main events are the 200s stroke and 400 IM, then the supporting events would be the stroke 100s and the 200 IM. If she swims a 4:52 in the 400 IM but can only muster a 2:25 in the 200, then it is safe to say that aerobically she is fine, but she must develop more speed before she can improve her long individual medley. So she works to bring down her time in the 200 to enable a breakthrough in her primary event. The same process can be used for the 200s stroke. If a swimmer aims to swim a 2:10 in the 200 fly, but his best time in the 100 is only a 1:04, his goal isn't happening. He needs more speed than he currently has if he wants to reach his primary goal. His secondary aim is to bring down his time in his supporting event, the 100 fly.

Ensure Needed Lessons Are Learned

For the most part, you are trying to set up swimmers to succeed. There are times, however, when a lesson badly needs learning for a swimmer to continue to develop and only failure will teach that lesson. Young swimmers are good at ignoring the obvious consequences of their behavior and refusing to see how their behavior does not correlate with their purported goals. When a coach's lectures run off a swimmer like water off a duck's back, a disastrous race can get the swimmer's attention. For example, entering a distance swimmer in his specialty when his practice attendance and performance have slipped and he is in no shape to swim well reminds him of why he succeeded in the past and what he needs to change if he wants to swim fast again. His race may be painful and a bit embarrassing, but the pain of taking one step backward right now is well worth the pleasure of taking several forward in the future.

Emphasize Making Cuts Early

When a swimmer repeatedly falls just short of the cuts for a major meet, the coach's careful and time-consuming planning is for naught. Falling short means getting locked into over-racing best events, draining the excitement out of those events by midseason and often creating performance plateaus. Further, instead of being excited about swimming fast, the swimmer worries, "I have to qualify, I have to qualify, I have to qualify," before every swim, increasing her anxiety and lowering her chances of reaching her goal. Soon making the cut, rather than swimming fast at the meet, becomes the goal.

Ideally, swimmers will have their championship meet cuts out of the way early so that coaches can plan entries for each meet intelligently and can focus their training and expectations for the target meet. By swimming fast early, swimmers have options: At meets, they can swim what you want them to rather than what they have to. It is helpful to have structures in place to encourage swimmers to make cuts early and often. First, emphasize the importance of swimming fast in the early season. This may seem to be an obvious strategy, but it is rarely used. Never lower expectations and tell kids that they will probably swim slow. Emphasize the opportunities if swimmers can get out of the gate quickly.

Second, find a midseason benchmark meet that has similar qualifying standards to the end-of-season championships so your swimmers are motivated to kill two birds with one stone. An example of this with my current team is the Missouri Grand Prix in mid-February. The cuts for Missouri are similar to the cuts for the short course YMCA Nationals, our season championship meet. Kids want to go to Missouri to race against the nation's best. But in order for kids to make the trip, we require them to have four cuts. By traveling to Missouri, they will have already qualified for the full complement of events at our season-ending target meet two months later. As a result, for the last few months of the season, we can focus our meet selection and training on our target meet. If a suitable benchmark meet isn't available midseason, you can encourage early qualifying in other ways. Post a list of championship qualifiers the day after your first meet of the season and update the list after each meet. Give the qualifiers public kudos at every opportunity. Competitive kids will swim faster to get their names on the wall.

Debriefing After a Meet

If you are going to get better, you need to evaluate what went right and what went wrong. All but the most self-aware and honest swimmers need the coach's eyes, brain, and experience to counsel them about a race's strengths and weaknesses. They need the coach to suggest changes for the next race and changes to make in practice for the next meet. Of course, after the last race coaches need to look at the big picture of their team's performance at a meet in order to ensure that any deviations from the planned course can be corrected in training immediately.

> All but the most self-aware and honest swimmers need the coach's eyes, brain, and experience to counsel them about a race's strengths and weaknesses.

Evaluating Swims

On our team it is a rule that swimmers talk with me or another coach immediately after each race, when the performance is still fresh in everyone's mind. This happens in the context of the two-minute drill, so our postrace talks are often short, with two or three focused points, and then we send them off to warm-down. This is a hectic time for all involved. The kids are exhausted and often emotional, and the coaches are doing 10 things at once. Often we are simultaneously watching one race with four kids in it, talking to a line of five or six kids about the races they just swam, and prepping two or three kids about the races they will be swimming in a few minutes. It gets overwhelming, even if one is a master at multitasking.

In this situation you must watch a race (or several swimmers in the same race) and try to immediately figure out what to say to each swimmer and how to say it as the swimmers get out of the pool and walk over to you. This means capturing in your mind the whole race and its parts and trying to figure out the *why* underneath, especially if it deviated much from what you talked about before the race or what you've been working on in practice.

One obvious decision is, what standard of judgment do you use when evaluating swims? Do you use a swimmer's previous best time? Often this time is old and not representative of the swimmer's current abilities. How about the components of the race? Often how the race was swum is crucial to the final time (e.g., good or poor splitting, tough racing or giving up, good technique under fatigue and stress or stroke falling apart at the end). Where the time is achieved? A result slightly off a best time can be just as impressive as a best time if achieved in particularly challenging conditions. Should you use the swimmer's potential in the race? Usually practice performances tell more about what a swimmer can do right now than her official best time. What about the swimmer's goal in the race? Often swimmers have different expectations of themselves than coaches have.

Coaches have different priorities for different swimmers. I tend to focus on a swimmer's potential, as determined by recent practices, and on the look of the race: how even the splitting, how tough the racing, how pretty the technique. But each coach will show the swimmers what is important to him by what he chooses to talk about and how he does it. Consistency is crucial: At a meet, ask for the same things you ask for at practice.

Using these standards, discuss the race. The controlling factors here are the purpose of the postrace talk and the swimmer's emotional state. No matter what you say to a swimmer, the race is over and there is nothing you can do to change it now. But what you say can affect the next race. No matter how you feel about the race, venting your emotions is probably not going to help a swimmer be better a half hour from now. The more a coach's postrace talk can be planned and strategic, the better. The key is the psychology of the swimmer, not the emotions of the coach.

Try to take your cue from the swimmer. No matter what you think of a swim, if the swimmer comes back overjoyed, having obviously met her goals, then you need to be overjoyed for her and your criticisms need to take a backseat to her satisfaction. Send her off to the warm-down pool with a high five and save your critique for the next practice. If a swimmer is dejected about a poor swim, then focus on what was good about the race and what concrete steps he can take to change the outcome next time. With some strong-willed swimmers, you may have to be insistent about this.

Start with what was good, especially if the race was poor and the swimmer is down. Then move to what you want the swimmer to do better the next time. Discuss concrete actions that can be improved upon; "poor turns with slow dolphins" can be comprehended and fixed much easier than "that was terrible" can. Talk to your swimmers about the need to think like a scientist and not take constructive criticism personally. You are not attacking them, just trying to fix their turns so they can swim faster. The point is not for them to feel bad or guilty about what they did wrong but to figure out what slowed them down and to fix it! Some kids grasp this point better than others; the ones who do tend to fix their mistakes and get better.

This is one area where I have improved and learned a lot over the last few years. I am calmer and more concise when talking with kids after the race, I am better able to keep a broad perspective about a meet, and I no longer think that how a nine-year-old races her 100 free this morning is career determining either for her or for me. For age-groupers, there is always a next time. Even if I did not see everything I thought a swimmer was capable of today, I know that the capacity is still inside him, and it will likely show the next time. The breakthrough will be that much bigger when it comes.

Evaluating Meets

Meets provide a coach with mounds of data about how the program is (or isn't) working and how each swimmer is (or isn't) working. The day after a meet, I sit down with three stacks of papers in front of me. First is a copy of the meet results organized by event and stroke; second is a copy of the results organized by swimmer; and third is my annotated copy of the heat sheet. For the heat sheet, during the meet I not only document the splits and final time for a swimmer, I also write down comments for later reflection about what was good and what was awful. These are simple and cryptic, such as, "Walls –" or "Stroke +," a minus sign denoting not so good and a plus sign very good. If I have time, I also note whether a swimmer fixed a problem that we have been focusing on in practice.

With these papers, I get to work, going through the meet from start to finish, looking for patterns both for the team and for individual swimmers. A pattern means that the training (physical, technical, and psychological) is producing certain tendencies. I use a simple list like the racing patterns checklist from chapter 12 as a starting point. Looking at events and strokes separately tells me which strokes are working well for the group and which are not, and it lets me know what I need to change before the next meet. Looking at the individual swimmer results gives insight into how each swimmer works. How is she following the common pattern of the group, and how is she different? How does this correlate with what I see in practice? What do we need to tweak to fix her problems? There will never be a perfect meet or a perfect program, so a coach will always have much to think about and suffer over in the quest for excellence.

Index

About the Author

Michael Brooks is the veteran of more than 20 years of year-round club, high school, summer league, and country club swim coaching. He has worked with all levels, from novice to Olympic Trial athletes. He coaches swimmers ages 8 to 18 so that he can keep the beginning, middle, and end of swimmer development in mind at all times.

Since October 2006 Brooks has been head coach of the York YMCA swimming team in York, Pennsylvania. Before that, he spent two years as the head age-group coach of the Brophy East swimming team in Phoenix, Arizona, and five years as head coach of the York site of the North Baltimore Aquatic Club (Michael Phelps' home club), where he worked with renowned coaches Murray Stephens and Bob Bowman.

Brooks was named both the state Age-Group Coach of the Year and the High School Coach of the Year two times, as well as Coach of the Meet at the YMCA National Championships. His swimmers have raced to well over 150 national top 16 and top 10 rankings, scores of Far Western and zone championships, and hundreds of state championships in all events on the program. Brooks resides in York, Pennsylvania.